The Last
Godfathers

Also by John Follain

A Dishonoured Society
Jackal
Zoya's Story
City of Secrets
Mussolini's Island

The Last Godfathers

Inside the Mafia's Most Infamous Family

John Follain

Thomas Dunne Books
St. Martin's Press
New York

THOMAS DUNNE BOOKS.
An imprint of St. Martin's Press.

THE LAST GODFATHERS. Copyright © 2008 by
John Follain. All rights reserved. Printed in the United
States of America. For information, address St. Martin's
Press, 175 Fifth Avenue, New York, N.Y. 10010.

www.thomasdunnebooks.com
www.stmartins.com

Library of Congress Cataloging-in-Publication Data

Follain, John.
    The last godfathers : inside the Mafia's most infamous
family / John Follain. — 1st U. S. ed.
        p. cm.
    Includes bibliographical references and index.
    ISBN-13: 978-0-312-56690-6
    ISBN-10: 0-312-56690-5
    1. Leggio, Luciano. 2. Riina, Salvatore. 3. Provenzano,
Bernardo, 1933– 4. Mafia—Italy—Sicily—History. I. Title.
HV6453.I82L36 2009
364.1092'2458—dc22

                                        2009006514

First published in Great Britain by Hodder & Stoughton,
an Hachette Livre UK company

First U.S. Edition: July 2009

10 9 8 7 6 5 4 3 2 1

To Sébastien

Contents

Prologue:

23 May 1992

Shortly after 4 p.m. on 23 May 1992, a Saturday, Italy's anti-mafia hero Judge Giovanni Falcone, his wife Francesca and an escort of bodyguards slice their way through Rome's ever-chaotic traffic. Blue warning lights flashing and sirens blaring, the motorcade skirts the Colosseum, decaying monument to man's cruelty, before heading south, bound for the airport and the city where Falcone was born – the Sicilian capital Palermo.

After scoring countless victories as a public prosecutor in Palermo – the biggest a trial which inflicted 19 life sentences and 2,665 years behind bars on no fewer than 338 mafiosi – the stout, mustachioed Falcone had moved to Rome a year earlier to take up the job of director of penal affairs at the justice ministry. With typical determination, the workaholic 53-year-old judge set up two new bodies that would coordinate both police and judicial investigations into the brotherhood across Italy. This finally gave the state the tools to tackle the spread of organised crime – assuming it wanted to do so.

But there is something spoiling Falcone's latest success. Now, as so many times in his career, the envy of his colleagues and the hostility of those who prefer to quietly ignore the mafia is causing him concern. His nerves are on edge. A sniping campaign has accused him of creating the new office of national anti-mafia prosecutor, known in the press as a 'super-prosecutor', simply so that he can fill it. A few days earlier, the judge had joked bitterly about his enemies' attacks, telling a colleague: 'After all, for someone like me who knows he's going to be killed, what do you think I care about being a super-prosecutor?'

Joking about his own death was typical of Falcone, who had a fatalistic attitude deep-rooted in Sicilians. One of Italy's most protected men – a helicopter often shadowed his motorcade – Falcone had twice been the target of assassination so far. The mafia first sent a gunman to shoot him in prison and when that failed it placed a bomb in a bag by his seaside villa; both attempts were discovered just in time. Asked in his bunker-like office in Rome seven months earlier about the constant risks he ran, Falcone had told the author matter-of-factly: 'Those who are doing something they believe is useful to society are more exposed than others, for many reasons – because of the inertia, cowardice and ignorance of others. And they are murdered – inexorably. That's all there is to it.'

As his motorcade races through the ancient walls of the Eternal City, Falcone and his wife have something to look forward to; Francesca, whose work as a judge prevented her moving to Rome with her husband, has just obtained a transfer to the city. The couple will soon be living together again and this is one of the last times Falcone will have to make a weekend trip to Sicily.

At 4.30 p.m., Falcone calls Giuseppe Costanza, his driver in Palermo, to warn him of his arrival. Costanza heads to Falcone's old home there to fetch the judge's armour-plated car. Half an hour later, a jet operated by the SISDE military intelligence service takes off from Rome's Ciampino airport on a secret, unscheduled flight carrying Falcone and Francesca to Palermo.

More than 300 miles to the south, in Palermo, a clan boss and wealthy businessman, the owner of a meat-processing company, a chain of restaurants and a butcher's shop, is enjoying a drink at Ciro's Bar on a broad, busy avenue opposite Falcone's block of flats. At about 4.45 p.m., the boss spots a white car he instantly recognises, an armour-plated Fiat Croma belonging to Falcone, leaving the garage opposite.

The boss guesses the car is headed for Palermo's airport to fetch Falcone and rushes to his butcher's shop nearby. His son is serving customers and the boss tells him urgently: 'Get moving, the car has gone, follow it!' Jumping on his Vespa scooter, the son catches up with Falcone's car and follows it to the access road to the motorway leading to the airport.

From then on, every element in an elaborate plan orchestrated by the mafia's godfather Salvatore Riina, head of the Corleonese crime family, clicks neatly into place, one by one.

The jet carrying Falcone touches down at Palermo's Punta Raisi airport a few yards from the Mediterranean coast at 5.43 p.m. Awaiting him and his wife on the runway are three armour-plated cars, their engines running, and six police bodyguards clutching their guns under their jackets. Falcone asks Costanza to let him drive his car and Costanza hands the keys over. Falcone likes to drive himself when he is with Francesca – snatching what he can of normal life. Francesca gets into the front passenger seat, Costanza in the back. The convoy speeds away, Falcone's car in the middle.

A lookout is stationed at the airport gate reserved for the police. He is under strict instructions from the chubby, friendly faced boss Giovanni Brusca, an expert at dissolving the bodies of victims in sulphuric acid. 'You must look inside Falcone's car. We have to be sure it isn't someone else inside. We can't screw things up. You must see him,' Brusca has told him. The lookout is concentrating so hard on obeying orders that he recognises Falcone sitting in the driver's seat as the car passes through the gate, but doesn't notice Francesca or the driver in the back – not that this is to make any difference. At 5.48 p.m. he calls an accomplice, Gioacchino La Barbera, to give a short, pre-arranged signal: 'Everything OK.'

One minute later, La Barbera calls another boss, Antonino Gioè, who is chain-smoking nervously as he watches a stretch of the motorway from a vantage point on a hillside three miles from the airport. At Gioè's side is Brusca himself, mastermind of the assassination plan, a remote control of the kind used by children to fly model aeroplanes in his hands. The simple device operates a bomb hidden in a narrow drain pipe that runs under the motorway –

some 770 pounds of explosives packed into 13 metal drums. The two mafiosi stand by an almond tree in flower. They have lopped a branch off another to give themselves a clear view of the motorway. They take turns to sit on a stool and peer through a telescope.

Gioè chats with La Barbera on a mobile phone. As they talk, La Barbera drives down a road which runs parallel to the motorway, shadowing Falcone's convoy. He worries that the call may be intercepted, so he chats about nothing in particular, jumping from one topic to another.

He can see the convoy so sharply he can make out the bodyguards holding their machine-guns at the ready.

From the back seat, Falcone's driver Costanza asks the judge when he will want him again.

'Monday morning,' Falcone replies.

'So, when we get to your flat, could you please give me my car keys so that on Monday morning I can get the car?' Costanza asks.

To his amazement, Falcone abruptly extracts the keys from the ignition and hands them to him. 'What are you doing? We're going to get killed!' Costanza rebukes Falcone as he feels the car, the gear still in fourth, slow down.

Falcone had apparently wanted to swap his bunch of keys, which included those for his flat, with Costanza's set there and then. Falcone turns towards Costanza, meeting Francesca's gaze as he does so. 'I'm sorry,' he says. 'I'm sorry.'

Still shadowing the convoy, La Barbera notices it is travelling at 50 m.p.h. – half the speed the death squad is expecting – and keeps his phone conversation going. He hopes that the two men on the hillside will realise from the length of the chat that the convoy is not approaching as fast as they expected.

'What are you up to this evening?' La Barbera asks.

'Nothing. If you're free we could go and have a pizza,' Gioè replies as he stares through the telescope.

'OK,' La Barbera says.

Shortly afterwards, La Barbera says suddenly: 'We'll talk later, *ciao*.' The five-minute call ends abruptly at 5.54 p.m.

Gioè understands. He can see the convoy nearing the bomb.

Brusca's plan is to flick the switch on the remote control as soon as he sees Falcone's car reach a fridge dumped on the edge of the motorway which he has chosen as a marker. Brusca hasn't yet seen the car when he hears Gioè urge him: '*Vai* (Go)!'

Brusca doesn't move.

'*Vai!*' Gioè repeats.

Brusca still doesn't move. He feels as if he's been embalmed, like an Egyptian mummy. A moment later, Brusca sees Falcone's white Croma at last and in that instant he realises to his surprise that the car has slowed down. It reaches the fridge but Brusca hesitates an instant.

'*Vai!*' Gioè urges a third and last time.

Brusca flicks the switch.

1

Corleone

1905–1963

Dr Michele Navarra, 'Our Father'

A grey-roofed town sunk in the mountains and desert-like plains south of Palermo, Corleone cowers as if in fear of being crushed by a gigantic black stone crag which falls sheer to the roofs of the dirty stone houses beneath it. An abandoned prison, built originally as a fortress, and a few straggly crows squat on top of the crag. A Saracen lookout tower is perched on another rocky outcrop, a relic from the time when the town was an important strategic point dominating the road from the Sicilian capital Palermo to the island's southern coast. Wedged into a hillside, the steep streets are as narrow and twisted as entrails, regularly turned into furnaces by the hot, humid *scirocco* wind blowing from the Sahara.

In his classic novel *The Leopard*, Giuseppe Tomasi di Lampedusa described the harsh environment, which peasants like those of Corleone depended upon for a living: 'this landscape which knows no mean between sensuous sag and hellish drought; which is never petty, never ordinary, never relaxed, as a country made for rational beings to live in should be ... this climate which inflicts us with six feverish months at a temperature of 104°'.

In Corleone, the landscape boasts another negative feature: it has much to recommend it to criminals. The thick Ficuzza wood nearby, once the hunting ground of Bourbon kings and ideal hiding-place for cattle-rustlers, has long been popular with those in need of a secluded spot to bury the bodies of their victims. Overlooking Corleone, the 5,300-foot high Rocca Busambra mountain, dotted with limestone caves and narrow gorges, promises safe refuge to fugitives.

Corleone, whose name is believed to derive from *Kurliyun* (Lionheart), an Arab fighter who conquered it in AD 840, has a proud tradition of standing up for its rights, and violently so; in the Sicilian Vespers of 1282, when the island rebelled against the French occupiers, Corleone killed more of the invaders than any other nearby town and earned the nickname 'the fiery one'. One of the figures most venerated by the town's 14,000 inhabitants is Saint Bernard, revered not just for his holiness but for his sword-wielding past. A seventeenth-century cobbler, he became Sicily's most skilled swordsman, defending the poor and the womenfolk against rich aristocrats whom he challenged to duels, before becoming a Capuchin monk and spending the rest of his life repenting the blood he had spilt.

The Catholic faith has always played an important role in the life of the town which once boasted some 60 churches and a dozen convents, and saw an incredible 74 saints paraded through the streets on the feast day of the Holy Sacrament. The crowds of the faithful walking behind each saint, borne shoulder-high, were so large that the dean and the mayor drew up in advance the order in which the saints were to be paraded and appointed a priest to regulate this holy traffic.

It's no coincidence that the townspeople called Don Michele Navarra, the founding father of the Corleonese clan which was to overwhelm the mafia like no other in its history, '*U Patri Nostru*' (Our Father) – just the way they referred to God. Like a deity the doctor, a short, corpulent figure with a bull-like neck and a broad, apparently kindly face, had the power of both life and death over every single one of them.

When Navarra was born in 1905, one of a land surveyor's eight children, life in Corleone hadn't changed for decades, even for centuries in many respects. His family was considered of a high social standing in a town of mainly peasants, shepherds and day-labourers. Poverty was so endemic that labourers who could boast ownership of not one but two mules were known as '*i borgesi*' – 'the bourgeois'. Most peasants lived in the same ground-floor room as their animals along with the odd pig or hen, often with only a curtain to separate them, allowing the smell of human sweat to mingle freely with the stench of the animals. Families cooked spaghetti and soup made from wild herbs in the bucket of water they also used to wash their feet. A goat was allowed to roam freely through the house as if it were a holy animal because its milk saved the children from dying of tuberculosis.

At dawn, long lines of men on foot or riding on their mules would thread their way out of Corleone along roads of clayey, light brown earth, often travelling for two or three hours in the rugged landscape until they reached a rocky holding of wheat, vines or olives of at most four of five hectares spread among the yellow hills which turned dark brown when the peasants set fire to the common meadow grass. In the evenings the procession of men and mules would return home in time for the *Ave Maria* prayer, the exhausted peasants stopping at watering places at the entrances to the town so that the animals could drink while the dirt was washed off their legs and hooves.

Navarra was considered privileged from birth not just because of his father's position, but also because of his family's links to a secret criminal association in Corleone. His uncle was a member of the Fratuzzi ('the Brothers'), a deceptively friendly label for the town's first mafiosi. First heard of in the early nineteenth century, the Fratuzzi's membership included authoritarian over-seers who managed the estates of absentee landowners who preferred to live in Palermo 22 miles to the north. Armed private militiamen, who enforced order on the estates and didn't hesi-tate to use violence, also became part of the Fratuzzi.

Navarra's uncle was among those who took part in an affili-ation ritual conducted in the presence of the association's bosses. With a dagger, a small incision was made on the new recruit's lower lip, his blood dripping onto a piece of paper on which a skull had been drawn. The recruit then took the membership oath, pledging fidelity to the association. Members made them-selves known to each other either with a password, or by touching the incisors in their upper jaw as if they had toothache. Such rituals would be quaint were it not for the misery the Fratuzzi inflicted on the town. They stole cattle, controlled the hiring of farmworkers and collected extortion money from landowners and shopkeepers in return for supposed 'protection'. Kidnapping and arson were common punishments for anyone who dared to rebel.

When and how, if at all, the Fratuzzi came to be part of the Sicilian mafia, itself born around 1860, remains a mystery. Even the origin of the word 'mafia' remains obscure. Some believe its roots lie in the Arab domination of Sicily from 827 to 1061 and the Arabic word *mahias* (daring) or *Ma àfir* (the name of a Saracen tribe). In 1658, a witch mentioned in an official Palermo document was nicknamed *Maffia*, meaning she had a fiery character. In 1863 Palermitans flocked to the Sant'Anna Theatre to see a new comedy, *I mafiusi di La Vicaria* ('The mafiosi of Vicaria Prison'), set in the city's jail and portraying members of a secret association – it was never named in the play – as virtually ruling the prison.

Two years later, Marquis Filippo Antonio Gualtiero, the government's envoy to Palermo, described 'the so-called Maffia or criminal association' as 'a large and long-standing sore'. From then on, the word was in common usage and in 1875 two Tuscan sociologists carried out the first-ever investigation into the society. One of them, Leopoldo Franchetti, was at first stunned by the beauty of the Sicilian landscape but stories of terrible violence made him feel 'everything change around him little by little. The colours change, the appearance of things is transformed . . . After a number of such stories, all that scent of orange and lemon blossom begins to smell of corpses.'

Navarra was only ten years old when his uncle is believed to have murdered, in 1915, the first local hero to have dared to take on the mafia. Corleone has given birth to a series of such courageous figures – more than any other Sicilian town of similar size – as if in proportion to the influence of its mafiosi. Bernardino Verro was a Socialist founder of the Sicilian peasants' movement which staged strikes and symbolic occupations of the land in an attempt to break the landowners' hold. His courage and better judgement failed him temporarily in 1893 when he allowed the Fratuzzi to persuade him that enemies were intent on killing him. Believing that the association would save his life if he agreed to join them he submitted to the lip-pricking initiation ritual.

It was a great coup for the Fratuzzi, anxious to preserve the established order which suited them well, and intent on crushing the rebellious peasant movements. But the coup soon backfired when Verro saw the methods they used. He promptly turned his back on the association and later described both the way it functioned and the secret ritual. Verro was the first to expose the mafia as a secret organisation with its own set of rules. Speaking to a crowd in a Corleone piazza, he courageously accused the mafiosi of turning it into 'the most wretched of Sicilian towns'. Triumphantly elected mayor, he was murdered one year later.

Those accused of his murder, among them Navarra's father, were all acquitted. Such courtroom victories were to become a triumphant trademark of the Fratuzzi's heirs – the clan of the Corleonesi.

Navarra's parents appear to have done what they could to discourage their son from following in his uncle's footsteps. They ensured he got a good schooling in Corleone before sending him to Palermo to study medicine. After passing his exams, Navarra soon had himself appointed district doctor for Corleone, at a time when the Fascist regime of Benito Mussolini was making the fight against malaria and tuberculosis a priority. A decree ordered that all public offices and schools be equipped with spittoons but, because it was short of funds, the town hall could afford only seven.

The young doctor returned to Corleone in time to witness another, much more ambitious campaign launched by Mussolini. Unable to tolerate any obstacle to his authority – the mafia was both a state within a state and a challenge to his totalitarian vision – the dictator pledged to rid Sicily of it once and for all. 'We must no longer tolerate that a few hundred blackguards overwhelm, impoverish and harm a magnificient people like yours,' he thundered during a short visit to Sicily.

Mussolini picked as his anti-mafia supremo Cesare Mori, known as 'the Iron Prefect' (a prefect is a government envoy) because of his brutal methods. When he galloped through the countryside hunting down bandits, he liked to shoot a few dead himself. He promised to eradicate the mafia 'as a surgeon penetrates the flesh with fire and steel, until he cauterises the pus sacks of the bubonic plague'. At dawn five days before Christmas 1926, Mori spoilt Corleone's festivities by sending police to seal off the town and hunt down 150 suspects. Lists of names in hand and led by an enthusiastic municipal police chief, Mori's squads knocked on the doors of the mafiosi. When they found their man, handcuffs were clamped on his wrists and the squad chief pronounced the ritual formula: 'By order of His Excellency the Prefect Cesare Mori, I declare you under arrest!'

In a display typical of 'the Iron Prefect', the column of prisoners, handcuffed and in chains, was paraded down the main street on their way to prison in Palermo. The display was not as impressive as Mori would have wished. The police had failed to find more than half those named on their lists. Many mafiosi had fled to hide in the mountains, and as news of Mori's exploits spread some had even chosen to emigrate as far as America; one murderer, who had more experience of death than most of his new compatriots, set up a lucrative funeral parlour.

Throughout Sicily, Mori exploited the mafiosi's so-called 'code of honour' to put pressure on prisoners to make them confess their crimes and to persuade fugitives to turn themselves in. Mori sent police squads to squat the mafiosi's homes, which in the absence of the head of the household were often inhabited only by women and children. The squads would often stay until the mafioso, exasperated by the threat to his honour implicit in the enforced promiscuity between his woman and the policemen, confessed or gave himself up. Prisoners were tortured, forced to drink jugfuls of salted water, beaten with coshes or whipped, hit repeatedly on the testicles or given electric shocks. The women of suspects who had gone into hiding were raped.

None of this appears to have shaken Dr Navarra's resolve to join the mafia. What exactly persuaded a young, small-town doctor with a safe, comfortable future ahead of him to take such a step – a medical career spent saving lives could not contrast more sharply with a criminal one spent taking them? Judging by his later actions one likely explanation is that Navarra's main ambition was power. And in Corleone, the mafia was the fast track to power. Discreetly at first and then with increasing self-assurance, Navarra started to lobby for influence among the criminal organisation's local bosses, exploiting his uncle's connections.

In an early display of unprincipled cunning, Navarra went to the Fascist authorities to inform on several bosses and 'soldiers' (low-ranking members of the mafia) in nearby towns. This not only cleared the field of potential rivals but also allowed him to ingratiate himself with ruling politicians. To build himself a force of his own, Navarra formed his own clan, recruiting petty criminals and ex-convicts who had slipped through Mussolini's net.

Plotting a criminal career didn't stop Navarra carrying out his more worthy duties at his surgery with professionalism and courtesy. He granted his patients many favours, readily referring them for a bed in a Palermo clinic or even waiving his fees. He willingly honoured families by acting as godfather at their children's baptisms and confirmations. Exploiting to the full the social prestige which his profession carried in a town as small and as poor as Corleone, he also made sure he had friends in the town hall and in the clergy, the latter always a force to reckon with there.

The doctor's attentions all had a price. Although he never said so in so many words, everyone knew he expected unwavering allegiance in exchange for his favours. He had understood early on that to gain power inside the mafia, he needed the support – or at least the tacit backing – not only of its members but also of outsiders, preferably the notables of the town. Every walk Navarra took through town became a yardstick of his increasing influence; as he paced the clean high street or the smaller alleys where children chased each other barefoot among smears of mule-dung and pig-droppings, only the animals ignored him. Acquaintances showed him their respect, bowing their heads before bending to kiss his ring. People began to say of him that he could *sciusciare* (blow), which in the local dialect meant he radiated so much ominous authority that the very air seemed to move in his presence – a quality usually only attributed to a mafioso.

Despite Navarra's treacherous contribution to Mussolini's onslaught, the Corleone mafia soon recovered. Thanks to an amnesty and a decree commuting their sentences, many mafiosi returned home from prison and from the islands to which they had been exiled. When Mussolini himself visited Corleone on a trip to Sicily in 1937, the police urged the local Fascist party secretary to throw a few bosses back into jail at least for the day of the visit. The request was rejected and the mafiosi, on horse-back, formed part of a welcoming party which escorted the dictator down the main street. Mussolini had repeatedly boasted that he had vanquished the mafia, but in Corleone the show of protection staged by the bosses demonstrated he had done no such thing. Corleone was theirs, and he was their guest.

Across Sicily, Mori's scalpel proved to have a blunt edge. Although he made thousands of arrests, these were mostly of low-ranking criminals. 'The Iron Prefect' realised that he had to aim higher and purge the Sicilian establishment of the mafia's friends. As he wrote in his memoirs: 'The mafia is an old whore who likes to rub herself ceremoniously and submissively against the authorities, trying to flatter, deceive and lull them into a false sense of security.' But when Mori started to pursue politicians and aristocrats, Mussolini sent him a terse telegram recalling him and transferred him to northern Italy – the dictator had no wish to launch an attack on his own party's blackshirts.

The 460,000 Anglo-American troops who liberated Sicily in 1943 – in what the US General George S. Patton proudly called 'the shortest Blitzkrieg in history' – are the latest in the island's bewilderingly long list of invaders through the centuries. They were given an exceptionally warm welcome. For once, Sicilians lined the streets to cheer, applaud and hug the foreign troops. The largest island in the Mediterranean and a stepping-stone between Europe and Africa, between the West and the Middle East, Sicily has played mostly unwilling host to Phoenicians, Greeks, Carthaginians, Romans, Vandals, Arabs, Normans, Spaniards, Bourbons and, in the Second World War, to German forces.

Most of them ruled the island from abroad and without consideration for the interests of the islanders, bartering it in exchange for other lands. The Italian author Luigi Barzini described how the legacy of these foreign occupations shaped what he called 'a philosophy of life . . . a moral code' among all Sicilians – although it would be fairer to say that such a stark outlook applies only to a certain number of them:

> They are taught in the cradle, or are born already knowing, that they must aid each other, side with their friends and fight the common enemies even when the friends are wrong and the enemies are right; each must defend his dignity at all costs and never allow the smallest slights and insults to go unavenged; they must keep secrets, and always beware of official authorities and laws.

The chaotic aftermath of the liberation of Sicily proved Mussolini's downfall – he was toppled by his own party – and Dr Navarra's golden opportunity. As in many towns across Sicily, the first move of the Allied military government (AMGOT) in Corleone was to appoint a mafioso of the pre-Fascist era as deputy-mayor and two more mafiosi as town councillors. In their anxiety to find anti Fascists to appoint to positions of power, and with a devastating lack of foresight and local knowledge, the liberators overlooked mafia connections. Across the island, 90 per cent of the 352 new mayors named by the Allies were either mafiosi or politicians close to the Separatist movement, closely linked to the mafia.

Lord Rennel, the head of AMGOT, reported back to London with only a touch of regret: 'I fear that in their enthusiasm to remove the Fascist *podestà* (mayors) and the municipal officials of rural towns, my officers, in some cases out of ignorance of local society, have chosen a number of mafia bosses or have authorised such persons to propose docile substitutes ready to obey them.' This cancelled the little impact which Mussolini's campaign had had on the mafia and catapulted the organisation into the heart of the state system. Perhaps reflecting this new dawn, mafiosi began to refer to their secret society as Cosa Nostra ('Our Thing'). Sicily has suffered from the consequences of AMGOT's actions ever since.

Navarra lacked any anti Fascist credentials, but he boasted privileged relations with the liberators thanks to his cousin Angelo Di Carlo, a mafioso who had been forced to flee Corleone when the Fascist police squad swept into town. Di Carlo had fled to America where he joined both the Marines and the American Cosa Nostra. Promoted to the rank of captain in the former, he built himself a reputation as one of the notorious gangster Charles 'Lucky' Luciano's most reliable killers. He forged ties with the Office of Strategic Services (the OSS, precursor of the CIA) to whom he pledged that, on his return to Corleone, he would ensure a peaceful transition from Fascism to liberation.

Back in Corleone, Di Carlo arranged for Navarra to meet a senior AMGOT official with the result that the doctor, despite any appropriate qualifications, was granted the exclusive right to all Allied military vehicles abandoned in Sicily. With road and rail transport across the island still suffering from the bombings and disruption of the war, Navarra lost no time in using Allied vehicles to set up a regional bus service which his brother headed. It is still in operation today, under the name AST, and is used by both Sicilians and tourists.

Shortly after the war's end, the Corleone boss Calogero Lo Bue died of natural causes in his bed. The battle for his succession pitted Navarra against Vincenzo Collura, who had emigrated in the 1920s to America where he had become close to two leading Italo-American gangsters, acting as best man at the wedding of Frank 'Three Fingers' Coppola and as godfather at the baptism of a child of Joe 'Olive Oil King' Profaci. Planning his return to Sicily following the boss's death, Collura lobbied friends to win support for his bid to succeed him. When he boarded the ship taking him home, Collura could be forgiven for believing that with such illustrious American sponsors, Corleone would fall into his hands with little effort.

But on his return in 1944 Collura found himself wrong-footed immediately by Navarra. The doctor moved quickly to summon influential mafiosi to his house before his opponent could build up a power base. Navarra's influence had grown so much that it was at his elegant home, on a piazza in the historic centre of the newly liberated Corleone, that the rebirth of the local clan was organised. Navarra won enough support to be appointed the new boss, at the same time seeking to placate the defeated Collura by putting him in charge of a section of the town, flanked uncomfortably by lieutenants loyal to the doctor. Collura accepted but made little effort to hide his resentment. Navarra didn't react; he would deal with that problem later.

Navarra had pulled off quite a feat. A provincial doctor just turning 40 and little known beyond his home town, he had managed to outwit his rivals and become a clan chief. His appointment marked not only a personal triumph, it also heralded the birth of what was to become known, and feared, as the Corleonese family.

Navarra's rule was a bloody one. In just four years, from 1944 to 1948, a total of 153 people were murdered in Corleone; an atmosphere of fear spread through the town and it was often said that 'people get murdered for no reason at all'. Often it was simply because the victim stood in Navarra's way, as in the case of the director of the local hospital. Navarra confided to his men that he wanted the job, saying with a sly smile: 'We'll find a solution . . .' Shortly afterwards, the director was murdered with a volley of buckshot. When investigators suspected him, Navarra dismissed the victim as a Don Giovanni, an incorrigible woman-iser. 'Everyone knew that, sooner or later, someone would make him pay for it,' he remarked before stepping into his dead colleague's shoes.

Navarra was always careful to keep his own hands as clean as possible, delegating to his henchmen crimes such as armed robbery, extortion and murder. One of their victims was the municipal policeman who had led Mussolini's squad to the mafiosi's houses. This vendetta took place on a piazza in the heart of town. Three shotgun bullets were fired into the man's stomach. As with most of the murders commissioned by Navarra, it proved impossible to identify the killers. Navarra was fond of joking that such deaths were due to 'a kick from a mule'.

Word soon spread of the doctor's criminal standing but his growing number of patients saw no change in his irreproachable bedside manner. Clearly not short of money, he went so far as to have many cared for in private clinics at his own expense. He was always ready to recommend an acquaintance for a job, to meet the cost of a lawyer for a mafioso who could not afford one, or even to find someone willing to lie in court to let a suspect off the hook.

What interested Navarra above all was not the money he earned from either his work or his crimes, but power. He owned only part of the house in which he lived and had inherited some modestly sized plots of land from his father. In contrast, he collected posts of responsibility in the community and beyond with passion. Apart from his post as director of the local hospital, he was also president of the local landowners' association and chief medical consultant to a national health insurance scheme – in which he set a record for the high number of patients under his responsibility – to the state railways, to an anti-tuberculosis centre, and to a health insurance scheme for small farmers. Not that all this satisfied him. When, despite all his influence, he failed to obtain the post of director of a second, new hospital in Corleone, Navarra took it as an affront to his authority and ensured that for as long as he lived, the hospital never opened its doors.

The doctor's fascination with power naturally led him to take more than a passing interest in politics but he revealed himself to be an unashamed opportunist. He backed, in turn, a party which advocated independence for Sicily, then the Liberals and lastly the Christian Democrats. To enable his henchmen to follow voters into the polling booth where they would make sure the locals cast the right ballot, Navarra signed hundreds of certificates declaring voters blind. When his Communist opponents discovered the scam and denounced him, a furious Navarra stormed off arm-in-arm with his wife to the polling station where he waved in the air a certificate he had signed himself declaring she was partially blind. He then escorted his spouse into a voting booth. Everyone knew she had perfect vision, but no one dared stop him. In exchange for such unorthodox canvassing tactics, relatives of mafiosi were given various positions of influence in local authorities, while politicians with underworld links were elected to the regional parliament.

Luciano Leggio

Luciano Leggio was by far the most faithful and promising of Navarra's young lieutenants. Born to an impoverished peasant family, Leggio was of more humble stock than the doctor. His parents were too poor to feed their ten sons and daughters and sent him to a seminary to train for the priesthood but this plan quickly collapsed when he refused to study. He dropped out of school at the age of nine. A few years later, he was to make up for this by threatening a schoolteacher with a gun and forcing her to teach him to read and write. Much of his religious teaching did stay with him, however; he was said to pray, on his knees, every evening before a crucifix and to list the 'injustices' he felt himself a victim to.

With a round, flabby face, full lips and a scornful stare, Leggio was referred to – only when safely out of hearing – as 'the Grain of Fire' because of his short temper or 'the Cripple' due to a slight limp. He suffered from Pott's disease, a tuberculosis of the spine which gave him back pain, fever and heavy sweats at night. Both during and after the war, Leggio earned far more than he would have done as a priest. As he testified in court later: 'How did I accumulate my fortune? I did the black market. Imagine! You could buy 200 pounds of grain from the Farm Board for 2,000–2,500 lire and sell it on the black market for 15,000.'

Leggio probably first came to Dr Navarra's attention at the age of 19 in 1944 when country wardens caught him red-handed stealing sheaves of wheat after the harvest and loading them onto mules with the help of an accomplice. When the wardens arrested the two thieves, Leggio made no show of resistance. But his eyes flashed with fury when one gave him a few kicks in the back-side for good measure. He stared hard at the wardens' faces, as if to impress them on his mind. After three months in jail, he was sentenced to a year and four months, but the sentence was suspended and he was released. Bent on revenge, Leggio recruited the help of Giovanni Pasqua, a soldier who lived next door to one of the wardens. 'Listen, my friend,' Leggio told him, 'the cops who arrested me mustn't get away with it. Starting with your neighbour, that Calogero Comaianni.'

One evening in March of the following year, the 45-year-old Comaianni was walking towards his home on the eastern edge of town, in the shadow of the crag that dominates Corleone, when he noticed two men following some way behind him. They were wearing blue woollen cloaks with hoods drawn over their heads. The sight was enough to unnerve him; it was popular knowledge that such cloaks were often used to hide a rifle. Comaianni walked faster, and so did the two men. He managed to reach his home before they could catch up with him. He told his wife Maddalena about the incident, telling her he thought he recognised one of the men as their neighbour Pasqua. 'What could anyone want with me?' he wondered aloud. 'I've never done anything wrong, only my duty.'

Early the next morning, Holy Friday, Comaianni cleared the ground-floor stable where he kept his horse – he, his wife and their five children slept on the floor above – and walked out to throw away the horse's dung in a nearby rubbish tip. He suddenly realised the same hooded figures as the previous evening were waiting for him. Comaianni looked around him, saw an open door and rushed towards it, only to have it slammed in his face. He turned, raced towards his home and had just managed to knock on the door when one of the two gunmen shot him twice. The door opened, and despite his wounds Comaianni managed to throw himself through it and drag himself up the first steps of the staircase. He then turned to face the gunmen. Recognising his neighbour, he shouted: 'Giovanni, what are you doing?' But the killers opened fire again and shot him dead. The oldest of

Comaianni's five children, in his early twenties, raced to fetch a rifle but his mother Maddalena stopped him and the gunmen fled.

Cradling her dead husband in her arms, Maddalena shouted to the neighbours, who were only now daring to approach, that she had recognised both the murderers – Giovanni Pasqua and Luciano Leggio. This was a rare example of defiance of *omertà*, the mafia-enforced law of silence; a Sicilian proverb says, 'He who is blind, deaf and keeps quiet will live a hundred years in peace.' Maddalena repeated her accusations to the police but the judicial system gave no weight whatsoever to a widow's evidence and the case was dropped.

It is likely Leggio joined the mafia at this time. Candidates for recruitment are routinely tested first and Leggio had shown his mettle. The initiation ritual has been set in stone for decades and would have seen Navarra himself preside over Leggio's admission and reveal to him the so-called 'code of honour' which mafiosi claim is based on traditional Sicilian values such as honour, family ties and friendship and which is supposed to govern their lives:

> Hear the commandments of Cosa Nostra. You will not touch the women of other men of honour. You will not steal, nor will you exploit prostitution. You will not kill other men of honour save in cases of absolute necessity. You will never speak of the affairs of Cosa Nostra in front of strangers, nor will you introduce yourself on your own to other men of honour.

This said, the boss then pricks the index finger of the recruit's hand with a thorn from an orange tree, his blood staining a paper image of the Virgin Mary at the Annunciation, the secret society's patron saint. The image is set alight and dropped into the recruit's cupped hands who, as he shifts the burning image from hand to hand, swears: 'As paper I burn you, as saint I adore you, just as this paper burns must my flesh burn if I betray Cosa Nostra.' The ritual made Leggio a low-ranking soldier of the organisation but, as Judge Falcone remarked, such soldiers 'are in fact generals. Or rather cardinals of a church which is much less indulgent than the Catholic Church.'

Leggio's first allegiance as a soldier was to his crime family in Corleone. At the base of the highly structured mafia pyramid, groups of ten or more soldiers – or 'men of honour' as they like to call themselves – are commanded by a *capodecina* (head of ten) who in turn answers to the family's elected head. Three or more neighbouring families are headed by a *capomandamento* (district boss), among whom the rulers of the organisation are chosen. A supergrass gave a rare glimpse of what becoming one of the 5,000 or so sworn members of the brotherhood must have meant to an otherwise-common criminal like Leggio:

> You must forgive me for this distinction I make between the mafia and common crime, but it's important to me. It's impor-tant to every mafioso. We are mafiosi, the others are just the rabble. We are men of honour. And not so much because we have sworn an oath, but because we are the elite of crime. We are very much superior to common criminals. We are the worst of all!

Five years after the death of the warden who had seized Leggio, the police arrested his accomplice Pasqua and obtained a confes-sion from him. 'Leggio and I hid not far from Comaianni's house to wait for him,' Pasqua said. 'As soon as he appeared we shot him. We'd already tried to do it the evening before.' Leggio was absolutely determined to avenge his arrest and had insisted on the killing. The thief arrested along with Leggio for stealing wheat confirmed: 'Leggio refused to let his mind rest and talked all the time about vendetta. He cursed and swore that he would make those bastards pay.'

When the case came to court, Pasqua abruptly withdrew his confession and accused the police of torturing him; the court acquitted both Leggio and Pasqua for lack of evidence. The verdict was upheld by an appeals court; the judges ruled that Maddalena's evidence was 'incoherent' and Pasqua's confession 'the fruit of intimidation'. Besides, the judges added, the murder took place too long after Leggio's arrest – eight months – to indicate a link between the two events. On hearing the verdict, the murdered man's widow Maddalena said only: 'They've killed my Calogero a second time.'

For the first time, the Corleonesi had defied and vanquished Italian justice, a feat they were to repeat again and again in the decades that followed. Leggio's victory won him much prestige in Corleone. He had not only proved that 'he wouldn't let a fly walk on his nose' – an old peasant saying used to describe a man worthy of respect, who would let no one walk all over him. In the eyes of many, he achieved the status of an untouchable.

Leggio quickly took advantage of this to get himself a job. After picking an estate he fancied and shooting its overseer from behind, Leggio went to see the landlord and told him: 'I will take the place of the dear departed.' No objection was raised – this method of brutal but instant promotion had been tried and tested by Navarra – and Leggio became the youngest overseer in all Sicily. Leggio was one of Navarra's ten underbosses and soldiers deployed as militiamen in as many estates, including the Ficuzza wood where bandits and mafiosi alike buried their victims, to ensure the doctor controlled not only the town but also the biggest estates surrounding it.

Navarra let it be known that Leggio was *cosa sua personale* (his own personal thing) – an echo of the name Cosa Nostra (Our Thing). Leggio would patrol the estate on horseback, a riding whip in his hand and a hunting rifle slung over his shoulder. His task was one that the mafia had fulfilled since its birth in the previous century: to guard the property of wealthy landowners, resorting to violence if necessary in the battle to stamp out any peasant demands for the right to own the land they worked on.

This battle to preserve the existing order was soon to come to a head in Corleone, pitting the doctor and his most ruthless henchman against a young, idealistic Resistance veteran.

Placido Rizzotto, 'the Northern Wind'

Like Dr Navarra, the slightly built Placido Rizzotto came from a mafia family. But unlike the doctor, Rizzotto was a rebel and never thought of following his father, an estate guard who had been jailed as a mafioso under Mussolini when the boy was just 11 years old, into the brotherhood. During the war, the semi-literate Rizzotto was forced to serve in the Fascist army but when Italy surrendered on 8 September 1943 after the fall of Sicily, he threw away his soldier's uniform and joined partisans waging a guerrilla war against Nazi forces in the Alps in the north-east. From the other young men who made up the Garibaldi Brigade, with their red handkerchiefs tied around their necks, he learnt how to cope with cold and hunger, and joined in long discussions of the ideals of liberty and equality.

When he returned to Corleone in 1945, his new fervent belief in revolutionary ideas earned him the nickname of 'the Northern Wind'. Rizzotto denounced the mafia's cattle-rustling and taught peasants not to bow their heads before great, titled landowners. He urged the peasants to take advantage of new decrees just passed by the government of national unity in Rome, granting peasant cooperatives the right to obtain concessions on land which their owners had failed to cultivate.

In a challenge not only to the landowners but also to the mafiosi who managed and guarded their estates, Rizzotto staged provocative occupations of the land. At dawn, Corleone saw a new, more joyful procession than the decades-old march of peasants and mules heading out to work distant patches of land. Often riding in the brightly coloured Sicilian carts still glimpsed today, peasants holding red flags aloft would follow Rizzotto, threading their way across the hills on their way to the neglected estate they had chosen for their protest. Once there, they would stick red flags into the earth to claim the land, if only symbolically. Rizzotto, a skilled speaker who could fire his listeners with enthusiasm, would then address them, telling them that their aim was to destroy once and for all a system that had done nothing but exploit them since ancient Roman times. This was their chance, he urged; since this estate was not being cultivated, they must come forward and claim it for themselves because they knew how to work it better than anyone.

Navarra sought to crush such protests while they were still in their infancy. On one estate, guards shot at the peasants with their rifles, and that night more shots were fired at the home of the Communist party secretary. In the worst example of such violence, on 1 May 1947, the legendary bandit Salvatore Giuliano and his men opened fire on peasants at Portella della Ginestra north of Corleone, killing 11 and wounding 27. In Corleone, Leggio indulged in violent reprisals against peasants; hundreds of mules and donkeys had their throats slit, and barns and straw stacks were destroyed by fire. No one came forward to report him to the police.

Rizzotto pressed on regardless. Again and again he made speeches attacking Leggio and his protectors, urging the peasants to tell the authorities what they knew. Navarra tried to talk him out of his struggle, but Rizzotto rebuffed him. In early 1948, the two men clashed on more mundane grounds. Seeking yet another title to add to his vast collection, the doctor asked to join the local association of ex-servicemen as an honorary member. Rizzotto happened to be its secretary and demanded to see details of Navarra's record. The doctor insisted he had all the official papers needed to prove that he was an ex-serviceman. He had indeed served as a reserve second lieutenant in a heavy artillery battalion, but only for a year. Recalled on the eve of the Second World War, he immediately had himself declared unfit for military service and was sent back home. Rizzotto turned down Navarra's request, which the doctor took as a personal offence.

Rizzotto soon gave Navarra more reason for displeasure. The young peasant made a point of leading his followers onto the estate which Leggio was supposed to be guarding. The protesters humiliated Leggio by chasing him away, raising the red flag on the castle dominating the property and then symbolically starting to plough the land to show it belonged to those who knew how to work it.

Rizzotto again gained the upper hand against Leggio when the two men fell to blows outside the municipal gardens at the entrance to Corleone. Leggio and several of his mafiosi friends had mocked the red handkerchiefs sported by Sicilian ex-partisans travelling through the town. The ex-partisans gave as good as they got and the incident turned into a brawl. Someone went to fetch Rizzotto in an attempt to stop the punch-up. The peasant leader appealed for calm but to no effect. Incensed by the mafiosi's taunts – he too had worn the red handkerchief during his years as a partisan – he sprang to the outsiders' defence. Grabbing hold of the frail Leggio, Rizzotto lifted him off his feet, slammed him against a wall and 'hung' him by his coat on the sharp bars of the gardens' wrought-iron gate.

Goaded by an incensed Leggio, Navarra began to spread the word that this young Rizzotto 'doesn't mind his own business' – a comment which had more than an edge of threat to it. Rizzotto knew enough about the ways of the mafia to realise he was in danger. But when his friends urged him to be careful, he replied: 'They can kill me but that won't solve anything. There'll be so many after me! It's not as if everything will stop just because I've been killed.' Rizzotto's elderly father, an ex-mafia convict himself, lost sleep over the risks he knew his son was taking and repeated to him again and again: 'If someone says he wants to talk to you, ask him to wait half an hour and come and tell me.'

Rizzotto simply played down the threat, telling his father: 'People respect me, even Dr Navarra!'

★

Rizzotto ignored his father's advice when word reached him that Navarra wanted to talk to him some three weeks after the fight in the square. Rizzotto agreed to a meeting on the evening of 10 March 1948 on the main street of Corleone, close to Navarra's home. It was a clear, cool evening and many people were out for a *passegiata* (stroll) following their dinner. But Navarra failed to turn up; while Rizzotto waited, he was approached by his childhood friend Pasquale Criscione, one of Navarra's men and the leaseholder of an estate which had been lost to the peasant movement. Criscione told Rizzotto they must talk, and they walked down the main street to the church of San Leonardo. There, Criscione related later, the two men separated.

The 33-year-old Rizzotto failed to return home. After a sleepless night waiting for her son, during which she kept walking out into the street to look for him, Rizzotto's mother found out that he had last been seen with Criscione.

She stopped Criscione in the street. 'What time did you leave him?' she asked.

'At ten past ten,' he replied.

'And what did he say to you?'

'That I must come and have a meal with him,' Criscione said.

Rizzotto's mother later confided that as Criscione talked to her, 'his ugly poisonous face turned white and he was trembling'. That evening she reported her son's disappearance to the *carabinieri*, the paramilitary police.

On the same night that Rizzotto disappeared, a 13-year-old shepherd boy died of a sudden and mysterious illness. The boy had been watching over his father's sheep outside Corleone when he was suddenly taken ill. He was taken to hospital and placed under Navarra's care. In a feverish state, the boy described seeing a peasant murdered that night on a path leading across fields at the foot of the Rocca Busambra mountain while he guarded the flock. The boy then lost consciousness and died shortly afterwards. The autopsy concluded he had been poisoned. Investigators established that unidentified 'friends' had brought the boy to Navarra's hospital, but they were unable to prove that, as local newspapers reported and many people believed, the boy had witnessed Rizzotto's murder and that Navarra had given the boy a fatal injection.

With Rizzotto's disappearance still a mystery, a rumour spread that he had been murdered in a fight 'over a woman', Leoluchina Sorisi. 'I'll eat the heart of whoever assassinated my Placido,' she was said to have sworn over his tomb. Nearly six decades later, the 86-year-old Leoluchina broke a lifelong silence to deny she had ever pledged to 'eat the heart' of the man who killed the peasant leader Rizzotto. He was just a friend of hers, she explained; he often came to her home because he was a close friend of her nephew. Her boyfriend was not Rizzotto but Criscione – who was seen with Rizzotto shortly before the latter disappeared.

They were engaged in the way that such matters were conducted then, with looks and a few words furtively exchanged while Criscione walked past her balcony. How could Leoluchina love a mafioso, her interviewer asked? 'But I didn't love him,' she protested. 'I knew I had to get married, that I had the right age to do it and that he could be a good match. That's how people thought in those days. From when they were small, girls were "trained" to be ready for marriage. And what's more it wasn't known that he was a mafioso. He behaved like a mafioso, that's for sure, but in the Corleone of those days lots of people behaved that way.'

Shortly after Rizzotto's disappearance, Criscione asked her to lie and tell the police that they had been together throughout that night. She refused and began to believe that he had become engaged to her as a way of getting close to Rizzotto, without raising suspicion. 'Wicked people are capable of such hateful things,' she reflected.

Seven days after Rizzotto vanished an anonymous letter, its grammar uncertain, reached the investigators. 'Beware of the people who I tell you was the executioners of Placido . . . first the Criscione brothers both of them, Leggio . . .' it ran. But this breach in the law of silence – an anonymous letter was traditionally the only way a Sicilian peasant would communicate with the police in the unlikely event he was willing to run this risk – led nowhere, as no evidence was found to incriminate the 'executioners' named in the letter.

The established order was now safe. The now-leaderless peasant movement ended overnight; no one any longer had the courage to unfurl the red flag over land controlled by the clan. Many peasants who had won the right to a plot of land renounced it for fear of reprisal. Not even Rizzotto's father's decision to defy the law of silence and tell the police all he knew about the mafia helped to resolve the mystery of his son's fate. But although the police had little on Leggio, nine months after the murder they demanded his exile to the mainland. Leggio failed to appear before the court hearing which was due to consider the proposal and that day he became a fugitive.

Leggio's notoriety as an untouchable grew and grew. Rumours said 'the Grain of Fire' was devilishly clever at disguises, that he could pass himself off as a priest, a police officer, a woman or even an American tourist. He was variously said to be hiding in an underground tunnel, a mountain hut, a Palermo clinic and a luxury seaside hotel. In fact he had no need to travel very far; he benefited from the generous protection of several local dignitaries, including a baron and his wife who employed an accomplice on their staff.

New testimony on Rizzotto's killing came from an unexpected source a year later. Giovanni Pasqua, a prisoner in a Palermo jail who had helped Leggio commit his first murder four years earlier, came forward to name the peasant leader's killers as Leggio, Criscione and Collura, Navarra's defeated rival for leadership of the Corleone clan.

Pasqua's testimony came on the heels of the arrival in Corleone of a dashing, strong-willed captain of the *carabinieri* police, Carlo Alberto Dalla Chiesa. A former partisan like Rizzotto, Captain Dalla Chiesa was from the northern Piedmont region, home of the Risorgimento movement which fathered a united kingdom of Italy in 1861. Dalla Chiesa was a courteous and brave officer who put loyalty to his corps and the state first and foremost. He was determined to do his utmost against the mafia, which he did not fear. He made a point of meeting Rizzotto's parents and promised them that he would do all he could to ensure that those who ordered and carried out the murder would be brought to trial 'partly because Rizzotto was a partisan like me'.

The murder was the captain's first big case and for five months he hunted for the three suspects. He finally found both Criscione and Collura, but not Leggio. Under interrogation, the pair confessed. They had brought Rizzotto to Leggio, who told him he wanted to talk; Leggio then took hold of Rizzotto's right arm and forced him to walk at his side, pressing a gun to his waist as they followed a path that led out of the town. On the Rocca Busambra peak, Leggio had shot him dead with a pistol, firing three times. The killers had then thrown the body into a crevice 'so that the crows wouldn't be attracted by the smell of decay and give away the place where he lay by circling overhead,' they explained.

Guided by the two murderers, Dalla Chiesa and his men trudged up the mountain. After a search which lasted several hours, they found the crevice. It took the captain a week to arrange for a fire brigade to come from Palermo to search it. The firemen took turns to lower themselves down to a depth of 160 feet, where, among the bones of mules, donkeys and horses, they found the remains of three bodies. Skull fragments, several other bones and various objects were brought up to the light. When Rizzotto's family examined them, they recognised a pair of rotting heavy boots and torn strips of material ripped from their son's clothes. The formal identification of his remains took place before an honorary lower court judge, who represented the rule of law in Corleone and who also happened to be Navarra's first cousin.

All Dalla Chiesa's efforts were gutted when at their trial Criscione and Collura withdrew their confessions, claiming they had been obtained by torture. Although the prosecution demanded life sentences for all the accused, a Palermo court acquitted them on the grounds of lack of evidence, and revoked a warrant for

Leggio's arrest. In effect, the judges had rejected as evidence both the family's recognition of the remains and the initial confessions of the two accused. The verdict, four years after the killings, was a slap in the face for Dalla Chiesa. Yet again, a Sicilian court had thrown away a chance to check the Corleonesi.

Omertà is so engrained in Corleone that it was 57 years after Rizzotto's murder before an 80-year-old pensioner admitted he had witnessed the kidnapping as a young man. The eyewitness, who gave his name as Luca and refused to have his surname published, had been walking past a church when he saw Rizzotto arguing heatedly with several other men. He heard Rizzotto shout: '*Basta* (enough)! Let me go!' The men then grabbed him and pushed him into a car waiting nearby with its engine running.

Frightened by what he had seen, Luca walked away as fast as he could and didn't even tell his family what he had seen. He reflected: 'People will think I was a coward, and maybe I really was. But in those days people like Leggio and his "friends" terrified everyone in Corleone. And I was only 20.' The fear had not left Luca – although he had recognised several of the men who had kidnapped Rizzotto, he refused to give any names.

As another eyewitness said in a rare indictment of the law of silence and fear which saw all that evening's strollers simply look elsewhere, walk faster and away and fail to save Rizzotto: 'He was our hero and we let him go. All we had to do, every one of us, was to have picked up a single stone from the street, and we'd have been too much for them.'

Although the killers went unpunished, his family never doubted who was to blame. At a ceremony marking the first anniversary of his son's death, Rizzotto's father appeared on the balcony of his home, a crowd looking up at him from below, to bravely denounce 'that fine gentleman' Dr Navarra for commissioning the murder. His index finger raised in anger and his voice rising to a shout, the ex-mafioso said he had no doubt that Leggio had 'silenced my son with lead'. 'Give me back my son's body!' he cried out. He then named several mafiosi and shouted how much he despised them, adding that he knew them well and knew what ferocity they were capable of. 'But soon you will fight each other like dogs and tear yourselves apart!' he predicted.

Events were soon to prove him right.

Exit 'Our Father'

As he celebrated his fiftieth birthday in 1955, Dr Navarra must have felt he could allow himself a smug smile. Everything was apparently going his way. The balding don, who now wore the few strands of hair he had left stuck over his broad scalp, had lost none of his passion for his favourite hobby – collecting titles, their number a reflection of the power he craved. The year before his birthday, he managed to have himself appointed district doctor for Palermo; but, his vanity apparently satisfied, he never took up the post.

Based on his brushes with the law so far, Corleone's leading citizen could rest assured that it would never be more than just a minor irritant. It was only in 1948 that police branded him the head of the Corleonese family; this led to a court sentencing him to five years of internal exile on the mainland, which was quashed on appeal. He was sentenced to exile once again, but Navarra's lawyers worked the system with such efficiency that he returned home after just one month's absence.

Turning 50 must have encouraged Navarra to feel it was time to settle his old scores with Collura, the only rival who had dared to challenge him for the post of clan chief. As if dealing with one of his sick patients, the doctor solved the problem in a measured, methodical way. First he had Collura's son murdered, then he waited all of six years before getting rid of Collura. By then, Navarra could be forgiven for thinking that his hold over Corleone was complete. He had politicians of the Christian Democratic party, a popular conservative movement backed by the Roman Catholic Church, in his debt; word that the doctor supported the party had enabled it to double its vote.

For all his cunning, Navarra underestimated the ambition of 'the Grain of Fire' Leggio, until then his most loyal henchman. Where the discreet Navarra ruled in the traditional mafia style, exploiting its influence over the country estates and infiltrating the political system, the brash Leggio thirsted after more aggressive and more lucrative schemes, such as stealing cattle, which he then butchered clandestinely. Leggio and a gang he created for the purpose stole animals from their owners and hid them in the Ficuzza wood. After killing and cutting up the cattle, they loaded the meat onto lorries and drove it off to Palermo for sale. The ever-more-entrepreneurial Leggio set up a road haulage company to make the frequent journeys to Sicily's capital more profitable.

Leggio's business plans – his first venture into potentially money-spinning public works contracts, an ambitious venture for the guard of an estate – set him on a head-on collision course with his superior Navarra. Leggio wanted to use his lorries to transport tonnes of equipment for a planned dam on the River Corleone and a reservoir that would supply citrus groves in the romantically named *Conca d'Oro* (Golden Shell) on Palermo's outskirts. But this threatened the bosses who for the past century had controlled the water supply to the orchards and charged inflated rates for it. They had a quiet word in Navarra's ear. It was enough to win his support and he spread the rumour that a dam of that size was dangerous, arguing that sooner or later the dam would burst and its waters submerge Corleone.

An embittered Leggio is said to have made one more journey to Palermo, but this time without any hunks of meat to sell. Officially sent as Navarra's representative, as one story goes, he attended an unusual conference at the city's plush Grand Hotel et des Palmes in October 1957. In attendance were Sicilian bosses and the most high-level American Cosa Nostra delegation ever to have crossed the Atlantic, headed by the Brooklyn-based Joe Bonnano. The summit lasted four days and took place under ornate, cut-glass chandeliers in the Wagner suite, where the German composer had written the third act of the opera *Parsifal*.

Police surveillance failed to establish what precisely was decided in the Grand Hotel, nor did any of the participants ever reveal the agenda. But it is widely assumed that the main topic, the only one that could have justified so many Italo-American heavy-weights travelling to Sicily, was drug-trafficking. Leggio has been said to have sought and obtained permission to eliminate Navarra on the grounds that he was too old and not cut out for Cosa Nostra's brave new world of international drug-trafficking.

It is most unlikely that Leggio was present. Navarra was simply too minor a figure in the Palermo-centred mafia of the day to be invited himself, let alone be able to send a junior delegate to rub shoulders with the American heavyweights. In addition, Corleone's clan had nothing to contribute to a discussion on drug-trafficking, assuming this was indeed what drew the Americans to Palermo. Nor was there any reason why the Americans, who were part of a separate brotherhood, should give the green light for the murder of a provincial Sicilian boss. There is, however, no doubt that the henchman was thirsting to take his boss's place. But a conference in a chic hotel was not the way he would achieve his goal.

For the time being, Leggio vented his fury with Navarra for wrecking his business project on Angelo Vintaloro, one of the doctor's lieutenants who was also a cattle-rustler. Vintaloro had good reason to oppose the dam as it would flood his wheatfields and vineyards. Leggio set out to put pressure on Vintaloro to sell up and leave. One morning in May 1958, Vintaloro walked into one of his cellars and the overpowering smell of wine made his head reel. Every barrel had been smashed to pieces, large scarlet puddles of spilt wine were slowly seeping into the ground. Word went round that Leggio was responsible for the vandalism – *omertà* was powerless to stifle rumours.

Despite his friendship with Navarra, a month later, when Vintaloro's wheat ripened, he had to plead for days with local peasants before any agreed to help him harvest it – such was the fear Leggio inspired. At last, just as the June sun was threatening to turn the wheat from gold to completely black, a few peasants worked secretly at night by the light of the moon and torches. They could have saved themselves the effort; they had hardly finished when the sheaves of wheat promptly vanished. This time, rumour had it that Leggio had loaded the entire harvest onto his trucks.

But Vintaloro still refused to sell up. He now received an anonymous letter of extortion, demanding that he hand over money or face more punishment. When Navarra heard of this, he hatched a plan to ambush the letter's mysterious author. The doctor refused to believe that Leggio could be responsible for such an affront to his authority. Vintaloro agreed to hand over the money and arranged a meeting near his farm in late June, with several soldiers sent by Navarra hiding in a cowshed. They saw a man approach, riding on the back of a mule, and opened fire immediately, wounding him in the arm. Leggio, for it was him, recognised one of his aggressors and shouted out: 'My friend, why are you shooting at me? Don't you recognise me?' Seeing that he was still alive was enough to make the soldiers flee.

When Navarra was told how the ambush had gone, he thought his lieutenant of some 14 years must have learnt his lesson. The fact that Leggio was wounded would make up for any loss of face Navarra had suffered. Or so the doctor believed.

Soon after lunch on 2 August 1958, a young doctor drove his older colleague Navarra towards Corleone, on their way back from Lercara Friddi, whose only claim to fame is as the birthplace of 'Lucky' Luciano. As usual, the supremely self-confident Navarra carried no weapon and had no bodyguard. That summer, his ego-fuelled, lifelong search for titles and awards culminated in a nomination for a knighthood in an order of the Italian Republic headed by the country's president, no less. The fact that the police had labelled him the boss of Corleone was apparently no obstacle to membership of this particular élite.

Under the early afternoon sun, the heat made worse by the *scirocco* wind, the car sped along the road which wound its way through fields parched by a drought that had seen no rain since

February. A small red lorry emerged from a side road, reversing into the path of Navarra's car. The car's driver slammed on the brakes and managed to slow down before hitting the lorry; the front of the car crumpled, its bonnet crushed into an upside-down 'V'.

Navarra had too much experience of ambush and murder – so far always under his orders – not to realise immediately what was happening; he started shouting even before another car, Leggio's Alfa Romeo, came up from behind and made it impossible for his car to reverse. But the doctor's shouts were quickly drowned out by a hail of bullets as gunmen jumped out from behind an awning covering the back of the lorry, and from Leggio's car. The killers fired again and again with a total of five weapons – two American and Italian sub-machine guns and three automatic pistols. Of 124 bullets fired, 92 thudded into Navarra's corpulent frame, which slid down into the seat as if a string had snapped. Several others struck his colleague who remained gripping the steering wheel, his head with a bullet-hole in the forehead lolling towards the window as the car rolled off the road and came to a halt in a field. As the killers fled, blood from the two doctors dripped down, splashes of crimson on the sunburnt gold of the short, dry stalks of wheat left behind after the harvest.

For Navarra's funeral two days later, the people of Corleone turned out as rarely before to pay tribute to the man they called 'Our Father'. Joining the crowd which filled the main piazza and all nearby streets were a battery of local dignitaries and delegations from clans across western Sicily. The mayor declared a day of public mourning and ordered the flag hanging from the balcony of the town hall to be flown at half-mast. By the coffin, inside the church of San Martino, dozens of wreaths were piled up in honour of 'the Benefactor'.

Neither Navarra's elevated status within the mafia nor his powerful friends outside it prevented his elimination by Leggio; the young challenger had defeated the boss with a combination of daring, skill, speed and devastating violence – a pattern that was to become a trademark of the Corleonesi.

The execution itself was more typical of gangland America than of rural Sicily. Leggio, modelling himself on American gangsters after quizzing emigrants who returned to Corleone, had preferred sub-machine guns and automatic pistols to the sawn-off shotgun, the mafia's trademark weapon. It was as if, amid the sun-parched fields where Navarra met his end, the traditional rural mafia and Al Capone-style gangsterism had suddenly come together with potentially devastating consequences for the secret society.

In the days that followed Navarra's death, police raided the homes of mafiosi – both enemies and friends of the doctor – but they found no one. The men had all vanished, fleeing to the hills to prepare for the feud that from now on – just as the father of the murdered peasant leader Rizzotto had predicted – would pit the mafiosi of Corleone against each other.

Leggio, Salvatore Riina and Bernardo Provenzano – 'the Holy Trinity'

At about 5 p.m. on 11 September 1943, as the 12-year-old Salvatore Riina, his two brothers and their father made their way home to Corleone with the family's mule down a rocky hillside track, sweating in the heat after working in the fields since dawn, they came across an unexploded bronze-coloured bomb which gleamed in the beating sun among clods of dry earth.

Unexploded bombs, mostly from American planes, were worth something; the explosive powder inside could be used to fill a rifle's cartridges, while the iron casing could be made into a ploughshare. After searching nearby, they also found a grey cylinder, a 16-inch long cannon shell which had shattered near the tip. It had apparently been abandoned by German soldiers who had camped in the area until the Allied invasion two months earlier. With the help of Salvatore, the most heavily built of his sons, the father gingerly took hold of the bomb and the cannon shell and slipped them into a jute bag, making sure they would not strike each other before tying the bag to the mule's back as securely as he could. Father and sons then restarted down the track that led home.

Born the second of six children – three boys and three girls – Salvatore Riina left school at the age of seven and helped work almost three hectares of land which had been owned by the family for three generations, yielding enough to feed them at least once a day in the desperate war years. It is likely that his father, who was listed in police files as 'capable of causing harm to people and to the property of others', made a point of teaching him early how to kill a hen or a lamb cleanly and quickly; peasant families wanted such tasks to become second nature.

An hour after finding the bomb and the cannon shell, father and sons reached Corleone and threaded their way through the dirty streets. In the alley outside the family home, a poor grey stone house with rickety tiles, Riina's father lifted the jute bag off the mule's back, slowly pulled out the unexploded bomb and began defusing it, his three sons watching in silence. After completing the task, he took the broken cannon shell into the house, followed by his sons who led the mule inside – the ground-floor room served as a stable on one side and was furnished with a bed, a rough wooden table and chairs on the other. Large terra-cotta jugs filled with fresh water – they were also used to store olive oil when the harvest had gone well – rested on the floor by the wall.

Riina's father peered inside the cannon shell; there was apparently no powder left inside so he started to strike the shell against a stone. The shell suddenly slipped from his grasp and exploded. Fragments ripped into him and his seven-year-old son, killing them both. Shrapnel wounded another son in the right leg, neck and cheeks. The mule died in the explosion. Riina himself didn't have even one scratch.

Shortly before sunset two days later, a long funeral procession followed the two coffins – one large, one small – to the cemetery west of the town. The black clothes of mourning made the bulge in the stomach of Riina's mother even more noticeable – she was eight months pregnant with her seventh child, a daughter. With his injured brother still recovering in hospital, Riina was the only male of the family walking at her side. As the procession neared the cemetery dotted with gaunt cypress trees, the wind rose, kicking up the dust of the dirty road and blowing the laments of the women over the fields. The funeral was the last time anyone saw Riina cry.

Despite the new responsibility weighing on his shoulders, Riina turned his back on the daily grind of a peasant's life within two years of his father's death. He preferred to lounge about the main piazza where he would vent his frustration on his friends, his high-pitched, whining voice filled with anger: 'I'm not going to stay in Corleone all my life. I'm not going to die poor. I don't want to live like a tramp.'

A short, squat figure with strong, calloused hands and arms too long for his build, Riina was nicknamed '*il Corto*' (Shorty) – he was five foot three – but never to his face; he spoke little, but the way he fixed his acquaintances with a steady glare from the narrow black cracks that were his eyes scared them. As a young man he had a handsome face, sporting a shock of thick, unruly dark hair and a pencil-thin moustache he trimmed obsessively over his thin lips.

Riina made friends with another rebellious peasant's son two years younger than him. Like Riina, Bernardo Provenzano – christened after the revered swordsman-turned-monk Saint Bernard – had left school early to work in the fields. But he too decided this was not the life for him; he had no intention of spending the rest of his days waiting at dawn in the main piazza of Corleone to be picked, or ignored, by overseers choosing who would work that day.

Riina and Provenzano soon became inseparable and were both recruited by Leggio. The trio carried out raids in the countryside, stealing cattle, butchering it clandestinely and burning the property of anyone who dared to stand in their way. They became known as Corleone's 'Holy Trinity', dominated by the older Leggio, and took to greeting each other with a kiss on the cheek – a gesture typical of mafiosi.

Locals saw Provenzano's older brother reprimand him; the family had never had anything to do with the mafia and the brother wanted to keep things that way. 'I'll split your head open!' he shouted at Provenzano. 'Mind your own business, it's got nothing to do with you,' Provenzano retorted. A police officer who similarly warned Riina against spending any time with Leggio had no more success. The teenage Riina replied defiantly: 'You of the state eat at our expense, you plot against us, you arrest us, you send us to jail and you send us into exile. I'd rather be dead than be a cop.'

Riina was 18 when he picked his first public fight on a May morning in 1949, the day Corleone celebrated a procession of a crucified Christ. Soon after the procession had ended Riina and several of his friends fought with Domenico Di Matteo, a young peasant, and his cousins. The teenagers went for each other with sticks and knuckle-dusters. The reason for the row has long been forgotten, but ten days later the two sides agreed to meet on a plot of packed earth where locals played bowls. They yelled insults at each other, then again started fighting, punching and kicking each other.

As the teenagers wrestled each other in the dust, one of Di Matteo's cousins pulled out a revolver. 'Everybody stop or I shoot!' he shouted.

Riina instantly whipped out an automatic pistol, took aim at the cousin and fired half a dozen shots in quick succession; he hit not the cousin but Di Matteo, in the right thigh. The cousin fired back, one bullet hitting Riina first in the right leg and then in the left. Di Matteo died that night of a haemorrhage caused by Riina's shot lacerating his femoral artery.

Interrogated three times over the next few days in his hospital bed, Riina initially swore that Di Matteo had wounded him first, but then admitted that Di Matteo had not been armed. Riina insisted however that he had fired only one shot, in self-defence. At his trial, as Riina stood in the dock, his wrists in chains, he glared at the court and snarled in a low voice when the judge started speaking: 'A lawyer or a cuckold of a judge never says the truth.' Sentenced to 12 years in jail, he served only six years before he was released for good behaviour in 1955. Semi-literate and hard-pushed even to sign his own name, Riina passed an exam in prison to reach the level of eight-year-old schoolchildren. He passed with high marks – including a surprising 9 out of 10 in 'moral education' – but his scholastic ambitions stopped there.

A year after his release, Riina first set eyes on the girl who was to become the love of his life. Visiting the house of his friend Calogero Bagarella, Riina was invited to stay for a meal. Calogero's 13-year-old sister Antonina, known to all as Ninetta, served at

table before disappearing behind a curtain where she sat down
to read a book. It's believed that the 26-year-old Riina decided
on the spot that this pretty girl less than half his age, with a fair,
oval face, shiny pitch-black eyes and long black hair she wore in
a pony tail, must one day be his wife.

Ninetta's peasant family was beyond reproach – at least in
Riina's eyes. Both her father and her two brothers, Calogero and
Leoluca, were mafiosi. Riina was particularly close to Calogero;
not only were they friends, but Calogero was also in love with
Riina's sister. At school Ninetta was well liked as a bright, happy
girl with a passion for reading. Too poor to afford books, she
borrowed them from the school library. 'I lived in poverty and
precisely for that reason I dreamt; I felt the need to become independent. I wanted to keep studying, to get myself a proper job,'
Ninetta said later. Her dedication contrasted sharply with Riina's
dismal record.

Riina wooed Ninetta the traditional way, known in Corleone
as 'waiting at the street corner'. Before 8 a.m. every morning
Riina, moustache always neatly trimmed, waited at the corner of
the alley where she lived, an alley so narrow no car could pass
through it, in a warren of tiny streets and houses made of tufa
rock. When she walked past, clutching her books, 'Shorty' drew
himself up as much as he could and hoped she would gratify
him with at least one look. Riina then followed her across town,
past the gate of the gardens where his mentor Leggio had once
been hung by his coat, until she reached the school. Respecting
the local custom, he never spoke to her as he followed her.

Bullets and the Law of Silence

After Navarra's murder, his heirs – such was the doctor's authority that those loyal to him were called 'the Navarra clan' even when he was dead and buried – sued for peace and Leggio agreed to a meeting a month after the funeral. The *scirocco* wind had started to blow the previous night and the mafiosi chose to meet under the pines and plane trees of the San Rocco bastion at dusk on 6 September 1958; the fountain around which old men and stray dogs liked to sit had long run dry and the grass in the flower-beds had been killed off by the sun but this was one of the only spots in Corleone which afforded some shelter from the heat.

Riina, alone and for once unarmed, was the first to arrive. Sent by Leggio to act as his representative, he stood with his back to a wall, waiting. When three of the late Navarra's henchmen arrived, Riina was the first to speak. 'Who is dead is dead, the dear-departed has gone away. Let's think of the living,' Riina said. He then crossed himself.

The old men sitting around the fountain, obeying an instinct born of fear, misery and death, slowly got to their feet and shuffled away. Only the dogs stayed to watch the scene. Riina spoke at length. Navarra's followers heard him out in silence and only when he had finished speaking did one of them hold out his hand in a sign of peace.

But Riina didn't shake hands. He had one more thing to say: 'There's just one more problem between us: you have to hand over to us those cuckolds who tried to rub out Leggio.'

Riina had no interest in the answer. In that moment, Provenzano and another mafioso emerged from under the trees and opened fire with sawn-off shotguns. One of Navarra's followers was shot in the face and died instantly; the other two fled. They raced through the heart of Corleone but were shot dead in the street, a stray bullet wounding a two-year-old girl. Shortly afterwards, Provenzano was shot and wounded in the head as he raced down the main street with a companion.

As Provenzano lay on the ground outside a tailor's shop, another of Navarra's followers urged an accomplice who had fired the shot: 'Shoot him, shoot him again!'

'Forget him. Can't you see he's dead? Let's take care of the other one,' the accomplice replied.

Further down the main street, they caught up with Provenzano's companion but he managed to find refuge in a shop. Navarra's followers failed to hit him but they wounded the shopkeeper's wife and her eight-year-old daughter, injured a woman who had been walking by, and shattered the shop window.

The police had an impossible time trying to piece together what had happened. One man they believed was a witness said: 'I didn't see anything and I didn't hear anything! A bit of a commotion, I thought it was young people fighting.' The man then sank to the ground, a patch of blood spreading through his shirt; three bullets had torn into his stomach.

The mother of the two-year-old girl told the police: 'I thought all those explosions were firecrackers for the feast day of the patron saint. My daughter must have been so frightened she hit her head against the railing.'

'What about the bullet which wounded your daughter?' she was asked.

'What bullet are you talking about?' she replied.

Provenzano, taken to hospital with a blood-sodden shirt, was also anything but helpful when a doctor asked him what had happened. 'I felt a strong pain in the head. I fainted, I didn't notice anything,' Provenzano lied. As one Sicilian proverb says: 'The man who is really a man never reveals anything, even when he is being stabbed.'

The doctor knew better than to ask any more questions.

The next day, Provenzano told police he had left home to go to the cinema but that before reaching it he had suffered a gunshot wound 'which caused me to lose consciousness immediately; so I've no idea what happened'. Provenzano's version was backed by a friend who said he had met Provenzano in the street shortly before he was wounded.

The only eyewitness account of any use was supplied by a police officer who said he had recognised Riina among the gunmen chasing each other. Several witnesses did testify that Provenzano had been among the killers. But a month later they suddenly went back on their testimony and left Corleone, emigrating to northern Italy.

Provenzano left hospital a free man. The *carabinieri* police captain Dalla Chiesa found out next to nothing about his crimes. Shortly after the shootout, Dalla Chiesa wrote Provenzano's name into his registers for the first time, accusing him of stealing six cows, 1,500 pounds of cheese, 2,800 pounds of cereals and a hunting rifle, as well as slaughtering cattle clandestinely and being part of a criminal association. The slim new file bore the letter 'M', for mafioso. Soon after that, Provenzano became a fugitive; decades later his life on the run was to set a new record.

The law of silence held. The Corleonesi had chosen to carry out their killings in broad daylight not only because they knew it would hold, but also because they wanted to be seen by the people of the town – a brazen demonstration of their increasing power.

From then on, there was no more talk of peace and Leggio ordered his men to destroy his enemies. Hardly a month went by without one of Navarra's followers being either wounded or killed. Even those who refused to take sides were fair game. Carmelo Lo Bue, a mafioso in his seventies who had been exiled under Mussolini, thought he could afford to ignore the feud as he was about to leave for America to join his sons. But as Lo Bue rode his horse home through the aptly named Calvary Street after a day in his vineyards and olive groves, Riina shot him first in the back and then in the mouth. Riina swiftly emerged as Leggio's most trusted killer, never hesitating to cut down rivals in the street or in shops where they had happened to seek refuge. 'We've got to always settle our scores; witnesses are always dangerous,' Riina told Provenzano and other accomplices.

Leggio's wrath also struck locals who had nothing to do with the mafia. Riina shot a fruit and olive oil trader in the back, heart and mouth – the last bullet a warning to anyone who witnessed Leggio's crimes to keep silent. The victim, a notorious chatterbox, had stood on the threshold of his home to watch the September shootout in the town centre and then blabbed to acquaintances about what he had seen.

Corleone's murder-toll climbed steadily. From 1943 to 1961, the town witnessed 52 murders and 22 attempted murders. Mafiosi were cut down, in the words of a Sicilian writer, 'in the streets of the centre or in those of the outskirts, inside houses or in the fields, at night and by day, treacherously or with a volley in the face, at the door of the bar, on the steps of the church or on the threshold of their home'.

One journalist went up to a mother crying as she walked behind a coffin in a funeral procession and asked her: 'Who was killed?' The mother replied: 'Why, is anyone dead?' As if a curfew had been decreed, locals stayed indoors after sunset, wary of witnessing a murder if they ventured outside. The authorities banned the use of white pointed hoods during the Good Friday procession, as killers used the sinister-looking hoods to hide their faces when they carried out murders during the march.

The only newspaper to give any importance to the Corleonesi at this time was the campaigning Palermo daily *L'Ora*, which ran a headline in capital letters '*PERICOLOSO* (DANGEROUS)' above a large picture of Leggio. The boss, the newspaper reported, was 'a rich man, fearsome and feared, a man capable of riding a horse with a sawn-off shotgun at the ready, a mix of old-style mafioso and modern gangster'. Two days after the article appeared, a bomb silenced the newspaper's printing presses.

From early 1961 onwards, Leggio used a more stealthy tactic than the usual street-shooting. This was the *lupara bianca* (white shotgun), which meant eliminating the victim without trace. This not only made police investigations even harder, it also made it impossible for relatives to swear vendetta in front of the corpse, let alone identify the killer. The method was usually reserved for those whom Leggio wanted to brand as particularly vile – men he considered spies or traitors, unworthy of being wept over by their loved ones. Friends of the late Navarra vanished apparently into oblivion, including a Christian Democrat town councillor.

Bodies were thrown into ravines or buried in the fresh concrete of new buildings. They were roasted on giant grills, an echo of the Spanish Inquisition which had terrified Sicily in the name of Catholic orthodoxy from the sixteenth to the eighteenth centuries and an exhausting task – getting rid of just one body took eight hours and a huge supply of wood to keep the flames going. Alternatively, the body was dumped in a grave; spadefuls of white lime powder were thrown over it, followed by a fertiliser used for trees which became corrosive when wet. After two or three months, depending on the rainfall, the remains were similar to an Egyptian mummy. Not even a wife or a mother could identify the victim.

A new figure made its appearance in the streets of Corleone: women who dressed in the black clothes of mourning after their menfolk disappeared but who, unlike other widows, had been unable to hold a funeral service for their loved ones. There was no grave for them to kneel in front of or leave flowers on. 'They burn those who do wrong and they don't even let you find the ashes,' people would murmur as the women in black walked by.

In 1963, Leggio planned to resort again to the 'white shotgun' for one of the last acts in the five-year feud – the elimination of Francesco Paolo Streva, the most feared Navarra lieutenant and described by police as 'sly, courageous and vindictive'. Before dawn one spring morning, Provenzano and another killer hid outside the home of Streva's lover, in the alley where Riina's girlfriend Ninetta also lived. A car waited nearby with its engine running to spirit Streva away, alive or dead. But he proved too fast for his enemies. When he slipped out of the house, he spotted them, quickly drew two pistols and fired; he wounded Provenzano in the shoulder before escaping. Provenzano, despite his blood dripping onto the ground, managed to walk home. Moments later, the doors of the houses he had passed opened and women darted out, wet rags in hand, to silently wipe the stone slabs. By the time the police arrived, there was no trail of blood for them to follow and, of course, no one had seen or heard anything.

Streva's quick instincts bought him a respite of only four more months, until he walked into a trap prepared by Leggio. Told that a member of Leggio's gang wanted to betray the boss with his help, Streva agreed to an evening meeting in the Ficuzza wood. Streva ventured cautiously into the wood, escorted by two bodyguards and a guard dog. Provenzano and an accomplice murdered all three men and threw their bodies into a ditch; they cut open the dog's chest and threw the animal into the ditch too, then, rifles slung over their shoulders, raced up the rocky slopes of the Rocca Busambra mountain to hide.

The feud, which ended with Leggio installed as undisputed boss of what were now known as the Corleonesi, was a formidable training ground for Riina and Provenzano, and they acted with impunity. It claimed so many lives that it got talked about not just in Palermo, but even in America, where bosses started to call the town 'Tombstone'. Norman Lewis, who visited Corleone in the early 1960s for his classic account of the mafia, *The Honoured Society*, wrote:

> In this world one occasionally stumbles upon a place which, in its physical presence and the atmosphere it distils, manages somehow to match its reputation for sinister happenings. Such

a town is Corleone . . . Men and women go perpetually in black, worn for old tragedies; for a father, five years; for a brother, three years; for a son, three years; a piled-up account of mourning that can never be settled.

Sorrow leaks from these people into the streets.

The Corleonesi were beginning to get noticed.

2
The Rise of 'The Peasants'
1963–1974

Palermo: Challenging the Establishment

Simply accumulating power in Corleone, as his predecessor Navarra had done, was just not enough for Leggio. Now in firm control of the town, he set his sights on a much bigger prize: Palermo. Swapping his meat-carrying trucks for a Mercedes more worthy of a boss, Leggio headed once more for the Sicilian capital.

Ringed by mountains and the sea, under Norman-Arab rulers the most civilised city in Europe, Palermo had for centuries sprawled across a lush valley of villas and palm, lemon, orange and olive groves known as the Golden Shell, which contrasted sharply with the rugged fields around Corleone, which were parched and desert-like by midsummer. A romantic but decaying city, Palermo was rich in historical and artistic treasures, from a Saracen centre of slum-like hovels to a Norman royal palace, Renaissance churches and extravagant Spanish baroque palaces that bore tribute to the flurry of invaders who had ruled Sicily. It had attracted philosophers and poets, one of whom had invented the sonnet there; the twelfth-century cathedral, a hotch-potch of Norman, Gothic and neo-classical features, was home to the remains of six emperors and kings.

When Leggio focused on Palermo, the city was one vast building site, in the throes of a money-spinning, anarchic and devastating building boom. As the capital of a Sicily declared a self-governing region after the war, Palermo was being transformed by a steady stream of subsidies from Rome. With tens of thousands of peasants from all over the island settling in Palermo, seeking homes and jobs, public authorities had earmarked huge sums for construction work. The number of inhabitants jumped by 20 per cent to 600,000 in the decade between 1951 and 1961.

In what became known as 'the sack of Palermo', dynamite blew up the wisteria-clad Liberty villas built for the wealthy in the *Belle Epoque* of the early nineteenth century, shattering their ornate turrets and decorative friezes and engulfing avenues of ficus and magnolia trees in clouds of dust. Throughout the Golden Shell, bulldozers tore up palm and citrus groves. The villas and groves were then replaced by ten-storey blocks of flats of grey steel and concrete, built so quickly and haphazardly that the new residents moved in often before the city hall had built sewers, tarmacked roads or installed street lighting. In contrast, piles of rubble from wartime bombings in the centre's dense web of alleys, which did not interest the developers, were left uncleared.

The building frenzy, which also saw monuments pulled down, was all in the name of 'making Palermo more beautiful' according to the slogan the overweight but slick mayor Salvo Lima, a Christian Democrat, loved to repeat – a sardonic smile played on his lips when he quoted the slogan to his friends. He was seen as so influential even among Sicilian emigrants that he was invited to America to participate in John F. Kennedy's bid for the presidency. Unknown to most of his electorate, Lima was the son of a mafioso and a mafioso himself. He and the boss Tommaso Buscetta went to see an opera at Palermo's Teatro Massimo together and Lima sent him tickets for the whole season as a present. On one official visit to America, a boss gave him a letter of introduction to meet Charles Gambino, the head of one of New York's five families. Such associations hadn't stopped Lima campaigning under another shameless slogan: 'For a democratic Sicily freed of the mafia'.

The Corleonesi had a potentially strong card to play in the city's politics, a privileged channel to the mayor, Vito Ciancimino, who as councillor for public works was responsible for the building boom. He was a key link between politicians awarding public works contracts, businesses doing the work and the mafia taking its cut. The son of a Corleone barber, Ciancimino had spent much of his childhood making lathers for his father's important customers – including Dr Navarra – before settling in Palermo at the age of 18. Scornful, thin and with a Hitler-style moustache, Ciancimino soon rose to become both a Christian Democrat party chief and a shrewd businessman, setting up a railway haulage company which had a monopoly in Sicily.

The mafia mattered to politicians like Lima and Ciancimino. A supergrass explained:

> The politicians have always come to look for us because we have a lot, a huge amount of votes at our disposal. To get an idea of how much weight the mafia has in elections, just think of the family of Santa Maria del Gesù (in Palermo), a family of 200 members. It's a terrifying strike force, especially if you consider that each man of honour can dispose of another 40–50 friends and relatives. There are between 1,500 and 2,000 men of honour in the province of Palermo. Multiply that by 50 and you get a fat bundle of 75,000–100,000 votes to steer towards friendly parties and candidates.

Under Lima and Ciancimino, in only five years between 1959 and 1963 the city hall released 4,205 building permits of which 80 per cent were granted to five strawmen, all of them retired, poor and with little or no experience in the building trade – the most 'qualified' of the five was a former bricklayer, who got himself a job as a porter in a block of flats he had, in theory, built himself. The Corleonesi arranged discreet meetings with Ciancimino. Leggio soon realised that he did not respond to intimidation, so the task of forging a working relationship with him was left to Provenzano, the least impulsive of the clan's 'Holy Trinity'. Slowly, Ciancimino began to see the light.

To obtain even a toe-hold in Palermo, Leggio needed allies among the bosses who ruled it. They were known as the *mammasantissima* (Holiest of Mothers), the most powerful of the fraternity's chieftains, and had a tight grip on the city, each of them in charge of a well-defined district. Their first reaction was to look down on the Corleonesi. They turned up their noses at the short, badly dressed and uncouth upstarts with calloused hands and berets, calling them *viddani* (villains, or peasants).

One of the most disdainful was Stefano 'the Prince' Bontate of Palermo's biggest clan, among the most charismatic of the bosses. A haughty mafioso's son whose family traded in oranges, tangerines and lemons, the handsome Bontate had studied with the Jesuits, was a smooth talker and loved the good life. He dressed elegantly, drove a Ferrari and had a weakness for champagne. A keen partridge-hunter, he was admired for his skill in shooting his quarry while on horseback on the estates of aristocratic friends, without losing control of his mount. For shooting humans, he used a pistol whose butt was gracefully inlaid with mother of pearl.

Bontate was one of the first to use a particularly awful way of getting rid of bodies. Having discovered the properties of acid while refining heroin, he would have his men fill a metal drum, of the kind normally used to store olive oil, with the liquid and then delicately plunge a body into it. The acid did its job almost perfectly; after a few hours, all that would remain at the bottom of the drum was an odd part of the pelvis, a bone fragment, gold tooth, necklace or bracelet engraved with the names of the victim's wife or children.

But it was short-sighted of 'the Prince' Bontate and others to mock the Corleonesi simply because of their rural origins. After all, the two godfathers of the 1940s and 1950s, Don Calò Vizzini and Giuseppe Genco Russo, were both from humble provincial origins – Vizzini was a day-labourer's son and Genco Russo a former shepherd. The two patriarchs may have dressed in ill-fitting clothes, a trouser belt embracing their vast paunches – Genco Russo had the habit of spitting on the floor, whoever he was talking to at the time – but they were respected, admired and feared. As one boss observed later with the benefit of hindsight: 'The Corleonesi were cunning, diabolic, clever and ferocious, a rare combination in Cosa Nostra.'

Leggio used a variety of disguises as he criss-crossed Palermo, dressing up as a policeman, a monk, a tourist and even a woman. He managed to spread beyond the meat market, which he had supplied for many years, to other sectors where he levied a commission of up to 20 per cent, from the grain market to snooker tables and pinball machines. He ran so many thousands of them that police estimated they earned him £800,000 a year. 'Leggio wasn't just rich himself,' a police investigator explained. 'Everybody who worked for him, covered for him, sheltered him, nursed him, was rich. The source of his power from the start was that fatal, lightning readiness to kill. But in the end, it was money too. The man *gushed* money.'

Being on the run didn't stop Leggio flaunting his wealth and connections. He left handsome tips at restaurants, gave flowers and perfume to nurses who treated him and readily accepted invitations to the villas of titled dignitaries. 'My life as an outlaw was spent in Palermo's salons,' Leggio said later – a remark which, however, must be taken with more than a pinch of salt, as with his comment that countesses and baronesses battled to seduce him.

One of Leggio's first moves was to make a pact with the Greco brothers, from a family in the coastal village of Ciaculli east of Palermo that had been producing bosses for generations. The new allies plotted to challenge the much more powerful La Barbera clan for control of the property boom. The boss Salvatore La Barbera, as head of the Palermo-centre area, controlled the neighbourhood that had become a property developer's dream. He was a close friend of the mayor, Lima.

But Leggio soon realised he was out of his depth when this confrontation spiralled into a war engulfing all the Palermo families. The murder of Salvatore La Barbera in 1963 prompted his brother to demand an explanation from bosses but they all said they had no idea who the killer was. A month later a car exploded outside the home of one of the Greco brothers in Ciaculli, destroying the house but failing to harm him as he was away at the time. Again, no one seemed to know who was behind it.

One of the commandments in the mafia's 'code of honour' is that members must always tell the truth to each other and the failure to identify those responsible for the two attacks fuelled suspicion among the Palermo clans, so much so that they turned against each other and unleashed what is known as the first mafia war of 1962–1963. It saw hundreds of bosses and soldiers shot down in Palermo's streets. Leggio and the Corleonesi watched from afar, careful not to take part in the massacre, as with each new body the clans slowly but steadily weakened each other.

The war ground to an abrupt halt on 30 June 1963 when someone called the police to report an Alfa Romeo car with a flat tyre abandoned on a dirt road running through a tangerine grove in Ciaculli. Shortly afterwards, another caller told the police: 'Don't touch the Alfa Romeo.' The police saw a gas canister lying on the backseat and electric wires leading from it. An army bomb-disposal expert was summoned as more police and soldiers deployed to isolate the area. In just a few minutes, the expert easily defused the device. Relieved officers who had previously been keeping their distance approached the car and one of them opened the boot. An explosion instantly ripped through the tangerine trees, killing five police officers and two military engineers; among their few remains were a gun, an officer's beret and a finger with a wedding ring.

Such was the public outrage caused by the killings that for the first time since the war started the state acted; the Ciaculli bomb violated the pact of peaceful co-existence between the two. Police surrounded entire districts of Palermo at night to search for suspects. Some 10,000 policemen were sent from the mainland to Sicily and more than 250 mafiosi were arrested in Palermo. Although the police net caught only lowly soldiers – bosses, and the entire Corleonese clan, slipped through unscathed – the arrests decimated so many families that it was forced to virtually suspend its activity. 'Cosa Nostra didn't exist any more in the Palermo area after 1963. It was completely knocked out,' one defector said.

'Be Wise' – Justice Mafia-Style

Leggio's poor health made him more vulnerable to capture than other bosses. In the autumn of 1963, he narrowly avoided arrest after an informer revealed that he was suffering from tuberculosis of the spine and was being treated at a hospital in Palermo where he had registered under a false name. When a hundred officers of the *carabinieri* police, led by Colonel Ignazio Milillo, a decorated veteran of Mussolini's wars, raided the clinic where they believed Leggio was staying, they searched the entire establishment for three hours, checking even the kitchens. But they found no sign of him.

It was only after a few days that Milillo realised he had got the wrong hospital; by the time he searched the right one, the only trace of the fugitive was a packet of his cigarettes on a bedside table. Leggio had lived there undisturbed for the past four months. Milillo did, however, seize an X-ray which showed three of Leggio's vertebrae were so crushed together they were close to falling apart.

Anxious not to be outdone by the *carabinieri*, their traditional rival, the police decided they too must seek Leggio. Angelo Mangano, a six-foot-two, unsmiling Sicilian with blue eyes, a square jaw and a pointed beard, was named the new police superintendent of Corleone. A marksman and a keen wrestler with an eye for newspaper headlines, Mangano had once arrested Leggio's brother. But a judge promptly ruled there was no case against the brother and he was released.

On the winter afternoon that Mangano arrived in Corleone, alighting from the Palermo bus in the main piazza and dressed immaculately as usual in a freshly pressed, double-breasted suit with a white silk handkerchief in his breastpocket, he handed over his luggage to a policeman who had been awaiting him. He then walked into a nearby bar where he introduced himself, to cold stares from the regulars, and ordered a glass of cold milk – not a macho drink, but Mangano couldn't care less what people thought.

After finishing his milk, Mangano started to walk slowly through the streets towards the police station 400 yards away. None of the men he passed lifted their berets to him in greeting; instead they simply looked away. This did nothing to discourage him; he took to stopping in bars and announcing in a loud voice that to catch Leggio 'all it takes is to follow his dribble of gold and blood'. Temporarily ignoring the traditional acrimony between their forces, Mangano and Colonel Milillo agreed to set up a joint team in the latter's offices in the centre of Palermo.

An unwritten rule is that bosses must be physically present to govern their territory effectively. But Leggio's self-confidence may also explain why he chose to return to Corleone only a few weeks after Mangano's arrival. Leggio's refuge was in the heart of the town, in a small tucked-away courtyard. This was the home of Leoluchina Sorisi, whom the rumour-mill still had down as the ex-lover of the peasant leader Rizzotto, murdered by Leggio himself 16 years earlier; in fact, her boyfriend was Leggio's henchman Criscione, who had been acquitted of the murder.

According to an account she gave much later, Leggio's soldiers persuaded Leoluchina to give him refuge by threatening to kill her relatives. When he moved in, Leggio himself sought to reassure her, telling her that he would not stay long and would 'leave you in peace'. He also hinted that she would be rewarded in some way. Leoluchina herself firmly believed that no one would ever find out; she had good reason to believe this, as no one would expect her to shelter the killer of a man people believed to be her former lover.

Police set up a few road-blocks around the town to make random checks on drivers, but this failed to catch Leggio. He rarely ventured outside. When he did, it was always as part of a three-car convoy; he would sit in the second car, and the first would be occupied by a couple of local notables who were beyond suspicion – they would stop and chat to police if ever they came across a road-block, allowing Leggio to drive on unchallenged.

The road-blocks did, however, yield a surprise catch on a December evening in 1963, when Leggio's henchman Riina was arrested just outside Corleone, sporting his usual pencil-thin moustache and wearing an overcoat against the cold. Riina tried to flee from the policemen on foot, sliding down a snowy slope, but they caught up with him and levelled their guns at him. Riina stared at them, his metallic eyes flashing with hatred. He told them his name was Giovanni Grande and that he was a farm-worker; he handed over a false driving licence to prove it.

At the police station, the superintendent Mangano questioned Riina well into the early hours of the morning; Mangano had no idea who his prisoner was, but he believed 'Grande' was a false name. Riina continued to insist his name was Grande, to the irritation of Mangano who saw himself condemned to spending a sleepless night for nothing, as he was convinced the man before him would not change his tune. Sipping at some cold milk – he offered a glass to the prisoner, who refused – Mangano tried again and again to catch him out, with no success.

At about 4 a.m., a policeman who, unlike Mangano, was born and bred in Corleone suddenly walked up to Riina.

'I know who you are . . .' the policeman said.

Riina stared at him but kept silent.

'You're Totò Riina!' the policeman exclaimed.

Riina's expression did not change and he remained tight-lipped. It was only at dawn that he finally admitted that yes, he was indeed Riina.

Riina's first taste of the Ucciardone prison in Palermo cannot have been too unpleasant. The jail built by the Bourbon dynasty in the early nineteenth century on the waterfront as a fortress was known to mafiosi as the Grand Hotel Ucciardone because all sorts of favours could be bought there. Dons paid guards handsomely to bring them fresh lobsters and champagne – 'Drugs were the only thing we didn't consume,' one former prisoner said – and paid doctors to deliver false medical certificates which assured them of a more comfortable bed in hospital. The jail indulged the bosses' every whim short of freedom; one insisted on wearing striped silk dressing gowns, another on smoking only with a silver cigarette-holder encrusted with precious gems.

Riina cut a poor figure in comparison, dressing as he always had in ill-fitting, creased jackets. He and his family were so poor that his mother could not afford the train journey to visit him in prison. What he saw of the Palermo dons' expensive tastes fed his ambition. 'When I get out of here I want to walk on a carpet of 100,000-lire banknotes,' Riina, who had shaved off his moustache and put on weight in custody, confided to one prisoner.

The Palermo dons still at liberty may have looked down their noses at the Corleonesi, but in jail Riina's closeness to Leggio earned him respect. Although the punishment for approaching another inmate's cell was three days' isolation, many prisoners took the risk just to glance at Riina through his door's spyhole; when they greeted him, Riina walked up to the door and, unable to offer his hand to be shaken, poked a finger through the small opening to be squeezed instead. The greeting was more dignified when Riina emerged for his daily stroll: prisoners bowed their heads as he passed.

Gaspare Mutolo, a young, cheerful tram conductor's son with a big, black drooping moustache, who shared Riina's cell, helped him kill time by playing draughts with him every evening. They made the draughts out of crumbs, darkening some with Nutella chocolate spread. Mutolo, a skilled player who easily beat all the other prisoners, was cunning enough to allow Riina to win. The losing tactic paid off, as Riina began to take him under his wing and granted him the 'honour', as Mutolo called it, of accompanying him on his walks.

A car-thief, Mutolo knew very little about the mafia. But before his arrest he worked as a mechanic in a garage run by a mafioso and was fascinated by the gatherings of bosses and soldiers he had witnessed. To coach Mutolo, Riina, who could barely read himself, told him to get a novel out of the prison library; the 800-page *I Beati Paoli* by William Galt, alias Luigi Natoli, featuring a legendary secret sect and swashbuckling tales of duels, kidnappings and assaults on nunneries in seventeenth-century Palermo. Another chronicler wrote of the sect's members: 'By day they would genuflect at the altar and pray . . . At night they would lie in wait, wrapped in their greatcoats, and roam the streets with a rosary in their hands and a dagger hidden close to their hearts.'

One day, Riina asked Mutolo about his thieving, testing him: 'When you go to rob things, if you've got to shoot someone, do you do it?'

'If it's the right moment,' Mutolo replied.

'If you've got to shoot someone you only need a second; but if you have to rob you waste more time,' Riina said.

Mutolo tried to explain that if he got involved in a row with someone then yes, he might shoot; but the idea of doing so without a reason was beyond him. Riina however couldn't understand why Mutolo found shooting a man harder than robbing him. For the benefit of his pupil, Riina set out the principle that guided his life in the mafia: 'You must use every means to reach your objective and all obstacles must be eliminated.'

The young prisoner came to idolise Riina. He was impressed by the way Riina kept calm at all times. 'Riina appears to be very gentle and humble. I've never seen him angry; sometimes I've seen him flush a bit, but he was never rude or aggressive,' Mutolo recalled. When Mutolo was transferred, Riina gave him a note for the governor of his new prison in southern Sicily; the note ensured that Mutolo was treated as an honoured guest there.

Six months after Riina began his tutorials in crime in the Palermo jail, the team hunting Leggio got lucky. After weeks of vain attempts, a police detective managed to recruit as an informer a young man whose family had watched over Leggio during one of his stays in the city. The source, whose reason for betraying

Leggio is unknown, revealed that he had driven Leggio from Palermo to a house in Corleone a few months earlier.

On a May evening in 1964 the superintendent Mangano and his rival Colonel Millilo accompanied the informant to Corleone; the house he led them to was that of Leoluchina, the woman who had agreed to hide Leggio. After surrounding the area, Mangano walked briskly up a short flight of steps and – in a polite anti-climax – knocked at the door. It was opened by Leoluchina.

Apparently knowing precisely where to look, Mangano walked up to a bedroom on the first floor where he found a puffy-faced Leggio lying in bed, wearing striped pyjamas and a leather brace over his chest. On the bedside table lay an assortment of pills and three books: Tolstoy's *War and Peace*, Kant's *Critique of Pure Reason* and a book of prayers entitled *Eternal Maxims*.

Mangano told one of his men to call Colonel Milillo, who on entering the bedroom had the good sense to walk up to the bed, bend down and start searching under the mattress.

'What do you want? What are you looking for?' a surprised Leggio remonstrated.

'Leggio, show me your gun,' Milillo replied.

Leggio smiled. 'I've got it here in the bedside table.' He made to reach for a drawer, but Milillo stopped his hand and grabbed the gun himself.

Leggio shook his head and said in a resentful tone: 'Colonel, there was no need for you to worry because I'd always have had to hand over the pistol to you. You fought me with honour, and it was right that honour should win.'

As Leggio finished speaking, he stared at Mangano with hate in his eyes. Leggio hissed: 'While that buffoon, that clown was capable only of capturing idiots like my brother. And now his mission is over.'

The implicit threat was left hanging in the air as Milillo ordered Leggio to follow him. With an apparently huge effort, Leggio managed to get out of bed and stand up, but he leant heavily on the bedside table to steady himself. Two officers helped to hold him up and get him dressed. Leoluchina, apparently no longer a reluctant guardian, combed his hair and stroked his cheek with her fingers while the two officers kept him on his feet.

Leggio, who had recovered his self-control, thanked them with a friendly smile. 'What can I do? I'm getting old,' he said. 'There's just one thing I ask of you: take me somewhere where the sun shines. I need a lot of sun if you want me to stay alive.'

An officer carried Leggio on his back down the stairs then set him down. As he was led outside, leaning on a stick, Mangano walked up to his side, took hold of Leggio's left hand which had been resting on an officer's shoulder and placed it on his own. The picture which made the front pages of the newspapers the next day portrayed Mangano as Leggio's captor.

Digging under the house, police found machine-guns, pistols and hand grenades; they found more weapons, well-oiled and wrapped in cellophane, in several tombs in the Corleone cemetery – the guns included the US-made Sten machine-gun which Leggio had used when he was still a humble henchman of Dr Navarra.

Shortly afterwards, the informer who had betrayed Leggio died in a bizarre road accident. Leoluchina was jailed for two years for hiding Leggio.

In the spring of 1966, Riina was summoned to a windowless room in the Palermo jail. Waiting to question him was a young prosecutor, Judge Cesare Terranova. Riina recognised the judge and immediately demanded to return to his cell. As Riina turned to leave, he spat out his anger: 'With you it's like with the Jews. You've always got something against me, there's an arrest warrant every five minutes. You and I, signor Judge Terranova, will meet only in court.'

Leggio gave Terranova just as hostile a reception when his turn came to be questioned. From a wheelchair, Leggio refused to talk, saying he couldn't remember his own name or that of his parents. Terranova turned to his assistant and said: 'Write that Leggio doesn't know whose son he is.' The judge saw that his remark incensed the prisoner. 'Leggio actually had foam on his lips; he would have killed me on the spot if he could,' Terranova told his wife. Leggio himself admitted: 'If I could have bitten him then, I would certainly have poisoned him.'

Terranova sent Leggio, Riina, Provenzano and another 61 mafiosi to trial in 1969. For the first time, the heavyweights of the Corleonesi were in the dock together, to answer charges of criminal conspiracy, murder and other crimes. The growing notoriety of the Corleonesi led to the trial being held on the mainland, in Bari in southern Italy; judicial authorities ruled that Palermo judges would be too vulnerable to intimidation.

Despite his poor health, Leggio, who was accused of nine murders, made a point of appearing regularly in court. He would arrive either using crutches, or lying on a stretcher, but he was always smartly dressed. When his turn came to speak, he smoothly attributed what he called his 'vicissitudes' to a vendetta by a police officer: 'He repeatedly suggested that I offer his wife the possibility of having some fun but I, for moral reasons, refused to take up this invitation. I had no relationship with this lady. Please, don't ask me to name names, I am a gentleman,' he said.

The only crime Leggio confessed to was black marketeering: 'During the war and immediately afterwards I dedicated myself to the black market and that transformed me from a poor peasant into someone who gradually drove Fiats and then custom-built cars. It's true I earned rivers of money.' His wealth, he continued, drew the attention of a corrupt police officer who asked him for money. 'I always refused and that's how I started being persecuted by the police,' he said. When, during a break in the trial, journalists asked him about the mafia, Leggio replied: 'In Corleone the mafia doesn't exist.'

Of the two witnesses called to testify against Leggio, one started ranting and raving and had to be taken to a psychiatric hospital where he was diagnosed as suffering from 'a form of psychogenic reaction', meaning he was terrified. The other, a barber, suddenly fell mute after crossing Leggio's gaze. Later, the barber found his voice again to shout to a journalist: 'I know nothing, nothing at all!'

As the trial drew to an end after three months, the prosecutor demanded a life sentence for Leggio, and a total of 300 years in jail for the accused. Shortly afterwards, someone stole a pistol which the prosecutor kept in his desk drawer. A few days before the verdict was due, the judges received an anonymous express letter sent from Palermo. The letter, written in black ink and full of spelling mistakes, read:

> You people of Bari haven't understood, or rather, you don't want to understand, what Corleone means. You are judging honest gentlemen of Corleone whom the police have accused out of whim. We simply want to warn you that if a single gentleman from Corleone is convicted you will be blown to pieces, you will be destroyed, you will be butchered and so will your relatives. Nobody must be convicted. Otherwise you will all be condemned to death – you and your families. A Sicilian proverb says: 'A man forewarned is a man half-saved.' It's up to you. Be wise.

The letter was signed with a cross.

When the verdict was announced, the presiding judge read out the names of the 64 accused and declared 64 acquittals. The judges ruled there was insufficient evidence to convict them of criminal conspiracy or murder. The court did acknowledge that the mafia existed, but explained that 'the equation mafia equals criminal association has no judicial impact'. As for Leggio himself, the judges decreed that his difficulty walking made it 'unlikely at the highest degree' that he had taken part directly in murders; he was convicted only of stealing grain two decades earlier and was given a suspended sentence. Riina was found guilty only of stealing the driving licence he had handed to police on the evening of his arrest and sentenced to a year and six months in jail. As it was his first conviction and he had already spent six months in prison, he knew he would be released immediately.

As the judge read the verdict, Leggio and Riina turned to each other and smiled. Fifty-five people had been killed in Corleone and it was as if, in the words of the late Dr Navarra, they had been kicked by a mule. 'If the mafia is everything they claimed I was – well then, the mafia doesn't exist,' Leggio said as he left the courtroom. The head of the police in Palermo immediately ordered his arrest on new accusations, but a senior judge ruled bizarrely that Leggio could be arrested again only in Corleone.

After five years in prison, Leggio made looking after his health his priority. He travelled to Rome where he booked himself into an exclusive clinic, suffering from a serious atrophy of the bladder. While he waited for an operation, he conducted business from his bed, visited by bosses, Neapolitan smugglers and a member of parliament. In what must have flattered his ego, he managed to ensure the operation was carried out by the personal doctor of no less a dignitary than Italy's president.

While Leggio attended to his health, Riina returned to Corleone. But Riina was promptly re-arrested by the police, who wanted him sent into internal exile on the grounds that his return could prompt more killings. A court ordered that Riina spend the next four years in San Giovanni in Persiceto, a small town in central Italy. Riina demanded a few days to settle his family affairs and returned home to formalise his engagement to his beloved Ninetta.

The girl Riina had first fallen in love with when she was barely a teenager was now a 26-year-old teacher. A model schoolgirl, she had always sat in the front row in class, studied Latin and Greek and read many novels; her favourites were about the oppressed and their oppressors. 'What I read in those books was life in Corleone,' Ninetta confided later. 'I was fascinated by Machiavelli. You know why? Because his principle, the end justifies the means, was applied to the letter by the local police.'

After setting her mind on becoming a schoolteacher – a profession usually reserved for those from wealthier families than hers – Ninetta enrolled at Palermo University to study literature and philosophy. She took the bus to the city virtually every day to attend lectures but two police officers followed her wherever she went, suspecting her of links to the mafia that were not simply sentimental. But she was forced to give up her studies and find work as a teacher in a private institute when one of her brothers was arrested and the other went on the run. The two had shot dead a cattle breeder who had boasted in public of his amorous exploits with Ninetta's sister, whom he had wooed until their father put a stop to the relationship.

Riina's silent tailing of Ninetta on her walks to school paid off. 'For years I followed her with my eyes, for years I never gave her a moment's rest until she decided to marry me,' Riina once confided. Before he was due to go into exile, Riina and his mother called at Ninetta's home for the 'clarification' which tradition required; the mothers of the two lovers discussed the dowry and where the couple would live once they had married. Riina was no rich suitor; a year earlier he had to ask some mafiosi to help meet a legal bill. But on the other hand, the mothers knew he could still make his fortune if he could stay out of jail.

Drinks were then served in the presence of the two lovers and Riina gave Ninetta a ring. 'We got engaged in the intimacy of our families,' Ninetta said later. 'It's not as if we said to each other "I love you" or "You're the light of my life"; we people are serious people.'

Shortly afterwards, Riina bid a chaste goodbye to Ninetta and left for exile in San Giovanni in Persiceto. At the local police station, he signed the register of people placed under special surveillance, only to disappear a few days later – a fugitive yet again.

Death of 'the Cobra'

Mafia bosses hate not knowing who is responsible for murdering any of their number and they spent more than six years trying to establish who had started the first mafia war and planted the car-bomb in a tangerine grove in Ciaculli that had caused a police crackdown. By late 1969, they were convinced they had found the culprit: Michele 'the Cobra' Cavataio, a boss and builder who owed his nickname to his deceitfulness and to the Colt Cobra revolver he always carried. 'If he wants to rid himself of an enemy,' a supergrass said, 'Cavataio is capable of knocking down a whole block of flats without a thought for the innocent victims.'

The Palermo bosses at first negotiated with Cavataio, or pretended to. During one round of talks, he committed the unforgivable error of reaching down into one of his socks to produce a map of the city with the names of each known family member written on it; he then demanded that some bosses be promoted and others demoted. Writing down anything concerning the clans was forbidden and at the time outsiders knew next to nothing about its structure and its members. At another meeting, Cavataio threatened to have a soldier killed within an hour if his demands were not met, describing just where the man would be ambushed; it was only after much pleading that he agreed to telephone his men and call off the murder.

The Palermo bosses decided that Cavataio was a loose cannon and must be eliminated. In a display of unity, they picked six mafiosi from different clans; Leggio suggested that Provenzano and Calogero Bagarella should be part of the hit squad and the offer was accepted. The Corleonesi now had a chance to prove their mettle to the Palermo patriarchs.

The death squad hit on the idea of copying the Chicago gangster Al Capone and his 1929 Saint Valentine's Day massacre, when his men dressed in stolen police uniforms and eliminated seven rivals in America's most notorious gangland slaying of the century. Shortly before 7 p.m. on 10 December 1969, Provenzano, Calogero Bagarella and four other mafiosi set off in two cars and drove through the rain to the offices of a construction company in northern Palermo which Cavataio used as his headquarters. Five of the six hitmen wore police uniforms and there were police warning lights on the roofs of the cars. The sixth, Gaetano Grado, stuck to his normal clothes; 'I'm risking my life, I don't want to die with a uniform on,' Grado protested. The gunmen were to get everyone together in one room, disarm them and then open fire. The squad brought jerry-cans full of petrol, as they were under orders to set fire to the offices as soon as they had shot their prey, in the hope of destroying the map Cavataio was believed to have hidden there.

As soon as the hitmen rushed out of their cars on reaching the offices, a single-storey building, Grado shouted to an employee standing outside: 'We're the police, come inside with us!'

The police uniforms were swiftly made pointless when Provenzano shot the employee before he could do as he had been told. Four hitmen rushed inside and opened fire. Grado recognised Cavataio, who had been warming himself in front of a radiator, and shot him in the shoulder. Cavataio crouched behind a desk and fired back with his Colt Cobra. His bullets shattered a window-pane and some splinters of glass lodged in Grado's eyes, blinding him temporarily. Grado managed to stumble out and shouted to the two killers who had remained outside: 'Go in, go in! I can't see any more!'

Cavataio managed to shoot Calogero Bagarella in the chest, fatally wounding him. Another of his bullets grazed Provenzano's hand, and another wounded one of his attackers in the arm. 'The Cobra' fell under the desk, apparently lifeless. After a shoot-out that lasted several minutes, what one mafioso later called 'an unreal silence' fell over the offices – cars could be heard swishing through the rain on the road outside. Provenzano walked up to Cavataio, grabbed hold of him and pulled him out from under the desk. Provenzano started searching inside his socks for the map of the Palermo clans. As he searched, Provenzano saw the supposedly dead Cavataio suddenly come to life and point a pistol at his face.

Cavataio pressed the trigger. But the pistol didn't fire; there were no more bullets. Provenzano turned his machine-gun, an Italian-made Beretta capable of firing 600 rounds a minute, on Cavataio and tried to fire. But the machine-gun jammed. With his bleeding hand, Provenzano was unable to unblock the machine-gun so he used its butt as a club to crush Cavataio's skull, kicking him at the same time. Then, picking up a loaded pistol lying nearby, Provenzano shot him once in the temple to finish him off. He then bent down to search the body, but he found only a single sheet of paper in the jacket pocket. Unknown to him, Cavataio had managed to tear up his list of mafiosi and throw it into the waste-paper basket before his attackers burst in. The list was later found by police, but investigators didn't realise its importance and it was never followed up. Two associates of Cavataio also died.

The wounded hitmen were in no condition to burn the offices as ordered. It was as much as they could do to carry away Bagarella's body, heave it into the boot of a car, and bury it secretly in a cemetery under someone else's tombstone. For several days afterwards, Riina wore a black tie in mourning for his brother-in-law's death.

The killing of Cavataio at first raised protests from clans across Sicily, who accused the Palermo families – and their accomplices, the Corleonesi – of duplicity in making him offers of peace. But within a couple of weeks the anger gave way to relief; so great was the clans' anxiety to put plots and wars behind them. Despite Provenzano's failure to keep to the plan for the murder, his reputation as a pitiless killer with more than his fair share of luck was established; this was the third shoot-out he had narrowly survived.

He now became known as 'the Tractor', as one mafioso explained: 'Because of the homicidal capacities he showed above all in the Cavataio massacre, in the sense that he just ground everything to bits and where he had been grass no longer grew.'

The Corleonesi took advantage of their new notoriety to ingratiate themselves with Palermo's bosses. They found an early ally in the capo Gaetano Badalamenti, who although he was of rough rural stock like them, still owning a herd of cows and selling cheese, had a passion for solid gold watches. The Corleonesi served him unquestioningly and as a favour purged his town of Cinisi, west of Palermo, of his enemies. Both Riina and Provenzano acted as Badalamenti's loyal servants. When Badalamenti served some time in prison he had no trouble continuing to enforce his authority; he sent his orders to Riina through an intermediary who visited him in jail and then briefed Riina and Provenzano over lunch in a restaurant. Riina carried out the murders ordered by Badalamenti without even asking the reason. 'Riina was just a little dog on a leash. Badalamenti would unleash him and, somewhere, a pair of eyes would be closed for ever. Then the dog went back to his kennel to wait for the next order,' said a boss who met Riina at the time.

But Riina soon began to do much more than simply act as executioner at Badalamenti's beck and call. He began to question mafiosi relentlessly to find out as much as he could about bosses and their clans. 'He found out the secrets, envies, ambitions and weaknesses of each man of honour,' the same boss added. 'He knew how much this or that soldier earned and how. He knew the scars and the resentments of each clan.' Riina took mental note of everything he learnt for future use. 'Riina was cold and attentive to every little detail. Mother Nature gave him a very precious gift: the memory of an elephant. If you'd told him something ten years earlier, you could be sure he'd never forget it. In fact, he'd remind you of it ten or twenty years later, in the same words,' another boss, Tommaso Buscetta, recalled. Riina was thirsty for information, but he revealed very little himself. Unlike other clans, the Corleonesi kept the identities of their soldiers secret – they were even more secretive than the mafia itself.

The word spread that the Corleonesi were always willing to help and didn't ask for anything in return – or at least not immediately. They even carried out favours for 'the Prince' Bontate, who had lost little of his disdain for them but wasn't above using them for his own ends. Unsuspecting bosses offered the Corleonesi a helping hand. When the Cavataio murder prompted police raids in and around Palermo, Badalamenti, who had left prison and was hiding Leggio in his fiefdom near the city, suggested he should seek refuge in Catania on Sicily's east coast, at the foot of Mount Etna. 'Wait for things to calm down, get some rest and take care of yourself,' Badalamenti told him. 'You can always leave one of your soldiers here. In any case you'll still be the one taking the important decisions. It's not as if Catania is at the end of the world; it's only two and a half hours from Palermo.'

Leggio took his friend's advice – the two had become so close that Leggio was godfather to Badalamenti's youngest child. Flanked by Riina and Provenzano, and wearing a light-coloured, double-breasted jacket, he set out in a Mercedes, four cars escorting him. That evening, they arrived at an arranged spot on an isolated country road outside Catania to be welcomed by, among others, Antonino Calderone, whose brother was the local capo. Leggio impressed Antonino Calderone immediately: he had 'a distinguished, proud bearing, he looked like a chief judge of the Supreme Court. He sat there, on a stone post beside that country road. And all of us stood there bewitched by this Leggio, as if the bee's knees had arrived. After all, he was the Number One in Sicily.'

Calderone's brother Pippo, known as 'Silver Throat' because of the microphone he spoke through after a larynx operation, was taken in by Riina's gentle and respectful manner. 'Riina pretended to be as meek as a lamb, all sugar and honey. He always had a grateful expression stamped on his face . . . as if he was thanking us because we were dealing with him, because we were allowing him – a rough peasant – to spend time with us,'

Pippo said. He even took pity on Riina: 'He had a sad light in his eyes and we thought: Jesus Christ! These peasants really have had a tough time. First they had to fight a war against Navarra, then they had to go on the run. Always keeping their eyes open, a pistol in their belt and a rifle across their shoulder, watching out for cops and enemies. Always out in the fields, in all weathers,' he reflected.

The awe Leggio inspired soon gave way to irritation as he began to make impossible demands of his hosts. Antonino Calderone thought him 'petulant like a child. He drove us round the bend.' After only a few days in the first country house chosen for his hideout, Leggio complained it was too cold and insisted on moving. He was convinced he could drink only a certain brand of mineral water following his prostate operation and forced Calderone to spend hours driving from one town to another looking for it.

Among Leggio's most insistent demands was that Calderone help him meet a woman who had first caught his eye during one of his hospital stays. 'Professor,' an exasperated Calderone told him bluntly, using the title Leggio loved, 'this is crazy. That woman knows who you are. Do you realise how dangerous this is?' Leggio eventually saw reason. Some time later, he asked his hosts for some sleeping pills; he had met two sisters and wanted to send one to sleep while he seduced the sister he fancied.

After moving a couple more times, and complaining that because he suffered from colic he needed plenty of fresh air, Leggio finally found a home further up Etna's slopes, close to the town of San Giovanni La Punta. Still flanked by Provenzano, who served as bodyguard and butler, Leggio settled in a villa with a view of the Mediterranean which the pair rented under false names, posing as brothers, both meat merchants. Leggio told shopkeepers he was convalescing after an illness. They ventured out freely for drives around the volcano, often accompanied by associates driving cars in front of and behind them to avoid any police road-blocks. Provenzano rarely took the wheel; his driving licence was a false one, and he was a notoriously poor driver. 'Those of us who had good cars were all very careful not to let him drive them,' Calderone said.

Leggio never paid for anything in Catania, from the Tuscan cigars he smoked to the villa where he lived. Despite his notoriety, in the late 1960s he didn't have even a penny in his pocket – or at least, that's what he told his hosts. When they themselves were short of money and could not afford to pay for his upkeep, they turned to Palermo bosses and extorted funds from wealthy businessmen. At the time, the whole of the mafia was short of money. Arrests had weighed heavily on its coffers; large sums had to be spent on lawyers' fees and on the upkeep of mafiosi families whose main breadwinner was behind bars.

Leggio's habit of sunbathing on the villa's terrace, sprawled naked on a deckchair, came close to ending his life on the run. The owner of a nearby block of flats complained to the police when the sight of the nude Leggio shocked a couple of potential buyers he was showing around. When two officers knocked at the door of the villa one morning, Provenzano was out and Leggio had little choice but to open the door, wearing a pair of shorts. The two officers greeted him politely and asked him to accompany them to their station.

Leggio unbuttoned his shorts to show he had a catheter and said: 'Right now? I'm waiting for the doctor who must come to take the catheter out. I'll come straight afterwards.'

The officers told him not to worry, he could come that afternoon.

As soon as they had left, an agitated Leggio telephoned Calderone. The boss reassured him: 'Listen, Professor. They didn't come because they know who you are. They wouldn't have come that way, just like that, knocking on the door. And I'm also sure that if they'd come any other way they wouldn't be alive now.'

When Provenzano returned to the villa, it was agreed that for caution's sake he would call on the police to find out what they wanted; he would explain that his 'brother' was ill and that he had come in his place. Leggio would wait in a car parked nearby. After a short while, Provenzano emerged from the police station and told Leggio of the complaint the officers had received.

Leggio pretended to take offence: 'Who is this cuckold who says I strip naked? It's not true. I don't sunbathe naked.'

'The police said all you needed to do was to put swimming trunks on in future, and that would be the end of the matter,' Provenzano said.

Leggio reflected for a moment and then exclaimed: 'Why move from here now? We're all right, we're not fugitives any more. The police know we're here, they don't suspect us and so they'll never come to bother us.'

Far from hiding in his villa and contenting himself with the odd spot of sunbathing, Leggio, bent on revenge, decided to seek out and murder the police superintendent Mangano who had arrested him six years earlier. He knew Mangano came from Riposto, a coastal town east of Mount Etna, and was convinced that the superintendent would return there to spend part of the summer by the sea. 'No better time to kill him than now,' Leggio confided.

Every morning at the height of the holiday season in August 1970, Leggio set off in a tiny, unobtrusive Fiat 500 driven by a young mafioso, to scan the streets of Riposto and nearby beaches for any sign of Mangano's distinctive, bearded, six-foot-two figure. Both men were armed with pistols, but Leggio also took with him a large knife, as he intended to kill Mangano slowly. Explaining to Calderone how he planned to do it, Leggio pulled his knife out and sliced it through an imaginary Mangano. 'You see how I want to do it? I want to cut him up this way and that way.' Despite Leggio's dogged searching, there was no sign of Mangano.

Calderone, who spent almost two years virtually waiting on Leggio, had no doubt the boss had been serious and explained just why even mafiosi feared him:

He was bloodthirsty. He liked killing. He had a way of looking at you which struck fear into everyone, including us mafiosi. The slightest thing was enough to make him get angry and a strange light would appear in his eyes which silenced everyone around him. When you were with him, you had to be careful what you said. The wrong tone of voice, a word misunderstood and there would be that sudden silence. Everyone was struck dumb and felt uncomfortable – you could smell death in the air.

That summer, Leggio was driven down the slopes of Mount Etna to the heart of the city of Catania, the chic Via Etnea paved with slabs of lava from the volcano and lined with fashion boutiques. He was shown into a vast apartment owned by the Calderone brothers, where he waited for several other bosses to arrive. The famously irascible Leggio burst out angrily when he learnt that Riina was in the street below with the Palermo boss Buscetta.

'What does Riina think he's doing, coming here with that sleazebag? Instead of pumping two bullets into his head, he walks around with him!' Leggio exclaimed.

Leggio considered Buscetta a Don Giovanni, a whoremonger. Inside the mafia, a passion for the female sex was seen not only as a sign of weakness, but also as a threat to the organisation. Leggio was hardly one to talk as he too fancied himself as a seducer. But unlike Buscetta, Leggio was unmarried and discreet about his conquests. When Buscetta walked in, Leggio betrayed no sign of his contempt and greeted him courteously. The bosses got down to the weighty business at hand: an ambitious plot led by a neo-Fascist aristocrat and descendant of Renaissance popes, Prince Junio Valerio Borghese, to stage no less than a *coup d'état*. Borghese, a Fascist war hero known as the 'Black Prince' because of his political sympathies, intended to seize government offices across Italy. He wanted to negotiate a pact with the brotherhood, guaranteeing that it would provide an escort for his envoys in Sicily. In return, the prince promised that the new regime would overturn a host of convictions that had sent many mafiosi to prison.

For the next three weeks Leggio and other bosses discussed whether or not to back the coup, their talks slotted in around the World Cup Finals in Mexico as Italy was about to reach the final. Leggio was in favour, hoping that his life sentence for Dr Navarra's murder would be cancelled. But several others were wary; they pointed out that the prince was a Fascist and that whatever fine promises he made, once in power he would deal with the mafia the way Mussolini had done – by handcuffing them. Nor did they like the prince's demand that they should wear armbands like the other plotters, to make them easily recognisable.

In order to judge the prince's real intentions, the Catania boss Pippo Calderone went to meet him in Rome. When the prince explained that he wanted the mafiosi to help arrest anyone who opposed the coup, the envoy protested in his metallic-sounding voice, microphone resting on his throat: 'We, mafiosi, should start arresting people? Look here, we don't do police work! If we have to kill someone, fine. We kill him. But police work is not our thing.'

The prince again pledged to overturn convictions against mafiosi, but the boss insisted: 'My dear prince, we're agreed. But you're not going to pull a fast one on us and repeat what Mussolini did?'

'No, no, don't worry. If you help us we won't turn on you. We'll respect the deal. But you have to understand that if there are murders when we are in government, the police and judges can't just do nothing. They will have to do their work,' the prince replied.

The mafia never did have reason to fear a new Fascist take-over. The prince launched the coup at night but it was aborted shortly after forestry guards, the prince's main troops, tried to take over the interior ministry in Rome.

On the Triumvirate

The Corleonesi's prestige and services rendered to several clans earned Leggio a place on a triumvirate set up in 1970 to rule the organisation. The two other members were his early ally Badalamenti and 'the Prince' Bontate; its first task was to reorganise and breathe new life into the mafia, which had been virtually suspended in the wake of the Ciaculli car-bomb that had killed seven officers.

Still hiding on the slopes of Mount Etna, Leggio was worried the other two bosses on the triumvirate would take decisions without consulting him. To prevent this, he appointed one of his two lieutenants to represent him. He didn't have a very high opinion of Provenzano's intelligence – 'Provenzano shoots like a god. It's a shame he has the brains of a hen,' Leggio said of him. But Leggio was also critical of Riina: 'Riina always wants to take bites that are bigger than his mouth.' Despite his misgivings Leggio's choice fell on Riina, an appointment that was the starting point for Riina's ascent to the heights of the mafia.

The Corleonesi now appeared to be on an equal footing with two of the most powerful Palermo bosses. But in fact they were lagging far behind, simply because they had yet to carve themselves a share of a business that was bringing unprecedented wealth to the rest of the mafia: drug-trafficking. Avid for money, Bontate was one of the first to bring drugs into Sicily. Throughout the 1960s and 1970s, Bontate and his allies controlled heroin trafficking, running refineries in Sicily and supplying the American market.

'When they started leaving jail in about 1968, the bosses of

Cosa Nostra were almost all penniless wretches. Then they all became millionaires, in a couple of years, thanks to drug-trafficking,' an informer said. Bosses took to buying designer clothes, including silk shirts by the dozen, from chic boutiques in the centre of Palermo. When asked how one could recognise a mafioso, the boss Buscetta, himself a dapper dresser, replied: 'By his silk shirt. By the car, which must be among the best, a Mercedes for example The tie is also very important. It must be flashy, very "Italian". Rings too, with a diamond. And the Rolex watch.' On his daily visit to the barber's, one boss had Moët et Chandon champagne served to customers and staff.

The refusal of Bontate and several other Palermo bosses to share the profits from the trade caused the first tension with the Corleonesi. The Corleonesi were both new to drug-trafficking and short of money, and when Riina attempted his first ventures he had to ask other mafiosi to invest funds with him. The impatient Corleonesi soon showed that they had no intention of playing by mafia rules. Forced to watch the drug-trafficking from the sidelines, they found another way of making money quickly – kidnapping. Riding roughshod over the unwritten rule requiring them to notify bosses before engaging in such activities, the Corleonesi kidnapped the sons of two Palermo industrialists and released them for ransoms. They wisely distributed the second ransom among the city's most needy mafia families, a move which won them popularity. However, the new tactic exasperated the other triumvirate bosses Bontate and Badalamenti; for them the kidnappings amounted to killing the goose that laid the golden eggs, as it targeted the very class – the rich businessmen – who were providing much of the profits from racketeering and kick-backs on contracts.

But the Corleonesi refused to stop. In August 1972, while three-quarters of Palermo's residents were seeking relief from the summer heat at the seaside, Riina kidnapped Arturo Cassina, the son of an elderly count. The nobleman was a friend of Bontate's, but as usual Riina did not bother to give any advance warning. Riina conducted negotiations himself, boasting that he talked to the count on the telephone while his feet rested on the hostage. This time he obtained a ransom of £1 million, which was collected by Father Agostino Coppola, a mafioso priest and the nephew of the Italo-American boss Frank 'Three Fingers' Coppola. The Corleonesi kept the money for themselves.

Just as they had done with their kidnappings, the Corleonesi notified no one before launching the first of their attacks against the Italian state, claiming the first in a long line of *cadaveri eccelenti* (distinguished corpses), victims who were eminent public figures. On a May morning in 1971 the chief Palermo prosecutor Judge Pietro Scaglione, a burly 65-year-old with heavy jowels and an aquiline nose, went to pray as he did every day in the chapel of the Capuchin cemetery where his wife was buried. Nearby are catacombs where almost 8,000 twisted, leering bodies preserved with arsenic and other chemicals are still on display – a practice continued as late as the 1920s. Scaglione emerged from the chapel to enter a car driven by his bodyguard, but it had gone only a few yards down a winding street flanked by cypress trees when another car blocked its way. Leggio himself was among the mafiosi who ambushed the judge and his bodyguard. Both the victims died before they reached hospital. The prosecutor's only crime had been to investigate Leggio.

In the early 1970s, Leggio abandoned his villa on the slopes of Mount Etna and settled in Milan, Italy's business and fashion capital, presumably wanting to distance himself from the triumvirate and enjoy a freer hand away from Sicily. He used at least six different identities in Milan, two of them a baron and a jeweller. His lifestyle was that of a wealthy businessman. He paid cash for a sixth-floor, five-bedroom apartment where he lived with his new girlfriend, a nurse, and the son she bore him. A chauffeur drove him around in a BMW and his shoes and clothes came from luxury boutiques.

Fine living didn't soften Leggio's vindictive edge, however. He ordered the murder of Damiano Caruso, a mafioso who dared to eliminate a young soldier Leggio had befriended. Leggio also ordered the murder of a lover in whom Caruso had confided. He then raped her teenage daughter and strangled her. 'The two women died because of Leggio's perversity, but also because they knew (about Caruso), and when there are women in the know there's the risk they'll talk. The men of Cosa Nostra are very careful about what they tell their wives,' a supergrass said. Leggio conducted most of his business, including kidnappings and drug-trafficking, from a wine shop and a restaurant where he met Riina, Provenzano and a string of other mafiosi. One informer who met Leggio at this time noted: 'I was stunned by the fact that no one managed to look him in the eyes. His manner was always violent and disdainful towards others.'

With Leggio in Milan, Riina swiftly became the Corleonesi's main envoy in Palermo. Even though he still answered to Leggio in the clan hierarchy, the less flamboyant and verbose Riina gradually built himself a solid base in the city, even forging new relationships with mafiosi across the island, often without the knowledge of clan heads. Riina wanted mafiosi to like him – he liked to joke with them and pat them on the back, and insisted they call him 'Uncle'. Flanked by Provenzano, who had now returned to Sicily, Riina increasingly dictated the Corleonesi's strategy without consulting Leggio.

Riina's growing influence did not go unnoticed. 'The Prince' Bontate openly mocked Riina, calling him the 'peasant' from Corleone. News of this made Riina's blood boil and he took to calling Bontate 'the Falcon', refusing to call him by his usual nickname, 'the Prince'. On one occasion Riina confronted Bontate. 'Me and the Corleonesi have given our lives for Cosa Nostra,' Riina told Bontate self-righteously. 'I helped you with the Cavataio killing, I lost my men and now you turn everyone against me and you want to send me back to Corleone without a cent?'

The other triumvirate boss Badalamenti, who had been the first to welcome the Corleonesi, now chose to back Bontate against them and went as far as to set Riina a trap. He arranged a meeting with him at an accountant's office in Palermo and then tipped off the police. Sensing something was wrong, Riina had stayed away and so avoided arrest. From then on, the Corleonesi grew extremely cautious. Riina would attend one meeting of the triumvirate and Provenzano the next; or they would invent a pretext to have the meeting postponed at the last minute.

As meetings of the triumvirate became virtually impossible to hold due to the tensions between its members, clans replaced it in the early 1970s with a much broader commission of more than a dozen bosses to rule over Palermo and its province. Headed by Badalamenti, it promised to respect the rules of the secret society, arbitrate disputes in a fair manner and put decisions to a vote. None of this was attractive to the Corleonesi and a furious Leggio stormed out of one of its first meetings shouting at the other bosses: 'You set up this commission. Fine, it's all yours! I don't want to be second to anyone.' In his place, the commission appointed Riina, with Provenzano due to replace him after two years. Leggio's two henchmen divided their new responsibilities between them. Riina concentrated on the building sector and drug-trafficking, while Provenzano focused on public works contracts.

Leggio's henchmen conducted their business without being bothered by the authorities. Riina and Provenzano featured only as tiny blips on the radars of investigators. One long 1970 report about their brotherhood dedicated only a few lines to them, in a paragraph entitled '*Second-rank individuals in the Corleone mafia context*'. The report was by an officer of the *carabinieri* police with first-hand experience of Corleone, Carlo Alberto Dalla Chiesa, who had been promoted to the rank of colonel with the job of commanding the force in Palermo. What struck him the most on his return to Sicily was that it was forging an ever-bigger empire, its networks reaching as far as France, Switzerland and America. The mafia was no longer a Sicilian or Italian problem but an international one.

The outspoken Colonel Dalla Chiesa bluntly pointed out to his superiors that one of the main ways the state had sought to crush the organisation – by sending convicted mafiosi into exile on the Italian mainland – had backfired. He complained that the

Corleonesi he had denounced as murderers back in 1949 had all been banished to a town near Milan, where he suspected they were up to no good. But now, when Dalla Chiesa asked for checks on them, he was told they were all living the lives of upright citizens.

Three years after Dalla Chiesa's report, Leonardo Vitale, the first mafioso to break the law of silence since the Second World War, gave investigators precious insight into the organisation as a whole and described the rise of the Corleonesi. The nephew of a boss, Vitale had been tested twice before he was recruited. First he was ordered to kill a horse, which he didn't have the nerve to do. Then, in 1960, the 20-year-old Vitale was ordered to kill a man, a key way of assessing a candidate. As Judge Falcone said: 'If a man of honour has to kill, he kills. Without questioning himself or anyone else. Without exhibiting compassion. If you hesitate over whether or not to kill, you'll be a dead man too.' Vitale performed the task well.

A modest soldier, Vitale betrayed the mafia's secrets when he was in the throes of an apparently mystical crisis of conscience. Vitale knew Riina personally and was the first to describe him as one of the most powerful bosses; he also talked of Riina's political links, named dozens of mafiosi and revealed plans to murder the prosecutor Judge Terranova. His testimony was significant simply because it demonstrated that the fraternity was active at a time when many experts believed it did not exist.

But Sicily was not ready for such evidence. The courts acquitted most of the people Vitale accused. Ironically, he was one of the few found guilty of murder, on the basis of his own confession. The courts ruled that since only an insane person could violate the law of silence, Vitale must be mad and a judge sentenced him to 25 years in a lunatic asylum. Released in 1984, Vitale was murdered in front of his mother and sister as they walked out of a church in Palermo after Sunday Mass seven months later.

'I Love Riina' – Ninetta Goes to Court

One hot July morning in 1971, an attractive schoolteacher from Corleone strode confidently into Palermo's law courts. There could have been no greater contrast between Riina's 27-year-old girlfriend Ninetta Bagarella and the traditional image of the Sicilian mafia wife, silent and dressed in austere black clothes. The boss Buscetta once described the typical spouse: 'The mafioso's wife is the pure and simple copy of her husband. She doesn't talk, because he's trained her not to. She must know nothing about his business. She has to remain locked up in her world. And, outside the home, people can't imagine how unhappy she is because she'll never admit it to anyone.' As she marched through the vast marble halls of the Palace of Justice, built under Mussolini in the Fascist style, the slender, tanned Ninetta held her head high and ignored the stares of the lawyers and clerks she passed. She wore a pastel blue linen dress printed with red and yellow flowers whose hem was above the knee and high-heeled shoes and she sported a diamond engagement ring.

Ninetta had travelled to Palermo to answer police accusations that she was 'dangerous' and 'the liaison officer for the Leggio clan, the link between the various fugitives'. She was the only member of the clan who had a diploma of any kind, the police said, adding that she arranged Leggio's stays in hospital. The previous year, when the police wanted to confiscate her passport, Ninetta sent it to them together with a letter branding them 'persecutors, tormentors, torturers'. Because of the insults, she was also accused of slander. The police had her sacked by the private school where she had taught physical education for the past four years. A prosecutor then called for her exile to the mainland for a minimum of four years, the first time a woman was the object of such a proposal.

As part of her defence, Ninetta had brought with her to the law courts a petition drawn up by the archpriest of Corleone and signed by dozens of her townfolk. The archpriest, a former colleague of Ninetta's at her private school, pronounced the Bagarellas 'an exemplary family dogged by misfortune and the law which today doesn't even respect the affairs of the heart and persecutes the schoolteacher only because she is engaged to Salvatore Riina'. He added: 'Her mother comes to Mass every morning and takes communion.' The truth was that Ninetta's 'exemplary' family consisted of a father and brother both exiled for mafia crimes, a brother who was officially a fugitive but who, unknown to police, had been killed two years earlier and a third brother who was a lieutenant of Riina's.

Sheltering from photographers in an office near the court where her trial hearing would soon begin, Ninetta gave an interview – the only one she ever gave – to the newspaper *Giornale di Sicilia*. 'I'm nervous, tremendously nervous, even if I'm making an effort to remain calm to explain my case to the judges. The flashes of the photographers' cameras don't help to calm me down. And I don't like publicity,' she began.

Her black eyes staring fixedly at the journalist, Ninetta made a spirited defence of her love for Riina. 'You'll think ill of me because I, a teacher, have fallen in love with and got engaged to a man like Salvatore Riina. But aren't I a woman? Haven't I got the right to love a man and to follow the laws of nature? I chose him first because I love him and love ignores lots of things, and then because I admire and trust him. I love Riina because I believe he's innocent,' she said.

She lowered her eyes and continued. 'Today I'm here for him. He's been away from me for two years, I haven't heard anything from him either directly or indirectly. I'm a woman. This silence makes me doubt whether he loves me. I feel alone and discouraged.' 'Riina,' she added in a public criticism that was unheard of for a mafioso's girlfriend, 'doesn't care about the feelings and needs of a woman.'

When the trial began, the presiding judge summoned Bagarella, who greeted the court politely, placed her bag on a table in front of her and stood waiting.

'Miss Bagarella, you know it has been proposed that you be sent into exile,' the judge said.

'I don't believe the court will want to send me into exile,' Ninetta said in a clear voice. 'If you have a conscience, if you have a heart, you won't do it. Only the women remain in our family. And we have to work for ourselves and for our men, fathers and brothers who are dogged by misfortune. I'm a woman and I'm guilty only of loving a man whom I esteem and in whom I trust. I have always loved Totò Riina. I was 13 years old and he was 26 when I first fell in love; he's never been out of my heart. That is all I'm guilty of, Your Honour.'

'Salvatore Riina isn't a lily-white little soul, Miss; he's wanted for many murders,' the judge said.

'A pack of lies. Slander. Salvatore is innocent.'

'Here you're accused of belonging to Leggio's clan.'

'I don't even know Leggio.'

Ninetta spoke in court for more than an hour, rejecting one by one the allegations made against her. As a guarantee of her good character, her lawyer pulled out of his briefcase dozens of letters from the headmaster of her school as well as from fellow-teachers and pupils' parents. 'The only thing I desire is to marry Riina,' Ninetta said. 'I don't want our relationship to remain platonic. But I haven't seen him for such a long time, I know nothing about him. I don't even know whether he still loves me.' When a journalist asked her after the hearing 'What is the mafia?', she shot back: 'The mafia is a phenomenon created by the newspapers to sell more newspapers.'

Ninetta's performance impressed the judges, but only to a limited extent. Although they rejected the demand that she be exiled to the mainland, they ordered her to be placed under police surveillance for the next two and a half years; they also banned her from leaving her house between 7.30 p.m. and 7 a.m. Once a week, she had to go to the police station and sign her name in a register. When Riina found out about the verdict, he exploded: 'I don't want other women. I want only Ninetta. They don't want to let me marry her? Well then, I'll carry out a massacre.'

Ninetta served her sentence until just one week before it was due to end on the last day of February 1974. When a policeman called at her home some two hours after her evening curfew, Ninetta was nowhere to be found. Her sister told the officer that Ninetta had found a job in Germany; in fact, she had joined Riina and from now on would share his life on the run.

Despite her status as a fugitive, Riina did manage to marry Ninetta, at least in a religious service, with the complicity of his friend Father Agostino Coppola, the priest so close to Riina that he addressed him as 'Dear brother' in his letters and hid ransom money from a kidnapping in a church sacristy. In the spring of 1974, 19 years after their engagement, Riina married Ninetta in secret before Coppola, two other priests, and a handful of guests to whom she had sent handwritten invitations. The altar was set up in the living-room of a seaside villa surrounded by pines near Cinisi west of Palermo, flower arrangements were supplied by a local boss and guests were given boxes with a small silver memento and sweets, a traditional gift.

When, that summer, in a safehouse that had been used by one of Ninetta's brothers, a policeman came across a gilded, hand-written card which read simply 'Antonietta and Salvatore married 16 April 1974' and Coppola's involvement became public, the priest tore up the marriage certificate. A furious Riina repri-manded him: 'You were scared because you celebrated my marriage and you tore up the evidence. You're a scoundrel.'

The marriage was never registered at the local town hall, which meant it was invalid. The couple spent their honeymoon in Venice, where Ninetta photographed a slightly overweight Riina as he posed in St Mark's Square. Apparently just another tourist, he stands with a smile on his face as he feeds the pigeons, two of them perched on the palm of his right hand. His shirt is stretched across a rotund stomach – a sign of his growing influence according to the old Sicilian saying: '*Omo de panza, omo de sostanza* (man with a belly, man of substance)'.

Nine months after the wedding, Ninetta gave birth to their first child, a daughter, at an exclusive clinic in Palermo. She registered under her maiden name. Neither she nor Riina was bothered by police during her stay there. According to one defector, who was a frequent overnight guest at the Riina home, the boss was careful to keep Ninetta in the dark about his crimes; he did, however, keep her informed about his wealth and properties. But Ninetta 'knew perfectly well that she belonged to a "family" of a certain kind', the supergrass said. She always remained fiercely loyal, 'she always followed her husband through thick and thin'. Riina never had any grounds to worry that she might talk out of turn. The informer found her so taciturn that he only half-jokingly observed to Riina: 'To make her talk, you need a pair of pliers.'

3

Forging a Dictatorship

1974–1983

Making Friends and Enemies

The greed that prompted Leggio to carry out one kidnapping after another from his Milan base proved his undoing. Victims included Eugene Paul Getty III, the 17-year-old grandson of one of the world's wealthiest men; the ransom paid for his release, shared between Leggio and gangs in southern Calabria, was some £1.3 million. Public prosecutors investigating several kidnappings in northern Italy became convinced they were linked. But they had no evidence to back their intuition until the spring of 1974 when, during a search for one hostage, an industrialist, they came across an isolated farmhouse east of Milan. From a trapdoor in a floor of the house emerged not the industrialist but another captive, an aristocrat.

The prosecutors learnt that the nobleman's kidnappers were talking with respect of a certain '*Signor* Antonio'. They managed to ascertain this was a Milanese resident, named Antonio Ferruggia, and put his top-floor flat under surveillance. They tapped his phone and realised time was running out when Ferruggia was heard saying that he planned to leave the following day and would be away for quite some time.

When, at dawn the next day, 14 May, a police officer rang the buzzer outside the flat, the first sound he heard was the noise of a child crying, then that of feet shuffling to the door. The moustachioed man wearing pyjamas who opened the door stared at the officer with a stunned expression on his big, round face.

The officer recognised Leggio instantly and opened his mouth: 'You are . . .'

Leggio did not let him finish, breaking in affably: 'Yes, I am.

There's no need for you to say my name. Can I at least get ready?'

The reason for Leggio's uncharacteristic show of discretion was that the girlfriend he lived with had no idea of his real name or of his criminal career. She knew him only as a businessman. 'Don't believe the horrible things people will say about me,' Leggio, now washed and dressed, advised her blithely as he left. Outside the block of flats, Leggio characteristically put on an upbeat performance for the benefit of waiting photographers. He waved, bowed and beamed before climbing into the police van.

Tradition dictated that a boss in jail was still a boss. But Riina quickly took advantage of Leggio's arrest to act as the head of the Corleonesi in his dealings with clan chiefs in Palermo and elsewhere. Riina's activism put a strain on his relationship with Leggio, who after a few months in prison made his disapproval known in a message to all bosses. 'Riina likes big meals, he likes to eat and has a few too many. And when he's drunk his fill he grabs his pistol and he kills a couple of people, or maybe three,' the message ran. From now on, Leggio ordered, mafiosi who wanted to deal with him must go through Provenzano, not Riina.

Thanks to his network of contacts, Riina soon heard about Leggio's message and never forgave him for it. When some over-enthusiastic recruits, thinking the idea would please Riina, suggested a plan to help Leggio escape from prison, Riina replied bluntly: 'Mind your own business. I'm in charge of this. If it becomes necessary I'll think things out and then I'll be the one to trouble you.' Whether out of spite or self-interest, Riina again ensured the failure a few years later of another plan for Leggio's escape. This time, Riina told Leggio that he would oversee the preparations. The result was that the plan was leaked to the police and Leggio was immediately transferred. 'If Riina had wanted it, Leggio would have escaped 150 times,' a supergrass said.

When Leggio was offered a place on a new commission of bosses set up in 1975, this time to rule over all the Sicilian clans, he decreed that both Riina and Provenzano would represent him on it. The regional commission, better known as the Cupola, was made up of representatives from all over the island and was supposed to enforce the brotherhood's unwritten rules and take decisions democratically, by vote. At its first meeting, the Cupola issued a ban on kidnapping in Sicily, on pain of death; a majority argued that kidnappings made the mafia unpopular and the pressure of police investigations harmed the clan on whose territory the kidnapping had taken place. Besides, all too often the wealthy victims, from nobles to businessmen, were either friends of the mafia or unwilling victims of its extortion racket.

The Cupola bosses saw Provenzano as more intelligent than Riina; he had 'a more refined mind' as one put it. But Provenzano was notorious for his inability, or his refusal, to take a decision. 'Every time there was a problem, Riina would tackle it,' an informer explained. 'He'd give a reply, positive or negative. But he decided. Provenzano isn't like that; he's slippery, a "philosopher" in the sense that he never takes a stand.' When asked for his opinion, Provenzano would invariably say that he would make it known at the next meeting. Bosses noticed that this irritated even Riina, but he never contradicted his companion.

Riina lost little time in showing what he thought of the kidnapping ban and went further than his mentor Leggio in challenging the Palermo bosses who still dominated the mafia establishment. That summer, Riina kidnapped Luigi Corleo, not only one of Sicily's richest men but also the father-in-law of Nino Salvo, a mafioso whose favourite motto was: 'Money breeds money and louses breed louses.' Salvo and his cousin were the state's tax-collectors for Sicily and friends of the bosses Badalamenti and Bontate. Until then they had been considered untouchable.

For all their wealth, the Salvos refused to pay the £16 million ransom. Not even the Salvos' friendship with the two Palermo bosses helped to save the hostage. He died, or was killed, during the kidnapping, and although pressed by the dead man's relatives an embarrassed Badalamenti and Bontate were unable to recover the body or to determine who had organised the kidnapping. The two supposed, but could not prove, that the Corleonesi were behind it.

If they had joined forces, Badalamenti and Bontate would have had all the military might they needed to counter-attack and break the Corleonesi while there was still time. But they failed to realise the significance of the Corleonesi's coup and did nothing. The 'peasants' had challenged the establishment and they got away with it.

Riina set out to conquer the mafia clan by clan, exploiting his charisma as a boss with a ready smile and the ability to recruit and inspire soldiers. In Palermo, Riina forged new alliances neighbourhood by neighbourhood. Gradually, he extended his network from Trapani in the west to Catania in the east. When one Cupola boss settled in Brazil, Riina plotted to have him replaced by a friend; and when another boss vanished, murdered without trace, Riina ensured that again an ally of his was appointed to the Cupola in the dead man's place. Riina is believed to have followed the example set by the most powerful bosses and to have become a freemason to help him widen his network, through contacts with masons in a host of professions from judges to bankers and doctors.

Riina did not limit himself to winning over bosses; he hit upon an ingenious way of infiltrating their clans as well. At a meeting of the Cupola, Riina asked that fellow-bosses place some soldiers at his disposal so that he could use them when he travelled across Sicily. The Cupola saw this as an innocent enough request, and granted what Riina asked. The result was that Riina created what amounted to a small mafia of his own, well outside the pyramid-like structure in which soldiers obeyed only their clan chief.

Only one boss became very quickly suspicious of Riina. Giuseppe Di Cristina, known as 'the Tiger' for his irascible character, was a mafioso of the rural school. Di Cristina had the pugnacious face of a boxer with thick eyebrows, small, deep-set eyes and full lips; deep creases ran down from the sides of his nose and the ends of his mouth so that he looked as if he was constantly looking for a fight. Both his father and his grandfather were bosses. His father had publicly anointed him as his successor on a Sunday afternoon when worshippers, bearing a plaster statue of the Madonna of the Chains through their town of Riesi in central Sicily, stopped below the boss's balcony. Watched by all, Di Cristina's father placed his hand on the young man's shoulder, a symbolic gesture which meant he was retiring.

The son proved a worthy heir, carrying out kidnappings, trafficking in drugs and earning the respect of Christian Democrat politicians. When a henchman sent to kill a victim managed only to wound him with a knife, Di Cristina, who had just finished reading *The Godfather* by Mario Puzo, copied an episode in the book: he sent the henchman and other hitmen, all dressed as doctors, into the hospital where the wounded man was being treated. They entered the ward where he lay in bed and finished him off with a pistol.

Di Cristina became a declared enemy of Riina's when, overriding the objections of several Cupola members, Riina ordered the murder of the *carabiniere* Colonel Giuseppe Russo. The officer had investigated kidnappings carried out by the Corleonesi, and was holidaying in woods near Corleone when he was shot dead in the summer of 1977. Many clans complained they had not been given any warning of the murder, with the result that several mafiosi had been arrested without having had the time to either go into hiding or prepare an alibi for that day.

Di Cristina tried to persuade the other Cupola bosses that it was high time they took action against the Corleonesi. Russo's murder was foolish, he argued; it reflected badly on the entire organisation. "'The Peasants" are at the gates of Palermo. Don't you understand?' Di Cristina urged them. But the chiefs underestimated Riina, and Di Cristina got nowhere. Behind Di Cristina's back, stooges promptly referred his comments back to the Corleonesi.

The boss Pippo Calderone, from Catania, did seek an explanation for the officer's murder from Michele Greco, the Cupola's secretary. Known as 'the Pope' because of his devotion and his bearing, which had the dignity of that of a man of the cloth, Greco liked to go hunting and pigeon-shooting and had bought himself a shooting range in order to keep in practice. He once told a court: 'They call me "the Pope" but I cannot compare myself to popes . . . But my conscience is serene, my faith is deep and I believe I am equal if not superior to them.'

To Calderone's questions, all Greco replied was: 'I asked Riina why the murder took place in the Corleone district and he told me that when a cop is killed no questions should be asked.'

A furious Di Cristina insulted Greco to his face: 'You're letting Riina treat you like a puppet; he just pulls the strings.' Greco said nothing.

Only two days later, Di Cristina narrowly escaped elimination. Two colleagues usually drove him to work at a mining company every morning, but that day he planned to leave home later. On their drive to work, the two colleagues – one of whom looked very much like Di Cristina and wore a blue beret similar to his – were ambushed and shot dead. Di Cristina instantly called a meeting of Palermo bosses, insisting that Greco's presence was essential. Greco failed to turn up for the meeting, sending 'the Prince' Bontate as his representative instead.

Di Cristina spoke first: 'I called this meeting and sent for Michele Greco because I want to say that you're listening to a dead man. This is a dead man talking. I'm dead. Now I want to know why on earth I was shot. Why did they shoot me? Why do they want to kill me? Can someone explain to me for what reason I have been condemned to death?'

'Michele Greco came to me,' Bontate replied, 'and asked me why you had called this meeting. And he told me he knew nothing about the murders, that perhaps it was the Cursotis who organised this. Maybe they are the ones who have something against you.' Bontate's reply was an evasive one as the Cursotis, a Catania clan, had nothing to do with Di Cristina.

The Last Stand of 'the Tiger'

One afternoon in the spring of 1977, bosses from western Sicily met on 'the Pope' Greco's Favarella estate, in his mansion surrounded by sprawling lemon and orange groves. 'It's quieter here, no one can see our cars from outside the estate and there's plenty of cool fresh air. We'll have a good meal and a good talk,' Greco had told bosses, at Riina's prompting.

By the late 1970s the mafia was doing well for itself. Never since the Ciaculli car-bomb of 1963 had the fraternity had it so good; it was making more money than ever, fugitives were sleeping soundly at home with their wives, judges could be counted on to deliver acquittals and politicians were obeying its orders. Few investigators bothered bosses; all the state worried about were the bombings and assassinations carried out by Red Brigade terrorists, who were carrying out murders and kidnappings during the so-called 'years of lead'. The Corleonesi were the only blot on an otherwise perfect picture.

At the meeting on Greco's estate, his brother Salvatore, known as 'the Senator' because of his ties to Sicilian politicians, waved a piece of paper in the air and then started reading aloud: 'Mafia crime is slowly transforming itself into a common form of organised crime . . . and its hold on the apparatus of formal power is slackening or even disappearing . . .'

The veteran Badalamenti interrupted. 'Who wrote that?'

'The Senator' replied with a half-smile: 'Parliament. It's the report of the anti-mafia commission.'

'And what's that piece of paper got to do with me?' Badalamenti asked.

'It means that in Rome they think the mafia doesn't exist any more. They think the mafiosi of old are becoming petty thieves.'

'Let them believe that.'

'Yes, all we need to do is to look after our business.'

'If only the Corleonesi could understand that . . .' Badalamenti sighed.

At the mention of the clan he hated most, Di Cristina exploded. 'The Corleonesi! The Corleonesi!' he shouted. 'They don't understand and they won't ever understand. Let's bump off that bastard Riina and then yes, we'll be fine – all of us will be fine.'

Never had a boss vented such rage against the Corleonesi. But not even this outburst managed to shake the family heads out of their lethargy.

'Riina can't do anything here in Palermo if we all stand together. Because as soon as he gets cocky we'll kick him in the teeth and send him packing back to Corleone to grow wheat,' an elderly boss said. The remark made the other bosses laugh, but Di Cristina didn't join in. Afterwards, as usual, the stooge Greco revealed to Riina what had been said.

There is an eloquent word in Sicilian dialect for Riina's favourite tactic in his power struggle – '*traggediare*' from the word for 'tragedy', meaning to plot behind someone's back, to fuel suspicion by telling lies about him. Riina's first victim was also one of the first who had taken the Corleonesi under his wing: Badalamenti. The ungrateful Riina accused him of setting up a drug-trafficking route which supplied American cities including Detroit, without telling other bosses.

It was hardly a life or death matter, but Riina plotted to cast Badalamenti in such an unfavourable light that the elderly boss increasingly found himself in a minority. At one meeting, Provenzano challenged him directly: 'Uncle Tano, what you're saying is wrong. I have the impression that your head has taken a bit of a knock.' Badalamenti's position became untenable, so much so that he was expelled from the mafia, a very rare sanction. He fled first to Spain and then to Brazil.

Frustrated by his failure to persuade Palermo bosses to confront the Corleonesi, Di Cristina acted alone. He managed to find out that Riina was hiding in Naples and sent five soldiers to look for him. Riina travelled regularly to Naples to discuss cigarette contraband with allies in the Camorra, the Neapolitan secret society. But the soldiers failed to find him. Di Cristina grew increasingly desperate; he knew his stand against the Corleonesi had turned him into a marked man.

In April 1978, the murder of a boss who was a close friend made Di Cristina realise that time was running out and he tried to enlist the help of the state in an attempt to deal a death-blow against his enemies. A week after his friend's death, he arranged to meet a police captain at night in an isolated farmhouse. The enemy of the Corleonesi and the officer talked alone. Although Di Cristina was at pains to hide his panic, the officer was struck by how terrified he was – like 'a hunted animal', he reported later.

The account Di Cristina gave the officer was undoubtedly biased: he made heavy accusations against the Corleonesi and their allies, taking care not to reveal his own role or that of his friends. But in that single, one-hour meeting he told the Italian state more about the Corleonesi than it had managed to find out in many years. He told the amazed officer that even from behind bars, Leggio was still in command through his lieutenants Riina and Provenzano. He accused Leggio of carrying out murders including that of Palermo's chief prosecutor; of planning to murder Judge Terranova; of setting up a team of 14 mercenary killers to eliminate his rivals; and of preparing to escape from jail soon. Leggio was also responsible for several kidnappings both in Sicily and in Calabria in southern Italy, which had helped make him a multi-billionaire.

Riina and Provenzano, Di Cristina continued, were known as 'the beasts' and were the most dangerous henchmen at Leggio's disposal, each responsible for at least 40 murders. No doubt hoping the state would arrest them, Di Cristina said Riina was probably in Naples, while Provenzano had been seen in a white Mercedes driven by the teenage son of the boss Bernardo Brusca, near Bagheria east of Palermo, only the previous week. Di Cristina also detailed the Corleonesi's network of alliances in Sicily and on the mainland.

The boss and the investigator parted, with Di Cristina trying to sound a confident note: 'By the end of next week I'll be taking delivery of the armour-plated car my friends have given me . . . You see, Captain, I've got a few venial sins on my conscience. And some mortal ones too.'

The Corleonesi forgave him neither. They never forgave and never forgot, as the supergrass Francesco Di Carlo, a former heroin trafficker, explained: 'Whether it's a prosecutor or a police officer, the Corleonesi have always condemned them to death. You understand? Even a journalist who writes something bad about them. The Corleonesi have always been like that. OK? They don't forgive anyone who gets in their way, not even after 50 years. That's what they've always done, with everyone. That's how the Corleonesi are, that's their nature.' Riina liked to tell his henchmen: 'The best forgiveness is vendetta.'

Through their web of spies, the Corleonesi found out that Di Cristina had broken the law of silence. The next month, Di Cristina was walking out of a block of flats in Palermo when two hitmen opened fire on him. Di Cristina pulled out his revolver, dropped to his knees – either because he was wounded or to dodge the bullets – and shot back. He managed to hit one of the killers in the leg. Surprised by Di Cristina's quick reflexes, they were about to flee when they realised that his revolver was jammed. They raced up and finished him off with six shots to the head. On the day of the funeral, 7,000 mourners including politicans and priests marched behind his coffin. Street-sweepers were ordered to drop their brooms and carry the dozens of wreaths.

Di Cristina's attempt to get the state to do his dirty work failed. The testimony was passed on to prosecutors, described as 'exceptional evidence' which underlined the threat posed by the Corleonesi and their allies. The very fact that he had shown that the mafia existed was shocking. One officer wrote: 'Di Cristina has revealed the horrifying *truth* that, next to the authority of the state, there exists a more incisive and more efficient power which is that of the mafia; a mafia which acts, makes money, kills and even judges, and all this behind the back of the public authorities.' But investigators failed to follow up his testimony. As in the case of the earlier defector Vitale, they simply could not believe that what a boss said could be credible. As for acting on his evidence, that was out of the question.

The Corleonesi chose to kill Di Cristina on the Palermitan territory belonging to the boss Salvatore Inzerillo, without telling him anything beforehand. This infuriated Inzerillo, an ally of 'the Prince' Bontate, as the murder brought police rushing into his territory. It took very little to send Inzerillo into a rage; he had once had a boy from his neighbourhood strangled because he had relieved himself on the wall of his villa when the boss's wife was just going out.

When Inzerillo demanded an explanation from Greco, the secretary of the Cupola, he was told the murder was of no great importance. Di Cristina was a police informer, 'killed for reasons that have to do with his family and are an internal matter', Greco lied. This was to become a trademark of the Corleonesi: eliminate a rival as soon as he commits an error and wrong-foot any friend or ally who could potentially seek revenge. This time the Corleonesi trampled over two rules – that the elimination of a boss must be approved unanimously by the Cupola and that a clan head must be warned in advance if a murder is to take place on his territory – and yet again, they got away with it.

Di Cristina's murder did jolt one Cupola boss, Bontate, into reacting, but it was to be too little, too late. He ordered his soldiers to kill Riina, but they could not find him. Instead, Bontate himself strangled Stefano Giaconia, an ally of Riina's. The job made Bontate an hour late for a meeting at a motel on the Catania–Palermo motorway. Bontate roared up in his Porsche Carrera and apologised with an annoyed look on his face: 'I'm sorry I'm late, but I had to change a flat tyre and I had to strangle Stefano Giaconia.'

'Don't worry, we waited for you. In any case, it's a very good thing you got Giaconia off our backs,' a boss said.

'That cuckold got on my nerves right until the end. After I'd killed him, we burnt his clothes and while they were burning there was an explosion. It was a .22 calibre pen-pistol which Giaconia had on him,' Bontate said.

'Hey, what a man of honour! He shoots even after his death!' another boss joked.

Bontate contented himself with Giaconia's murder. He trusted in his own strength and kept repeating that the Corleonesi could never defeat him and his allies. But the Corleonesi were already making a mockery of the way the mafia was governed. The blatant disregard with which the Corleonesi treated the Cupola robbed it of any authority. The Catania boss Pippo Calderone complained that it had become useless: 'You're there for hours, you talk and talk, you agree on something and then . . . The Corleonesi appear with their faces of stone, silent and humble. They don't say anything and you think they agree with you. As soon as they leave the meeting they do whatever they want. Who would have thought that oaf Riina would cause so much trouble?'

Pippo Calderone regretted the day two decades ago when he had helped hide Riina and Provenzano who, on first arriving in Palermo, were mocked as 'peasants': 'The way they dressed was a joke. We fitted them out from head to toe. And while we were spending millions on hiding and helping them, those snakes were already thinking about how to eliminate us. It took me a lot of time to understand Riina, but it's not easy to realise immediately what a fox he is.'

The boss's brother Antonino could only agree: 'Riina's incredibly ignorant, but he's got the gifts of intuition and extraordinary intelligence, he's very difficult to understand and to catch out. And at the same time he's like an animal. His philosophy is that if someone's finger hurts, it's better to cut his arm off; that way, you're sure you've solved the problem.'

In the summer of 1978, less than two months after Di Cristina's murder, Pippo Calderone found a bomb hidden under his car seat. There was no indication as to who had planted the bomb, but Calderone and his brother Antonino were in no doubt. Antonino pleaded with Bontate and other Palermo chiefs to stop the Corleonesi. Didn't they realise that the Corleonesi's strategy was to first clean up areas away from Palermo, such as Catania, and then strike in the Sicilian capital? How much time did they think they still had?

The Palermo bosses heard him out and then, after an embarrassed pause, one of them replied: 'We can't intervene openly in your favour now. We have to be cautious, we have to hide our true feelings. We have to keep pretending to be friendly. If we don't, they will go on the rampage.'

Late the following month, Pippo Calderone was shot and seriously wounded in the stomach, dying of his injuries in hospital three days later. An ally of the Corleonesi explained to Antonino that his brother had been killed because he had broken a rule: he had ordered a mafioso's murder without warning the head of the area where it took place. The ally was parroting a lesson learnt from the Corleonesi, Antonino reflected bitterly: 'Kill enemies one by one every time there is a favourable opportunity to eliminate them. And do everything in a "formally" correct way so that not even the victim's closest friends can react, given that they are in the wrong.'

A few weeks later, Riina insisted on paying tribute to Pippo Calderone in front of the Cupola. He talked of the dead man's reputation as a magnanimous and generous man of honour, of his efforts to make the mafia more orderly and harmonious. His only mistake had been to become friends with that rat Di Cristina – but of course Pippo had done so in good faith, Riina said. The time had come to let bygones be bygones, Riina concluded, to forget discord and spite, and to get to like each other again.

Riina spoke with such fervour that one friend of the victim wept. But the dead man's brother thought Riina was perhaps putting on an act. 'I couldn't decide whether those noble words came from a feeling of sincere mourning or whether he was like a victor who has just eliminated a dangerous enemy and is proud of his victim's importance,' he said later.

The increasingly assertive Corleonesi settled old and new scores both inside and outside the mafia. The journalist Mario Francese, of the Palermo newspaper *Giornale di Sicilia*, had written about the Corleonesi for most of the past decade, detailing more than any other reporter their killings, business dealings and spread to Palermo. Among his scoops was the interview with Riina's girl-friend Ninetta in which she complained that he was neglecting her. Eight years later, in 1979, Ninetta's brother Leduca shot him five times as he made his way home. A few minutes later Francese's son Giulio, also a journalist, arrived to write about the killing; he didn't know who the victim was. The head of the flying squad spotted Giulio, took him aside and told him who the victim lying under a sheet was. Giulio had never seen a body before and didn't have the heart to lift the sheet; he didn't want to see the state his father was in.

Despite being on the run from the state and at the same time having to hide from enemies seeking his elimination, Riina now unleashed an offensive without precedent – a series of murders whose victims were 'distinguished corpses' and that, uniquely in a democracy, saw organised crime decapitate state institutions. The years 1979–1980 saw the killings of Michele Reina, provincial secretary of the Christian Democrats; Boris Giuliano, Palermo's deputy police chief; Judge Cesare Terranova, president of the appeals court; Pier Santi Mattarella, the Christian Democrat president of the regional government; and Emanuele Basile, a captain in the *carabinieri* police. The Corleonesi failed to either consult or warn the Cupola before any of the murders.

According to a supergrass, the murder of Mattarella by the Corleonesi in January 1980, shot dead beside his wife and son as they walked to Mass, prompted a tense confrontation between Bontate and the Christian Democrat ex-prime minister Giulio Andreotti, affectionately known to mafiosi as 'Uncle Giulio'. Andreotti allegedly met Bontate in a small villa. Bontate's henchman Francesco Marino Mannoia testified that he was made to wait outside during the talks, but he heard shouts coming from inside. Afterwards, Bontate told Mannoia that Andreotti had demanded an explanation for Mattarella's murder. Bontate had allegedly replied to Andreotti: 'In Sicily we're the ones who command and if you don't want the Christian Democrats to be completely wiped out, you have to do as we say. Otherwise we'll take away your votes not only in Sicily but also in the whole of southern Italy. You'll be able to count only on votes in the north, where they all vote Communist.'

When the evidence of the eight supergrasses denouncing him as the mafia's 'most powerful political patron' was first made public, Andreotti denied any links with mafiosi and accused the brotherhood of launching a vendetta to punish him for the measures his governments had taken against it – Andreotti had served seven times as prime minister and 33 times as a minister. In a 2004 ruling, the Supreme Court found that Andreotti had forged links with the mafia and was guilty of participation in a criminal association up to the spring of 1980. They found that Andreotti had cultivated friendly relations with several bosses, had met them, shown himself ready to help them and asked them for favours. But the judges acquitted Andreotti on the grounds that the offence had been committed so long ago he was legally no longer answerable for it. The judges also dismissed an account by one informer that Andreotti had met Riina, the two men exchanging a kiss on the cheek as a sign of respect. The court ordered Andreotti to pay legal costs.

Tommaso Buscetta, 'the Boss of Two Worlds'

In early 1980, the future of the Corleonesi hinged for a few hours on a meeting in the luxurious Hotel Flora on Rome's Via Veneto, where, at the height of the *Dolce Vita* (Sweet Life) two decades earlier, paparazzi photographers had chased Elizabeth Taylor and Richard Burton. In a discreet corner of the hotel's lobby, an envoy of the Palermo allies Bontate and Inzerillo did his utmost to persuade the fugitive boss Tommaso Buscetta to help them put paid to the clan known with increasing venom as 'The Peasants' – by either peaceful or violent means.

The quiet-spoken, well-mannered Buscetta was one of the most charismatic bosses and he could turn many mafiosi against the Corleonesi. There was a snag: he was frowned upon by some of the older mafiosi for riding roughshod over the fraternity's diktats whenever affairs of the heart were concerned. Born in one of Palermo's poorest neighbourhoods to a glass cutter – and the youngest of 17 children – he was only 16 when he married his first wife Melchiorra Cavallaro. He joined the mafia a year later, attracted by the respect this would bring him. A mafioso, he claimed, 'had to act within the norms of a man of honour, because all the things that I have known inside Cosa Nostra are beautiful – with the exception of murder, which is a necessity.'

He met Vera Girotti at a casino in 1963, left his first wife and their three children but didn't divorce her, and married Girotti in Mexico. He then moved to New York, arranging for his first wife and their children to settle in the city while he continued to live with Girotti. After giving Buscetta two daughters, however, Girotti abandoned him and left him with the two girls.

Buscetta moved to Brazil in 1971. On Rio de Janeiro's long Copacabana beach of white sand and palm trees, he spotted a beautiful young blonde. The 21-year-old Maria Cristina Almeida de Guimaraes was 19 years Buscetta's junior and the daughter of a wealthy lawyer whose friends included a former president, Joao Goulart; she spoke five languages and was studying psychology at university. To his credit, Buscetta did tell her that he was wanted by the police, but failed to mention that he was a mafioso. Knowing he was a fugitive did not stop Maria Cristina falling in love with him; she promptly dropped out of university, as the jealous Buscetta could not stand the idea of her chatting and drinking with her fellow-students. 'He wanted me to be just a wife,' she reflected later. They married in 1978 and she was to give him seven children.

In the traditional-minded mafia, it was enough to make any mafioso's head whirl. 'A man who abandons his wife, takes a mistress, and then two other wives, isn't a man of honour,' the Palermo boss Antonino Camporeale objected. However, Buscetta was spared any drastic punishment for his turbulent private life; the brotherhood did decide to expel him after he abandoned his first wife, but the measure was never enforced and it did not harm his career. Buscetta started out as an efficient killer, moved on to cigarette smuggling and then, according to Italian investigators, the US Federal Bureau of Investigation and the US Bureau of Narcotics, he became a leading heroin and cocaine trafficker on routes stretching from America to Mexico and from Canada to Brazil – something he always denied but which earned him the nickname 'the Boss of Two Worlds'.

Buscetta never had any difficulty crossing the Atlantic. He obtained his first passport thanks to the intervention of a Christian Democrat member of parliament who sent a personal message to Palermo's police chief: 'Buscetta is someone I am very interested in.' Soon afterwards, the anti-mafia commission of the Italian parliament described Buscetta as 'a qualified killer ... wicked, aggressive, engaged in a vast criminal activity . . . a mafioso of the highest rank in league with the big shots of the American underworld'. When Buscetta was arrested in Brazil in 1972, the police tortured him to make him admit to drug-trafficking charges; officers gave him electric shocks on his genitals, backside, teeth and ears and ripped the nails off his feet, but he said only: 'My name is Tommaso Buscetta.' The police then forced him and his third wife Cristina to board an aeroplane designed for parachuting; officers grabbed Cristina, who was pregnant, and, holding her by the hair, suspended her from the plane above Sâo Paulo. She fainted. Again Buscetta refused to talk. He spent eight years in jail.

Now, in the elegant surroundings of Rome's Hotel Flora, a free man again, he listened attentively to his friends' envoy Nino Salvo, whose father-in-law had been kidnapped and killed by the Corleonesi five years earlier. 'The Corleonesi have taken over everything,' Salvo complained, 'the mafia's internal affairs and its relations with politicians, its "clean" and its "dirty" business. They lord it over everyone,' he said.

'We need to stop those peasants, otherwise we're all going to die,' Salvo continued. 'Someone has to stop them spreading everywhere. Masino, you've got to agree to get onto the Palermo commission. Only you can win this game. Tell us what you need and we'll see to it that you get it,' Salvo said. With Buscetta on board, the Palermitans hoped they would carry enough weight to defeat the Corleonesi.

'I realise things have become tough; the Corleonesi are very strong,' Buscetta replied. But he was more concerned about what he saw as a great change for the worse within the mafia itself. 'Cosa Nostra has degenerated,' he went on. 'Everybody is thinking about money and few are ready to fight for a just cause. I doubt they'll listen to me. I doubt I can start a constructive discussion with people who are deaf. The men of honour are obsessed by their craving to make money. That's the only music they listen to. They've lost their way.' Buscetta concluded: 'I can't help you. Anyway, I've got a promise to keep to my children. I'm going to

Brazil. And I wish you good luck against "the peasants". You know very well I never liked them.'

Over the months that followed, the Corleonesi's enemies invited him to Palermo and did their best to change his mind. One of the first to offer Buscetta a safe house was Rosario 'the Terrorist' Riccobono, who owed his nickname to his habit of condemning people to death on a whim and to his fondness for watching the sentence being carried out. He offered Buscetta a hideout in the seaside resort of Mondello on Palermo's outskirts, which thanks to the Sicilian climate, stays busy right up to the end of October.

'No one will look for you here,' Riccobono assured his friend.

'What do you mean, you have the power to guarantee such a thing?' an incredulous Buscetta asked.

Riccobono told him he had a mole at the Palermo police head-quarters: Bruno Contrada, the head of the flying squad and a member of the military secret service. 'I've got Contrada, who will warn me if there are raids or searches for fugitives in this area, so here you'll be safe and sound,' he said.

The boss was proud of his alleged mole. 'Contrada is at our disposal,' he told another mafioso. 'Actually, if the police stop you and take you to the Palermo HQ, ask for him immediately, I've already given your name to him.' Riccobono explained that Contrada always gave him advance warning of police raids to catch him. In return, the boss said he paid Contrada handsomely; when Contrada wanted to give a girlfriend a car as a Christmas present, Riccobono boasted he had footed the bill.

When some 20 supergrasses testified against him years later, Contrada denied all charges and challenged prosecutors to prove he had ever known Riccobono. 'I only ever came into contact with mafiosi during questioning or when they were lying dead in front of me, when they had been reduced to corpses,' he said. But Italy's highest appeals court convicted him of helping the mafia and sentenced him to ten years in prison.

Buscetta preferred to divide his time between two other hide-outs – a house outside Palermo and the country villa of his friend

Bontate. To avoid arrest he simply made sure that he only ventured out between 1.30 p.m. and 4.30 p.m. – a time when Palermo and its police patrols ground to a halt for the afternoon siesta. He and Bontate talked at length about the Corleonesi and what to do about them.

One day at the country villa, a vast residence ringed by security cameras, Bontate unveiled what he called 'a no-nonsense, simple way to stop the peasants walking all over us'. Bontate explained: 'I think we can avoid a war. If I kill Riina with my own hands at one of the next meetings of the commission, they'll calm down. They'll understand we're ready for war and how strong we are. My family alone has more than a hundred men of honour ready to shoot at one nod from me.'

Buscetta was appalled. He thought Bontate was highly intelligent and he found his friend's lack of lucidity baffling. 'You're talking rubbish, Stefano,' Buscetta said. 'The commission is full of friends of Riina's who would rub you out a second later. And anyway these things have to be done immediately, and no talk beforehand, or they're better not done. Riina's like a dog: he sniffs out what people are saying and he understands there's something against him in the air. But you people talk and talk. In the meantime it's the Corleonesi who get things done; they're knocking us down one by one like skittles. My dear friend, I think that you're a dead man already.' Buscetta said the last words on impulse, without thinking they could soon become true.

On the eve of Buscetta's departure for Brazil in early 1981, his closest friends organised a farewell dinner in Bontate's villa. Buscetta had decided to build himself a new life outside the mafia but there were no hard feelings – they gave him a gift of £250,000 to help him. The dinner was a moving occasion for Buscetta; at the age of 53, he felt he was leaving 'with my head held high, and for ever'.

With characteristic lack of modesty, and talking of himself in the third person as if he was some sort of mafioso monarch, Buscetta later boasted: 'Tommaso Buscetta was not more or less aggressive than Riina. He was – and is – much more intelligent. He would have cut him down to size, reducing him to the rank of an ordinary district boss. My charisma and my following inside Cosa Nostra were such that if I had put myself at the head of a fraction of it, I would have destroyed the Corleonesi in the cradle. I would have annihilated them when it was still possible to do so,' Buscetta explained.

The Corleonesi were soon to show that it was now too late for Buscetta or anyone else to annihilate them. They would themselves do the annihilating.

While the Corleonesi's foes struggled to fight them with increasing desperation, a tenacious 41-year-old investigator who was to become their worst enemy was burning the midnight oil on his first big mafia case. A few words from his superior had been enough to change the life of the shy, taciturn Judge Giovanni Falcone. 'This case here, it's very delicate. You have to do it,' was all Rocco Chinnici, the head of Palermo's team of investigating magistrates, told him in the spring of 1980.

Falcone's father was a chemist so austere he prided himself on never having drunk a coffee in a bar and his mother was a devout Catholic from Corleone. Falcone was born in the historic heart of Palermo where he was raised, save for a period when Allied bombing raids forced his family to seek refuge near Corleone. His father, in Falcone's words, taught him 'to work hard, to respect commitments'. His energetic, authoritarian mother showed him few signs of affection and taught him that little boys, let alone men, don't cry. When he slipped and cut his head open in the bath at the age of four, he didn't shout or cry but calmly went to tell his family what had happened, the blood running down his face.

Growing up in Palermo, Falcone learnt about the mafia early on. Falcone said later that 'as a child I breathed the air of the mafia with every breath – the extortions, the assassinations'. A boy he played table tennis with became a drug-trafficker. As a young man, he was horrified by the violence – it seemed to him that the secret society was 'like a seven-headed Hydra, or an inexorable lava-flow, responsible for all the evils of the world'. He was dismayed that the big trials, including those against the Corleonesi, ended in acquittals and all the time officials denied the very existence of the mafia.

After studying law at university, he took on the job of public prosecutor in Marsala in western Sicily, and his first case saw him investigate an entire clan for ten murders. Falcone, who was married but childless, began to receive postcards with coffins and crosses drawn on them. Falcone shrugged this off: 'This is something that happens to all beginners and I wasn't unduly disturbed by them,' he wrote in his memoirs. The trial was a disappointing start for him: the judges were threatened and acquitted the mafiosi.

Thinking of death became second nature to Falcone, but he was also able to joke about it. 'Of course you stay on your guard, you calculate, you observe, you organise your life, avoid getting into a situation where you're not in control. But you also acquire a large dose of fatalism, because there are so many ways to die, let's face it: a car crash, your plane might be blown up, an overdose, cancer, or even no reason at all!'

When Falcone moved to Palermo in the summer of 1978, he spent more than a year working on bankruptcy cases. When Judge Terranova was shot dead as he left his home, Falcone knew what he had to do. Terranova was the worst enemy of Leggio and the Corleonesi – he had kept a photograph of Leggio on display in his office which his colleagues had given him as a joke. The day after the murder, Falcone asked to be transferred to the section Terranova had headed – which meant prosecuting mafia cases. When Falcone's sister Maria asked him why he had changed jobs, he replied: 'You only live once.'

The mafia case Falcone was assigned by the chief prosecutor Chinnici in the spring of 1980 was a big and complex one. The main accused were the bosses Bontate and Inzerillo, the 'Cherry Hill Gambinos' gangsters in Brooklyn and the wealthy Palermitan builder Rosario Spatola, together with heroin-traffickers, money launderers and freemasons on both sides of the Atlantic. For Falcone, it was an eye-opener: 'The mafia, seen through the Spatola trial, appeared to me as a world that was enormous, boundless and unexplored,' he said later.

Falcone fired off an unprecedented flurry of letters to Palermo banks demanding details of suspicious money transfers, including all receipts for foreign exchange operations, and he pored through reams of banking records. Working his way through a pile of photocopies of cheques, he would spend hours spreading them out on his desk, scrutinising them, comparing signatures and trying to find links between them. He knew he needed solid evidence to make any charges stick. As he explained: 'Investigating the mafia is like crossing minefields: never take a step before making sure that you are not going to put your foot on an anti-personnel mine.' The evidence he assembled so painstakingly persuaded a court to convict 74 accused, a rare achievement in Sicily.

Falcone's hard work ruffled feathers in the law courts, where mafia cases invariably ended in acquittals for lack of evidence. The president of the appeal court summoned Chinnici, Falcone's superior, and accused him of ruining Palermo's economy by allowing such an investigation into the city's financial system. 'Bury Falcone under mountains of minor trials, that way he won't be able to discover anything,' the high-ranking judge recommended.

That summer, the boss Inzerillo claimed a 'distinguished corpse' of his own – Judge Gaetano Costa, killed while he browsed through books at a bookstall in the centre of Palermo – simply to show that he existed. 'I had to do something big. I had to show my opponents that my family is strong and powerful. That I could order anybody I wanted killed and when I wanted, just like the Corleonesi,' Inzerillo said.

Falcone was among the first to reach the scene. As Costa lay dying on the pavement, a colleague rushed up to Falcone and shook his hand warmly. 'Just think of it; I was sure they'd got you.' From then on, Falcone was assigned an escort – a police car and three police bodyguards. To his family, he played down its importance. 'It's a technical necessity more than anything else, there's no reason to worry,' he said.

But he started carrying a gun in his briefcase.

Purges and Banquets

Early in 1981, Riina received an unexpected visit at the Palermo villa where he was lying low with his family. A mafioso brought him a message: the police had discovered his address and planned to raid the villa the following morning.

'Let's go, let's go!' Riina exclaimed. He turned to his wife: 'Ninetta, get the children and pack our clothes, we're going immediately.' Riina drove his family away in a white Mercedes with the mafioso driving ahead in a small Fiat 500. He swiftly found a new refuge for his family, which now consisted of two sons and two daughters, the youngest of whom, Lucia, was only a few months old. The children were all born at the same Palermo clinic, with the help of the same midwife. When Lucia was born, Ninetta was so confident the police wouldn't find out about it that she added her married name to her maiden one in the clinic's register.

Rising to the top of Italy's 16,000-strong most-wanted list did nothing to stop Riina planning a new offensive unlike any the mafia had ever seen. What the Corleonesi now carrried out was, in the words of the defector Antonino Giuffrè, 'a detailed study to find out, district by district, who was close to Bontate . . . and then proceed to their systematic elimination'. In each neighbourhood, the Corleonesi set up hit squads of ambitious young soldiers, ready to carry out a murder as soon as a quarry was spotted. Giuffrè himself was surprised to see a whole gang of youths waiting in a safe house; 'there were numerous weapons ready to hand on the table and they were ready to move at very short notice to carry out murders,' he said.

Bontate also had a plan of his own – typically, it involved

waiting. He would wait before eliminating Riina; to avoid retaliation, he must first get rid of Riina's favourite killer, Giuseppe 'Little Shoe' Greco, who was so feared within the secret society it was said he had been born with a Kalashnikov rifle in his hand. No brainless brute, 'Little Shoe' – a reference to his short stature – had passed his end-of-school examinations in Latin and Greek with marks that were among the highest of his year. He started killing at the age of 16 and was in the habit of sniffing cocaine shortly before committing a murder.

Both Riina and 'Little Shoe' proved much faster than Bontate in the race against time that would decide who was to survive. 'Little Shoe' and another five men Riina had selected to eliminate Bontate 'went to the mattresses', as American mafiosi would put it: they hid in a Palermo flat where they spent the days chatting, playing cards and cleaning their weapons, which included two Kalashnikovs – an innovation the Corleonesi borrowed from the Red Brigade terrorists.

On his forty-second birthday in the spring of 1981, Bontate left his home after blowing out the candles on his birthday cake with his wife and children, who had given him a tie and some eau de Cologne; he was bound for his country villa. 'Little Shoe', who followed Bontate's brand-new Alfa Romeo on a motorbike, caught up with him at a traffic light and stood up to fire with a machine-gun. Bontate had no time to reach for the pistol in his belt. As the body of 'the Prince' slumped sideways, a luxury Vacheron Constantin pen, which matched the watch of the same make he was wearing, slipped from the breast-pocket of his suit. A shot fired from two feet away left the boss so disfigured it took police several hours to identify him.

The Corleonesi had begun their bid for supremacy by eliminating as many of Bontate's closest allies as they could, with the aim of leaving him isolated and helpless; when they came to murder Bontate himself, the Corleonesi reasoned, there would be no one left alive to avenge him. Bontate's error, in what Judge Falcone called 'a tragic game of chess', was not to understand the perverse plan in time.

On the evening of Bontate's death, Riina talked with his friend, the patriarch Bernardo Brusca, as he munched some cheese on the terrace of a villa half-way between Palermo and Corleone where he was now hiding. 'The Palermitans haven't yet understood who the Corleonesi are. And when they do understand, it'll be too late for them. Palermo will already be ours. The whole of Sicily will be ours,' Riina said.

Riina was tired – he stood up and yawned. He started to walk back into the house but turned to look back at Brusca and added in a near-whisper: 'Bontate's dead, now it's the other one's turn.' His friend knew who would be next – Bontate's ally Salvatore Inzerillo.

The charismatic capo Buscetta guessed who would be next on Riina's deathlist. From Brazil, Buscetta called Inzerillo and told him not to leave his house, not to fix any appointments and not to speak to anyone. He should concentrate exclusively on the counter-offensive he planned to launch, Buscetta advised. But Inzerillo shrugged this off. He had ordered an armour-plated version of an Alfa Romeo, which he believed would protect him. To another mafioso who pressed him to be careful, Inzerillo confided: 'They won't touch me. I'm certain they won't try anything against me. I've sent fifty kilos of drugs to America on behalf of the Corleonesi and I'm safe until I receive the payment for that batch. This way I've got time to organise the war against these bastards.'

The Corleonesi were fond of money, but they prized power above all else. Inzerillo took delivery of his new car and had still not received the payment for the drugs – some £2 million – when he was ambushed in May 1981. He was walking towards his car after a rendezvous with his mistress when four killers hiding inside a van opened fire; not even bothering to get out of the van they fired through the windscreen, shattering it. One of the soldiers sitting in front felt the bullets whistle past his ears and saw a trail of sparks in the air. Like Bontate, Inzerillo was shot in the face; police only managed to identify him after five hours thanks to his fingerprints and the initials 'S.I.' on a gold medallion hanging from his neck.

Shortly afterwards, before a celebratory meal with the killers, Riina toasted Inzerillo's death with Moët et Chandon champagne. 'So much for those who wanted me dead!' he exclaimed.

Buscetta commented: 'Inzerillo was killed "like a fool" because he had an armoured car but he forgot that it protects you only as long as you're inside.' The Corleonesi made sure they were not left out of pocket by Inzerillo's murder, obtaining from his former associates the money for the drugs he had sent. The Corleonesi suggested a meeting with Inzerillo's right-hand man; he turned up with three other mafiosi and all four were eliminated. A few days after Inzerillo's murder, 'Little Shoe' Greco and other hitmen seized his brother Santo and a friend. As the killers prepared to eliminate them, the friend wept in anger rather than in fear. Santo reprimanded him sharply: 'Stop crying and tell those bastards to hurry up.' The killers obliged.

To protect the Corleonesi from retaliation, no explanation was given for Inzerillo's murder and, for many weeks afterwards, his relatives had no idea who had committed the crime. Another brother of his called Santino, escorted by his uncle Calogero Di Maggio, demanded to be told at a meeting of underbosses and soldiers on the Favarella estate.

'Someone has to pay! Someone has to pay!' Santino shouted.

The other mafiosi tried to calm him down. 'Come on, Santino, don't get angry, no one knows who killed your brother,' one said.

'Stop being hypocrites. Who killed Salvatore? You have to tell me, now!' Santino railed, banging his fist on a desk. 'You'd better talk because I'll find out how things went anyway and then we'll have it out.'

Realising the danger his nephew was putting himself in, Di Maggio also tried to placate him.

'No, Uncle, for God's sake they have to tell me who did it!' Santino shouted. He banged the desk a second time and then a third.

A couple of mafiosi signalled to each other. Whipping out cords, they rushed to grab hold of both Santino and Di Maggio, slipped the cords around their necks and strangled them.

The two bodies were stripped of their clothes and trussed up before being stuffed into large rubbish bags and driven away in the boots of two cars. Outside a country house, the bodies were burnt on a giant grill and then buried under a pergola.

Eventually, Inzerillo's family did find out who had killed him. His 16-year-old son swore to seek revenge for his father's death. 'The man who killed my father is Salvatore Riina, and when I'm a man I will kill him,' the boy pledged. The Corleonesi heard about his promise, and 'Little Shoe' Greco was sent to seize him. The killer slowly sliced off the boy's right arm with a knife used for cutting sea urchins, shouting in his ear as the boy fainted: 'You won't be able to use this to shoot Salvatore Riina any more.' Then he pressed the muzzle of his gun to the back of the boy's neck and fired. Salvatore Inzerillo's brother Pietro was found tied up in the boot of a Cadillac in New York, with 20-dollar bills stuffed into his mouth and on his testicles.

For the supergrass Mutolo, the bloodletting usually known as the second mafia war of 1981–1983 was no such thing. He explained: 'A war is when two or more families arm themselves and know that one group is fighting another. In Palermo this mafia war never happened. What happened was a massacre. There was only Riina's strategy of terror. We got to the point of being scared of talking even among friends because we'd think, "He's not here, but he hears everything."' An estimated 1,000 mafiosi died in the purges. None of them were Corleonesi. Some 300 people simply vanished, victims of the *lupara bianca* ('white shotgun'), which ensured no trace of their bodies was ever found.

Mystery also surrounded the killers themselves. Riina kept the identities of the new hitmen he hired secret even from the other clans. As Judge Falcone remarked: 'The real strength of the

Corleonesi is their almost complete control of the province of Palermo. They've got men everywhere and we don't know them. That allows them to have at their disposal a real and proper ghost army which arrives in the city, shoots and leaves undisturbed.' The Corleonesi were never short of soldiers. As an informer explained: 'The word killer doesn't exist in Cosa Nostra. Those who join Cosa Nostra are all killers. We have hit squads made up of the most ferocious men.'

The purges struck a broad range of victims. As Riina's brother-in-law Bagarella explained: 'It's not only those who openly take a stand against Riina who risk being murdered at any moment, but also those who find out about measures against him, or about people being dissatisfied with him and who don't inform him immediately.'

Riina's favourite way of cutting short any debate on a mafioso's fate was to turn to one of his henchmen and say, in Sicilian dialect: '*Niscemunnine* (Let's get it over with)', which meant a death sentence. There is only one known case of Riina backing down after ordering a murder. After discovering that two soldiers were trafficking in drugs behind his back, Riina did not stop to consider that he and the soldiers' fathers were godfathers of each other's children. Riina told a lieutenant: 'These two have to be caught and suffocated because they're two horses who can't be controlled.'

The lieutenant hesitated all of ten seconds before replying. 'Can't we think about it? I'll call them, I'll talk to them. Your friends are in jail; it would be a shame if they lost their sons . . . If it turns out they don't obey, we'll grab them and get the job done.'

Riina stared at him briefly. 'Ah, that's how you see it? OK, let's do that.'

To carry out death sentences, the Corleonesi used soldiers they had recruited from clans all over Sicily and even managed to persuade close relatives to turn against each other. '*Piano piano* (Little by little), the Corleonesi had everyone killed. We even did the killing ourselves; one soldier would kill his brother, another would kill his brother-in-law. We became a bit infatu-ated with the Corleonesi. Because we thought that by getting rid of the old bosses we'd take their place,' a supergrass testified.

Victims were eliminated with the old-fashioned shotgun, or with the more modern Kalashnikov. A popular alternative was strangulation, considered 'clean' as it makes little noise and leaves no blood behind. But as one defector with 25 murders to his name told Falcone: 'Do you realise how much strength is needed to strangle a man? It can take up to ten minutes and the victim writhes, bites and kicks. Some even manage to break free from the rope. But at least it's a professional way of doing the job.' Once the job was done and before rigor mortis stiffened the corpse, the dead victim's wrists and feet were tied together behind his back, the rope also going around the neck; the body could then be fitted more easily into a car boot – a practice borrowed from rural Sicily and known as *incaprettamento* (literally, goat strangling).

Victims were stabbed, strangled or shot in the street, in bars or in pizzerias. One was cut down by 'Little Shoe' Greco as police escorted him from one prison to another on Palermo's ring road. 'Little Shoe' jumped onto the front bonnet of the car carrying the prisoner and fired through the windscreen, killing him and all three policemen guarding him.

Not even a prison cell was beyond the Corleonesi's reach. At the Palermo jail, the soldier Vincenzo Puccio dared to criticise Riina's methods, telling a fellow-prisoner: 'As soon as I get out, I'll tear that cuckold's head off.' At dawn one spring morning two of Puccio's cellmates first immobilised him in his bed with a blanket wrapped tightly around him, and then murdered him with blows from a cast-iron frying pan used to grill steaks. One of Puccio's fellow-prisoners explained: 'Puccio blabbed that he didn't agree with Riina's methods. That's why his elimination was decided: the whingeing made Riina think there was a plot against him.'

The cellmates claimed they had got into a fight with Puccio

over what to watch on television – a football match or the quiz game *Colpo Grosso*, in which housewives strip to score extra points. Their justification collapsed when an hour later, a brother of Puccio's was shot dead in a cemetery. With Machiavellian cunning, Riina not only eliminated Puccio and his brother but also ensured the cellmates whom he didn't trust served longer sentences – even from outside prison, Riina was pulling the strings of his puppets.

The Corleonesi routinely made their victims' bodies vanish by dissolving them in acid. The capo Giovanni Brusca estimated that several hundred victims met such an end during the purges. Brusca was in a good position to give such an estimate; so many were despatched by him that he was nicknamed *lo scannacristiani* (the man who cuts Christians' throats). Acid was a precious commodity for Brusca and he stocked up on it whenever he could obtain it, chiefly from fellow-mafiosi or friends on building sites. 'I was always on the lookout for acid. It was like finding a shotgun, a pistol,' he explained. It took 11 gallons of acid to dissolve a body in three hours; sometimes Brusca would use a burner to warm the acid and make it more effective. He usually threw any remains into a stream at San Giuseppe Jato. When the Palermo mafiosi mocked Brusca and the Corleonesi, calling them 'peasants' and 'louts', or joked about their shoes being caked with mud, he would reply: 'And what about you? What lovely water you drink in Palermo . . .' – the stream Brusca threw the human remains into fed a dam which was one of the main reservoirs supplying the island capital.

If no acid was available, Brusca and his men would dig a grave some five metres deep and bury the body in that. But after several such bodies were found by police, he used a mechanical digger to dig graves 50 feet deep which, he noted with satisfaction, made it impossible to find the bodies.

Only one enemy of the Corleonesi managed to survive an attempt on his life. The ex-butcher Salvatore Contorno, a former bodyguard of Bontate's who went on to heroin-trafficking, was famed for keeping his nerve at all times and for his shooting skills. As he drove home through Palermo, giving a lift to a friend's 11-year-old son, Contorno recognised a mafioso driving slowly in the car in front. Then he spotted two other mafiosi clearly keeping watch, one from a top-floor window and the other from behind a garden gate. 'Only the motorcycle's missing,' Contorno whispered to himself. As he did so, a motorcyle appeared in front of his car and swept down on him.

Contorno braked hard and threw himself sideways to shield the boy sitting next to him. The windscreen shattered as bullets fired by 'Little Shoe' Greco's Kalashnikov wounded the boy in the cheek, grazed Contorno's forehead and shaved a lock of hair off his head. As the motorcycle turned on them again, Contorno pushed the boy out into the street, threw himself out of the car and kneeled down behind its engine, thinking it would ward off bullets. When 'Little Shoe' opened fire again, Contorno managed to shoot him, toppling him off the motorbike, but the killer was saved by his bulletproof vest. The hit squad fled. Unable to track down Contorno and eliminate him, the Corleonesi instead murdered those who helped him hide – from the father of a cousin to a doctor who had treated him after the failed murder attempt.

After that, Contorno bought himself two armour-plated cars, each one of them equipped with an electronic device that allowed him to start the engine from a distance.

Mafiosi not allied to the Corleonesi grew to dread receiving a message that Riina wanted to see them; they knew they had little choice but to obey the invitation, as failing to do so amounted to signing their own death warrant. Even Riina's invitations to lunch were feared; he became notorious for plying a lunch guest with plentiful and excellent food, keeping up a jolly banter throughout the meal – and then giving his guest a gruesome surprise. As a supergrass explained:

> If you talk to Salvatore Riina, you'll ask yourself: 'Is it possible that this is Salvatore Riina?'

He's a very educated person, with such a gentle expression. He was the first person to invent the method, before killing someone, of inviting him for a meal, making him eat and relax and making him enjoy himself.

After eating, you would strangle him and that would be the end of it . . . You eat, you have fun and then you kill. That's the novelty Salvatore Riina introduced.

Both Riina and Provenzano participated willingly in the mafia's lively social life. As the informer Brusca explained, all mafiosi considered themselves part of an extended family. He added rather plaintively: 'It may seem strange but although we killed hundreds and hundreds of people that wasn't the only way we passed the time. We had fun too . . . It wasn't just dictatorship and silence.'

To celebrate the initiation of a new soldier, mafiosi would hold huge open-air banquets at country villas. Women were never invited; their role limited itself to preparing the food which their husbands and boyfriends – soldiers and bosses alike – contributed to the meal. 'Watching them arrive was like seeing the Three Kings. Everyone brought something. Everyone *had* to bring something,' Brusca recalled.

For the next six or seven hours, the mafiosi would gorge themselves on a rich assortment of starters, from cured ham and mozzarella cheese to stuffed peppers and aubergines, followed by pasta boiled in large copper pans, fresh fish and meat, prepared on a barbecue, and finally cakes and cannoli – typical Sicilian pastries filled with fresh ricotta cheese, chocolate chips and candied fruit – all accompanied by red and white wine, champagne and strong black coffee. 'When the food was ready, we'd sit down at table and we never stopped: we'd gobble up everything and we had to accept everything. Those who refused a dish or two were disapproved of,' Brusca recalled.

At these banquets, Riina would be relaxed and good-humoured, even playful at times. When Brusca and a few friends were spotted secretly gorging themselves on prawns while the other guests waited for meat to cook, Riina and Provenzano chased them, shouting: 'Hey cuckolds, you gave us meat to eat while you pinched the prawns!'

At one banquet, Riina, who had a passion for cooking game, served a dish he had prepared himself. When the bosses asked what it was, Riina replied: 'You eat and afterwards I'll reveal the secret.' When Riina told them after the meal that they had eaten fox meat, a couple of guests left the table to be sick.

Riina chatted jovially with young soldiers and pulled their legs. 'Would you like a beautiful yacht, with you stretched out in the sun next to a beautiful girl?' he'd ask.

'Yes, Uncle Totò, of course I'd love a beautiful yacht,' a soldier would reply.

'Unfortunately, I can't give it to you . . . because you'd sell it,' Riina would say. Riina was so obsessed with saving money, Brusca noted, that even if he had only one big banknote he would hide it under his mattress.

The banquets almost invariably ended with soldiers and bosses throwing bucketfuls of water over each other across the table, shattering plates and glasses in the process. But no one ever forgot Riina's status. One banquet ended with four soldiers rounding on Mariano Agate (a 'born comic', according to Brusca, and also good at killing) to tickle him so mercilessly that he sought refuge on the table, where he thrashed about trying to dodge them. As the soldiers' antics sent cutlery, plates, bottles and glasses flying, Agate appealed to Riina: 'They're killing me . . . Please do something.'

'Mariano, I can't get involved. I can't help you,' Riina replied, for once declaring himself powerless.

Brusca drew a serious conclusion from such frivolous antics: 'People have to understand that never, at any time, have men of honour realised what they really were. Bosses and soldiers always believed they belonged to an "army" at war and that they had the best reasons in the world to do so. They always thought the others were in the wrong.' Brusca himself saw mafiosi as making up their own state and himself as a soldier at its loyal service: 'I have never committed crimes for reasons other than to obey the interests of Cosa Nostra. In my twisted brain the mafia helped the weak.'

General Dalla Chiesa

In the autumn of 1981, Pio La Torre, a Communist member of parliament, returned to Sicily to lead his party on the island. As a member of the anti-mafia commission in parliament, he didn't hesitate to denounce corrupt politicians. Before taking up his new post in Palermo, he unveiled a draft bill which was revolutionary in a country where many officials still believed that the mafia didn't exist. La Torre's bill would introduce the specific crime of mafia association, allow the state to seize the property of bosses and ban public works contractors from passing on business to other firms, usually mafia-controlled ones. The bill would hit the bosses where it hurt – in their wallets. On the morning of 30 April 1982, 'Little Shoe' Greco ensured La Torre never saw his bill become law, shooting him dead as he drove to work.

That very evening, a *carabiniere* General returned to Sicily. Carlo Alberto Dalla Chiesa, who as a captain had served in Corleone more than 30 years earlier, arrived in a taxi to take up his new job as prefect, the state's chief envoy, in Palermo. The government had decreed a month earlier that General Dalla Chiesa, who had successfully campaigned against Italian terrorism, would 'coordinate both nationally and locally' the fight against the mafia.

When Dalla Chiesa was first sounded out about the Palermo job, he made it clear that he was not interested in an ordinary prefect's job. What interested him was the fight against the mafia and he wanted the powers and the means to win that fight. Among the senior politicians he talked to before he set out was the former prime minister Giulio Andreotti – at the latter's request. Andreotti was not in government at the time, but given his strong electoral following in Sicily, Dalla Chiesa agreed to call on him. The General noted afterwards in his diary: 'I was very clear and I left him in no doubt that I would do no favours to that part of the electorate on which his political supporters draw.' When he told Andreotti all he knew about his lieutenants in Sicily, the former premier blanched. Andreotti then told the General a story about a boss who had died in America and had been sent back to Italy in a coffin with a ten-dollar banknote stuffed into his mouth. Andreotti later denied having had this exchange with Dalla Chiesa, saying they only discussed drug-trafficking.

Anxious to appear to be doing something in the wake of La Torre's murder, the government sent Dalla Chiesa to Palermo a week earlier than planned. But it did not grant him the powers he requested. His first official engagement was La Torre's funeral and he noticed that the president of the regional government, whom he had denounced as a mafioso years earlier, gave the funeral speech.

The General was deeply worried about his new Palermo job. Shortly after his arrival, he confided his concern to his diary in the form of an imaginary conversation with his late mother. 'I find myself asked to perform a truly difficult and even dangerous task,' he wrote. 'In just a few hours I have been catapulted into a treacherous, mysterious world; the struggle ahead does some-times make me feel exhilarated but I don't have anyone close to me, I don't have the help of a friend. All of a sudden I find myself in someone else's home and in an environment which on the one hand expects miracles from your Carlo and on the other curses my arrival.' After referring again to the 'physical risks' he was running, he assured his late mother: 'Today I'm certainly not prey to panic or to terror.'

But he swiftly took measures to improve his security. He moved his desk away from the window of his office so that he couldn't be shot from outside; he checked on two cleaners and found out that they were related to mafiosi; he began planning a small apartment in the mansion where his office was situated so that he wouldn't have to make four trips a day through Palermo; he never drank coffee on his own, fearing he might be poisoned.

Dalla Chiesa didn't believe in armour-plated cars or body-guards and insisted instead on keeping his appointments and the routes he took secret. When fighting terrorists, he had twice foiled plans to assassinate him by turning up on foot or in a car driven by his late wife. In Palermo, he often took the bus and early one morning he walked through the fish market in a mafia-infested neighbourhood to show people that he did not fear his enemies. The General believed that the brotherhood's power was based not on Sicilians having a mafioso outlook on life, as some officials argued, but on the fear it inspired. To one of his school audiences, he said: 'I myself can be afraid, but as prefect I mustn't show I'm afraid, I mustn't pass it on to other people.' As his son Nando later remarked: 'What poor devil would stop being afraid if he saw that even General Dalla Chiesa was afraid and went around with escorts and sirens blaring? He chose to be an example, while knowing that he was more at risk than anyone else.'

A few days after his arrival, Dalla Chiesa invited several journalists to his office. The journalists thought they had been invited to a press conference, but he told them he had no news to give them. He just wanted to sound them out, he said, to find out whether he could count on their support in the fight against the mafia, which he said would be much tougher than that against terrorism. Pressed by the journalists, he agreed to give them a statement: he told them that one town held the key to the mafia's mysteries – Corleone.

In a symbolic challenge, the General hosted a meeting of 15 mayors in Corleone and urged them to fearlessly report directly to him anyone who put pressure on them over public works contracts or any other local issues. If they needed something for their community, he told them, they should appeal to him and not to mafioso intermediaries. 'To be able to look at our inter-locutor without lowering our eyes, to be able to laugh, talk, listen, face our sons and their sons without self-reproach, to be able to pass a life on to the young made up of sacrifice and renunciation – but clean – we can do that if we are together,' Dalla Chiesa said.

Back in Palermo, he took to visiting schools, arriving unannounced to talk to pupils about the mafia; when the pupils of one school realised who had come to see them, they gave him a standing ovation. His fighting spirit struck a chord among Sicilians; hundreds wrote to him to denounce abuses, from illegal building projects to a local authority's failure to supply a town with water. But at the same time rumours began to spread in Palermo that the General was power-hungry and 'criminalising all Sicilians'. One successful Palermo lawyer protested:

> General Dalla Chiesa can be a disaster for Sicily. If he gets to be a superpoliceman against drug trafficking, he'll end by ruining this city. Imagine everybody who lives off drugs being thrown out of work. They'll sack our homes. They'll hold us up, break into our stores and offices. Restaurants won't be safe. Our wives won't be able to go out in furs. We won't be able to go out at night. There'll be no more peace, believe me. No, beware of what he does, this Piedmontese General.

That July, Dalla Chiesa, a widower, married Emanuela Setti Carraro, a Red Cross worker. The newly-weds kept a low profile in Palermo; Dalla Chiesa always refused invitations to dinner parties, wary of meeting people linked to the mafia. He was still anxious, perhaps more so than before. During the summer holidays with his family, he insisted on showing his son Nando land that his mother had left them and talked of the need to clear some trees.

'But Dad, there's no hurry, you can deal with that when you retire,' Nando said.

His father replied in thinly veiled terms that he might not live that long.

A few days later, when Nando asked him point-blank where

he found the courage to stay in Palermo, Dalla Chiesa replied: 'Nando, there are things you don't do out of courage. You do them so that you can continue to look your children and your children's children serenely in the eyes.' He added: 'There are too many honest people, so many ordinary people who trust in me. I can't let them down.'

But the General failed to get into his stride in Palermo; his demands for stronger powers fell again and again on deaf ears in Rome and there was little echo of his victorious crusade against the Red Brigades. His frustration mounted as mafia killings continued unabated. The newspaper *L'Ora* gave up trying to find new headlines in its reporting of them and instead printed only a number: that of victims since the start of that year, 1982. By the end of the summer, the toll was above 100.

Dismayed by what he called displays of 'mafia arrogance', Dalla Chiesa gave an interview to a newspaper, in which he protested: 'They kill in the middle of the day, they carry bodies around, mutilate them and deposit them near the police head-quarters of the regional government offices, they burn them at 3 p.m. in a street in the centre of Palermo.' And yet, he complained publicly for the first time, he was still waiting for the govern-ment to give him the means to do the job it had asked him to do, that of coordinating the fight against the fraternity.

Asked how he felt set against bosses, he replied: 'We're studying each other, making the first moves as if in a game of chess. The mafia is cautious, slow, it judges you, listens to what you say, checks on you from a distance.' He explained:

> For instance, a friend who had done business with you or worked in your office says as if by chance: 'Why don't we go and have coffee at so-and-so's house?' The name is illustrious. If I don't know that heroin is flowing in rivers through that house, I'll go, and serve as their cover. If I know it and go, it's a signal that I'm prepared to give my sanction.

Clearly aware of what might lie in store for him, the General confided he had studied the new tactic of killing the powerful –

the 'distinguished corpses': 'I think I've understood the new rules of the game: the powerful man is killed when two factors come together to make a fatal combination, when he has become too dangerous but can be killed because he's isolated.' The interview shocked Palermo; representatives of the state simply didn't speak with such frankness.

A new remark drew cynical smiles among Palermo's establishment: 'If Dalla Chiesa goes on like that, he won't last beyond the winter.'

Exasperated by Rome's failure to hear his appeals and by the complicity of Christian Democrat politicians with the mafia, Dalla Chiesa turned for help to Ralph Jones, the US consul in Palermo. The two met secretly on 3 September 1982, with the General telling Jones that only the US government, at the highest level, could do something 'to make things move on'. Jones later related a story Dalla Chiesa told him at their meeting:

> While a *carabinieri* commander in Sicily in the mid-1970s, he said, he received a call from the force's captain in the west Sicilian village of Palma di Montechiaro, who had been getting threats from the local mafia boss. General Dalla Chiesa drove up to the village. It was the time of the late afternoon stroll. The General took the captain's arm and began walking slowly with him up the main street, then down it, then back up again. Everyone was looking at them. Then this strange couple stopped outside the house of the village mafia boss. They stood there until the point had been made that the young captain was not alone. 'All I'm asking for is someone to take my arm and walk with me,' the General said.

After working late in his office that evening, Dalla Chiesa called a seaside restaurant near Palermo and booked a table for two for dinner; he told an aide that he was taking his wife Emanuela out to enjoy some fresh fish. Later that evening, he and his wife got into his small personal car while his bodyguard followed in the official Alfa Romeo – he believed this was safest, as any killers would expect him to be in the Alfa. In any case, he thought, riding in an armoured car wouldn't stop bullets hitting him.

The mafia sent eight hitmen armed with Kalashnikovs to rid itself of the General. Shortly before nine o'clock, in a small street near Palermo's main piazza, 'Little Shoe' Greco opened fire on the bodyguard from a motorcycle driven by another mafioso. 'Little Shoe' then turned his attention to the car carrying Dalla Chiesa and his wife. He was furious to see another soldier do the job before he could reach the car.

The General barely had time to throw himself across his wife's body in an attempt to shield her. He was already dead when one of the killers raised his weapon to shoot him repeatedly in the face and disfigure him. His wife's face was also riddled with bullets. The bodyguard, found unconscious and seriously injured, died later of his wounds.

Dalla Chiesa had kept a diary of his hundred days in Palermo. But on the night of his assassination, a former employee whom he had sacked on his arrival entered his residence with an unidentified companion. The pair were allowed in because they claimed they had come to fetch sheets to cover the victims' bodies. That night, the key to Dalla Chiesa's safe, where he was believed to have kept his diary, disappeared. The key was found much later, in a drawer which had already been searched; but by then the safe was empty.

When news of the assassination reached the Palermo prison, jailed mafiosi toasted the General's death with red wine. 'So much for Dalla Chiesa, let's get drunk!' one shouted. However, that night, 'Little Shoe' was not in a celebratory mood. He ranted for hours against the soldier who had shot Dalla Chiesa before he could, shouting that he and he alone was supposed to kill the General; the soldier had robbed him of a prestigious quarry. 'Little Shoe' twice aimed his pistol at him, a hair's breadth away from adding his accomplice to his long list of victims.

Under a shrine to a powerless saint near the spot where Dalla

Chiesa and his wife were killed, someone left a note which read: 'Here dies the hope of honest Palermitans.'

Ten days later, parliament rushed through the La Torre law. In making membership of the mafia a crime, the state had finally recognised that the fraternity existed.

Buscetta Plays for Time

Half-way through the purges he had launched, and with many of his enemies having managed to flee Sicily, Riina turned against their relatives. Tommaso Buscetta, 'the Boss of Two Worlds', was top of Riina's deathlist and the first victim was the brother of Buscetta's first wife. Buscetta saw it as a clear sign that, as he put it: 'The Corleonese noose was starting to tighten around my neck.'

In early 1982, the Corleonesi picked the frail, 60-year-old veteran Antonino Salamone, a close friend of Buscetta's, to murder him. Salamone had settled in Brazil, and was ordered to contact Buscetta, arrange a meeting and kill him. On paper the plan was foolproof; one unwritten rule is that no mafioso can refuse an order to carry out a murder, and Salamone was the last person Buscetta would suspect. But even after a lifetime in the secret society, Salamone couldn't kill his friend. He was, however, too shrewd to betray even a hint of hesitation in carrying out the order. Buscetta said of his friend: 'He's a sphinx. No one can tell what he's thinking. He's too subtle.' With the pretext that he had some urgent business to clear up, Salamone fled to the mainland and gave himself up to the police. 'Officer, don't say that I turned myself in; say that you arrested me. You'll look like a hero,' Salamone said. When he was placed under house arrest, he promptly disappeared, shaking off anyone sent to punish him for his disobedience.

That summer, Buscetta received a visit not from a murderer but from a patriarch still hopeful that the Corleonesi could be defeated. Badalamenti, who had lost several relatives in the purges, flew to Rio de Janeiro to try to persuade Buscetta, who now bred workhorses and cows on a 65,000-acre farm near the mouth of the Amazon, to return to Sicily and take on the Corleonesi.

'We have to launch the attack on the Corleonesi by killing Leggio. You must use the friends you made in jail. Find a safe way of killing him,' Badalamenti urged.

'That's crazy,' Buscetta replied. 'Stop thinking you can wage war on 'the Peasants' . . . Come and settle in Brazil, you're safe here. Bring your family and wait five, six, seven years. Let everybody know you don't want to have anything more to do with Sicily and that you're letting the best man win. That will give you time to get stronger, study how things stand and prepare a formidable counterattack.

'Then, when you're ready,' Buscetta went on, 'you go back to Sicily. You find your enemies unprepared. You catch them by surprise and you do what you want with them. They won't be able to defend themselves.' Buscetta reminded him of the Greco clan, which 40 years earlier had pretended it had been broken up; the men of honour made sure they were seen with prostitutes, and left their property in the hands of their enemies. After five years, however, the clan had slain 40 of its enemies in just one night, sealing its return.

Badalamenti at first accepted Buscetta's plan, and travelled with him to Belém del Parà where he owned an estate of equatorial forest he was in the process of clearing to convert to pasture and crop-planting. Badalamenti kept talking about the need to stop the Corleonesi but failed to convince Buscetta. Not even the news that his brother had disappeared swayed him. It was during Badalamenti's visit that Buscetta and his third wife Maria Cristina learnt of her brother's disappearance; a farmer, he had nothing to do with the underworld. Buscetta again felt the Corleonesi's noose tightening round his neck.

Shortly afterwards, Buscetta was told that two of his sons, who ran a pizzeria in Palermo and were not mafiosi, had disappeared. He realised immediately that the Corleonesi had struck again. 'The blow was such that since then I have no longer been able to laugh, or to be happy,' he said years later. Riina was 'a bastard, a hyena', Buscetta said. 'He didn't even allow me to recover their bodies. He must have roasted them on a grating or dissolved them in acid.' Buscetta also blamed Leggio:

I'm better than him. I know where his son is, but I didn't go and kill him because he had done nothing to me and then, who knows, maybe he will become a good person. If I had the possibility, I'd kill him anywhere, even in court. If somebody brought me a gun, I'd do him in in front of the judge. It's not fury, it's not anger; it's just that I'm a father. I accept any kind of battle waged against me, but I'm not going to fight someone who has nothing to do with it.

Years later, the supergrass Salvatore Cancemi confessed that he had tricked Buscetta's two sons into getting into his car, telling them a friend wanted to talk to them. The sons were then driven away to a remote spot where they were strangled to death on Riina's orders. After turning state's evidence, Cancemi asked to see Buscetta, looked him straight in the eyes and confessed that he had helped to strangle Buscetta's sons. Far from striking him in anger, Buscetta embraced Cancemi, kissing him on both cheeks. 'You couldn't refuse. I forgive you because I know what Cosa Nostra means,' Buscetta said.

There was more mourning for Buscetta. In quick succession, his son-in-law was killed and then, at the Palermo pizzeria where they worked, his brother and his nephew. The killers spared Buscetta's daughter, who was sitting at the till. Finally, on the Fort Lauderdale beach in Florida, killers believed to have come from New York shot dead, as he lay sunbathing, an old friend who had served as the best man at Buscetta's second wedding.

Badalamenti offered his sympathy and once again tried to persuade Buscetta to act. 'Let's counter-attack,' Badalamenti said. 'Let's rebel. Whatever the cost. We too should use the scorched-earth policy around them.' There was no doubting Badalamenti's application: in 1969, he had ordered the murder of a man who

– two decades earlier – had dared slap the gangster 'Lucky' Luciano in the face at a race-course.

'It's useless,' Buscetta replied. 'My sons are dead now. If I don't react, the Corleonesi will interpret my inertia as surrender and they will stop tormenting me. I've got two other children who could be hit. I will take my revenge on them, but I have to think things out first. And I don't believe this is the right time to fight the Corleonesi.'

Badalamenti eventually returned to Sicily, but Buscetta stayed put. If he had given in to his hatred and flown to Sicily to kill Riina, it could have taken him weeks or even months to find his enemy – during which time he would be extremely vulnerable. He thought of killing Leggio's son, or Riina's children, but immediately felt ashamed of the idea.

Buscetta compared the Corleonesi to the Nazi army: 'They didn't limit themselves to attacking cities, they also blew up the bridges to prevent supplies reaching them. They applied a scorched-earth policy around their enemies, massacring anyone who showed even a hint of sympathy for them.' Riina, Buscetta said, eliminated several people simply because they had met Buscetta in prison and said afterwards that he had made a good impression on them. Some of them were not even men of honour, but common criminals. Riina's aim was to ensure that if ever Buscetta did return to Italy and needed a safehouse, he would find all doors closed to him. 'They were all terrorised,' Buscetta said.

A few weeks before Christmas 1982, Riina hosted a festive lunch at Bernardo Brusca's villa. Among the bosses and soldiers whom Riina invited was 'the Terrorist' Riccobono, whose Palermo clan Riina had never managed to infiltrate. Riccobono suspected nothing and accepted the invitation.

Riina, more jovial than ever and apparently full of seasonal goodwill, greeted Riccobono with a broad smile. 'Welcome among us. Today we'll chase away all bad thoughts and we'll think only of filling our stomachs,' Riina told him.

After enjoying a rich meal with many bottles of good wine, the guests settled into armchairs for an afternoon siesta. As 'the Terrorist' slept, someone whistled. Three mafiosi who had been careful not to eat or drink too much crept up on him. As they slipped a rope around his neck and strangled him, one of them shouted: 'Your story ends here!' In the next room, the same fate befell Riccobono's three bodyguards. The bodies were then dissolved in acid.

That afternoon and evening, Riina oversaw the murders of 20 mafiosi; some were Riccobono's followers and the rest were from another Palermo clan. Several, invited to another Christmas celebration at the Favarella estate owned by 'the Pope' Greco, Riina's stooge, were cut down while they strolled through the gardens. Others were shot at their homes or vanished without trace. Some bodies were thrown into drums filled with acid, others were scattered with corrosive chemicals and buried in the grounds of the estate. Body parts that survived such treatment were poured down a drain or thrown into the sea.

Riina was euphoric. 'We did better even than the Americans and their Saint Valentine's Day massacre,' he said smugly – Al Capone had limited himself to just seven executions. The Corleonesi ordered that none of their enemies should be allowed to flee Sicily. When the New York boss John Gambino, sent by the patriarch Paul Castellano, visited Palermo and asked what reception any fugitives to New York should be given, Riina gave a clear answer: kill them all. Back in New York, Gambino advised his friends to think not of the dead in Sicily, but of the living. Riina did, however, give several relatives of mafiosi on the losing side a choice: they could either settle in New York with the help of the city's clans, never to return to Sicily, or face execution if they remained. Many chose to emigrate and eventually became allies of the Gambino family, which Riina tolerated.

In the spring of 1983, at a banquet held in a villa near Agrigento's famed Valley of the Temples, which date back to ancient Greece, bosses from across Sicily paid homage to Riina as the new god-father, the *capo di tutti capi* (boss of bosses). By now, the Corleonesi had completed their rise to supremacy, which according to Falcone cost a thousand lives. No boss would dare to call the Corleonesi 'the Peasants' any more. At the banquet, Riina made a speech thanking all those present and through them 'all the people of Cosa Nostra'. Its 5,000 sworn members were now at his command.

The supergrass Calderone painted this portrait of Riina at the height of his career:

Riina is as powerful as Jesus Christ because he has supreme power. He holds men's lives in his hands. He can take away or spare anyone's life with just a nod. He's above everyone. But at the same time he's reduced to misery because he can't go for a walk, he can't move, he can't sleep, he can't sit in a garden of orange trees in the evening and enjoy the cool breeze and the smell of orange-blossom: he has no peace and quiet ... He's consumed by the terror of getting killed ... A life of tension and fear, a tragic life.

Corleone Inc.

Until Riina rose to power, the mafia had at least paid lip service to its 'democratic' principles. The clans elected their bosses; the Cupola 'parliament' met regularly, discussed issues openly and then took a decision, often by vote. As a rule, bosses sought to reach a consensus. To mark Christian celebrations like Easter or Christmas, the Cupola could pardon mafiosi who had been suspended for some shortcoming or other. But the mafia that emerged from the purges was, in the words of Judge Falcone, 'stronger than ever, more compact, monolithic, watertight, rigidly hierarchical and more clandestine than ever. The rebels and recalcitrants had been winkled out and eliminated one by one.'

Riina turned the fraternity into a dictatorship based exclusively on terror. From now on, bosses were imposed from above and chosen for their links to the Corleonesi – filling first of all the jobs left vacant by the purges. Mafiosi who had been suspended were no longer pardoned; often their only possible fate was death. Summits became rare and when Riina did summon bosses to a meeting, he would spend much of the time alone with each of them to keep secrecy at a maximum. Riina and Provenzano made a point of never appearing together at such summits. 'Provenzano and me, it's as if he was me and I was him,' Riina would explain. 'So if you don't see us together it's so that the two of us can't be arrested at the same time and can't be killed at the same time either.'

In the eyes of many mafiosi, the Corleonesi trampled over supposedly sacred principles, such as the 'code of honour'. The informer Mutolo explained that in the past, mafiosi were murdered according to set guidelines. 'You killed those who behaved badly and who didn't respect the rules. The end justified the means. You'd follow the "code of honour" even in eliminating the worst traitor,' Mutolo said. To avoid triggering a crackdown by the state, the organisation rarely murdered police officers and judges as the Corleonesi did; 'Above all it never touched women or children.' He added: 'I'm not a saint or a hero, but I'm proud that with my clan we refused to take part in the slaughter (carried out by the Corleonesi); we were convinced that to shoot, to strangle, to wipe out a life there had to be a good reason, always.'

When the Corleonesi seized power, Mutolo complained, 'There was no more pity, let alone honour. Everyone was killed so they could remain in power: men, women and alas even children.' Riina – with whom Mutolo had once shared a cell – had no principles whatsoever: 'They could kill Jesus Christ all over again and Riina wouldn't bat an eyelid,' Mutolo said of him. In fact, the 'code of honour' had always been a myth as the mafia didn't hesitate to kill women or children when necessary. But mafiosi still deluded themselves that these rules existed; they were a useful tool in winning consensus, as they helped persuade outsiders that the brotherhood was at their service.

Riina didn't stop at creating a dictatorship. He was also set on imposing his will on every means it had of earning money. Soon after the purges ended, Riina asked Pino Lipari, a fellow-mafioso, to arrange a meeting for him with the Corleone-born Vito Ciancimino, a former mayor of Palermo – his term in office lasted only three months, cut short by a scandal after his mafia links were exposed, but he remained an influential member of the Christian Democrats. Riina wanted to ensure that a new conference centre in the Sicilian capital would be built by Carmelo Costanzo, a builder from Catania in eastern Sicily whom Riina was backing. A Palermo faction had also made a rival bid.

When Riina called at Ciancimino's luxurious seventh-floor apartment, wearing a cashmere coat on top of a navy-blue suit that sat oddly with his stocky build and rough-looking face, he was shown not into the sitting-room but into Ciancimino's bedroom. The city councillor was sitting up in bed, wearing his pyjamas – that was the way he liked to do business. Being received by a man in pyjamas and in bed annoyed Riina but he hid his irritation and began to argue his case. There was worse to come: Riina had spoken only a few words when Ciancimino interrupted him in an imperious tone. The matter was settled, Ciancimino said; it had been decided 'politically' that the contract would go to the Palermitans.

Riina again betrayed no anger – he would no doubt have dearly liked to at least slap Ciancimino in the face for his arrogance – but he made one last attempt as he prepared to go. 'I leave convinced that this conference centre must be built by Costanzo. I hope you'll think about it so we can conclude the matter success-fully,' Riina said.

As soon as he stepped into the lift, Riina vented his exasper-ation on the unfortunate Lipari. Riina grabbed him by the collar and hissed: 'I asked you to bring me to Ciancimino, it wasn't your doing. But if I should ever have a fit of madness and ask you for another appointment with Ciancimino you mustn't bring me to him because if you do, when I come back to my senses again, you're dead.'

Lipari did, however, go back to see Ciancimino and warn him that he should never again decide on such contracts without consulting Riina first. The conference centre was never built; after Provenzano intervened to press Riina's case, Ciancimino decided the safest option was to simply shelve the project.

To prevent such setbacks, Riina revolutionised the mafia's hold on the economy, appointing *consiglieri* (advisers) who answered only to him. The most influential of these was the mafioso Angelo Siino, a builder, amateur rally driver and freemason, who was nick-named 'Charles Bronson' because of his big moustache. Siino's job was to oversee the handing out of public works contracts. Previously, clans competed for contracts through companies they controlled; if they lost, they demanded protection money from the winning businesses. But under the system Siino invented, a clan would first obtain a list of tenders and the companies taking part, then it decided which firm should win and what kick-back it should pay the mafia. A mafioso appointed to oversee the process would visit each firm in turn and impose the level at which each should price its bid. This ensured the clan decided who won.

Everyone involved in the scam benefited: 2–3 per cent of the value of the contract went to the local clan, another 2 per cent went to politicians and yet another 2 per cent went to Riina. The clan would muscle in again after the tender had been awarded, dictating which firms should act as suppliers and subcontractors and who should be hired as security guards and other staff. A defector explained how businesses found the system useful:

> For entrepreneurs, having the mafia on their side meant ... being able to work in peace and make a lot of money without running the risk of having motor vehicles damaged, or strikes, or demands for kick-backs which even the most low-ranking mafioso feels he has the right to make of anyone who invests on his territory.

Gradually, the Corleonesi built themselves a monopoly over public works contracts in Sicily. Siino himself was rewarded handsomely and spent his wealth on luxury cars, hunting rifles and Cartier watches, always with gold straps.

Riina invested part of his fortune in a financial institution more secretive even than a Swiss bank – Rome's Institute for Religious Works, better known as the Vatican Bank. In the summer of 1982, the financier Roberto Calvi, whose links to the Vatican Bank earned him the nickname 'God's Banker', was found hanging under Blackfriars Bridge in London. According to a supergrass, he was murdered by the Corleonesi because he failed to return funds he had been asked to recycle. But a court has acquitted two mafiosi and three other suspects of killing Calvi and his death remains a mystery.

Provenzano ran much of the Corleonesi's rapidly expanding business from the first-floor offices of an iron and metals depot outside Bagheria near Palermo. His number-crunching desk work at the depot, dividing up dirty money between various clans, together with his habit of making notes in pencil of everything people said to him earned Provenzano – who had until then been known as 'the Tractor' – the new nickname of 'the Accountant'.

The depot was no ordinary office. Giuffrè, Provenzano's former right-hand man, testified: 'Appointments would be set there for people who were no longer considered trustworthy and once they turned up, they never went home again – they'd be killed. So this place had a double function: first it was like an extermination camp: one of Cosa Nostra's, and in particular Provenzano's, extermination camps. And secondly it was a place for him to meet people closest to him.'

Dozens of Provenzano's execution orders were carried out just across the courtyard from his office, in the warehouse furthest away from the road. Provenzano had no need to ask whether such an order had been carried out; sniffing the air was enough to tell him all he needed to know as the pungent, nauseating stench of a body dissolving in acid would spread throughout the depot, which became known as 'the Bagheria extermination camp'.

As far as business was concerned, Provenzano had his hands full. From the depot, the Corleonesi trafficked in drugs as part of the so-called 'Pizza Connection' ring and gave orders for morphine base to be imported from Turkey for refining in a nearby laboratory and then exported to America. The mafia had a finger in every conceivable pie in Sicily, ensuring businesses won the contracts and paid extortion money for a host of projects from relaying town piazzas to building schools, council housing, hospitals, waste-recycling plants, roads, aqueducts, dams and airports – the mafia came to control the entire concrete-making sector in Sicily and made a profit even from the construction of law courts.

Through relatives and friends acting as strawmen, Provenzano set up four different companies which supplied everything from syringes to medicine and laboratory equipment, at artificially high prices and in a virtual monopoly, to Palermo's health authorities, which were all in the hands of Christian Democratic factions.

The 'peasant' from Corleone with no business experience was able to do this by relying on other mafiosi and on outsiders, from doctors to construction entrepreneurs, who acted as his advisers.

The five-foot-six Provenzano dressed shabbily, like a modest Sicilian farmer – corduroy trousers, a polo-shirt, a V-neck sweater, a heavy jacket and the typical *coppola* (beret). He confided to other bosses that he had no trouble getting around, as everyone took him for a farmer. One summer, police set up road-blocks near Bagheria, acting on a tip-off that Provenzano was in the area. The police stopped the car he was travelling in, an old Fiat loaded with hay. But Provenzano passed himself off as an old farmworker, handing over false identity papers to prove it. He was waved on.

Like any office-worker, he would drive home every evening to the home in Bagheria where he lived with his family, a villa decorated with frescoes and stuccoes set in a garden filled with plants and flowers. Provenzano is believed to have fallen in love with Saveria Benedetta Palazzolo, a shirt-maker 12 years younger than himself, in the late 1960s. Despite her humble profession, investigators later estimated her to be worth at least £170 million in shares, buildings and land, including a former feudal estate. In 1973, when Saveria was 27 years old, police may have wrecked a plan by the couple to build themselves a house in the town where she was born; as soon as investigators found out she had bought a plot of land, Saveria hurriedly sold it and then vanished.

Two years later and pregnant with Provenzano's first son, she showed some of her spirit when a policeman challenged her. 'Excuse me,' he asked her, 'but how can you say that you don't know where Provenzano is, given your condition?'

Saveria retorted: 'Excuse me, you can have children only with your husband? Isn't it possible to have them with other men too?' When Saveria, who was not even married to Provenzano, told her parish priest what she had said, she laughed out loud, clearly proud of her audacity. The two sons she bore Provenzano, Angelo and Francesco, had their births registered in Palermo, but then disappeared for many years afterwards.

The police repeatedly investigated Saveria. In 1983, they called at her home in Cinisi to arrest her on suspicion of criminal conspiracy and complicity in murder. But she had already gone and from then on was a fugitive like her husband. A prosecutor issued a warrant for her arrest as a suspected accomplice of the Corleonesi and she was sentenced in her absence to three years in prison for money laundering and for helping to cover up Provenzano's affairs. Later, she benefited from an amnesty.

For guidance on his investments, Provenzano turned to Giuseppe Provenzano – no relation of his – a business consultant and professor of banking from Corleone. Arrested and accused of administrating Saveria's assets, the consultant was described as 'a kind of adviser to the Corleonesi family'. Cleared for lack of evidence, he enjoyed a lightning political career: elected as a conservative member of the regional parliament, he became president of the regional government.

4

The 'Servants' of the State Fight Back

1983–1992

Judge Falcone in 'Enemy Territory'

In the summer of 1983, the Corleonesi used a car-bomb to claim a 'distinguished corpse' for the first time. A small Fiat 500 packed with more than 200 pounds of TNT exploded as Rocco Chinnici, the chief prosecutor, walked out of his block of flats in Palermo. The blast killed Chinnici, two bodyguards and the porter of the block and wounded another 20 people. It punched cars up as high as the third floor before they tumbled back down. Experts concluded later that the victims had been killed both by the blast and by a rain of thousands of red-hot metal fragments. With Chinnici's murder, the Corleonesi pioneered the use of terrorist-style car-bombs; the Sicilian newspapers began comparing Palermo to Beirut. Only three weeks earlier, with Chinnici's approval, Judge Falcone had ordered the arrests of Riina, Provenzano and a dozen other mafiosi for the murder of General Dalla Chiesa.

From now on Falcone's personal security was drastically re-inforced. He had long paid close attention to such arrangements. When, shortly before Chinnici was killed, the justice ministry sent Falcone a special 'bulletproof raincoat', the prosecutor took his bodyguards out into open country on a Sunday afternoon and had them test it; they riddled it with bullet-holes. After the death of his superior, Falcone doggedly scrutinised arrangements at his office and his home and for his trips across Palermo. 'I believe this is the first rule, when one takes on the job of fighting the mafia . . . I know the risks that I run doing the job I do, and I don't believe I should give a gift to the mafia by offering myself as an easy target,' he wrote.

Whenever Falcone ventured out, four escort cars travelled with him, sirens blaring, tyres screeching as the motorcade sped through the city, his bodyguards wearing bulletproof vests and carrying machine-guns. A helicopter, flying so low the noise was deafening for passers-by, flew overhead. Arriving at the law courts, he would be driven up the steep ramp that leads to the top of the large flight of steps in front of the building and be escorted in through the main entrance. Access to his office was through armour-plated doors. Of the 70 bodyguards at his disposal, he chose eight every day, whom he picked at the last moment.

A sentry box with bulletproof glass was set up outside Falcone's block of flats. A bodyguard was stationed inside his front door even at night. The only exercise he took was some gymnastics when he got up in the morning at 5 a.m. and daily visits to a swimming-pool, early in the morning or late at night. He gave up going to the cinema, as it meant freeing four rows of seats to create a security cordon around him. Falcone was now the most protected man in Sicily.

Several of his neighbours wrote to a local newspaper complaining they were afraid they might get hurt or killed if the mafia tried to murder him. One neighbour, calling herself 'an honest citizen who pays taxes regularly and works eight hours a day' also protested that the noise of the sirens disturbed her during her afternoon siesta and in the evening when she watched television. Wouldn't it be best, she suggested, if Falcone and other judges were housed in specially built houses on Palermo's outskirts? The complaints saddened Falcone. He was getting used to criticism from politicians and from his colleagues, but such hostility from ordinary people weighed on him; he counted on their sense of solidarity. 'In the end, my brother was practically condemned to a sad life,' his sister Maria said. 'He was alone in this war. He had a handful of friends and that's all.'

Chinnici's death was the source of deep personal sorrow for Falcone, who didn't only lose a superior he respected. Concern for Falcone's safety had tormented his mother Luisa ever since he was first assigned an armed escort. She never spoke to her son about her fear that he might be killed but she confided to a friend: 'I will die of grief.' A few days after General Dalla Chiesa's murder in 1982, she suffered a heart attack. She never recovered completely, made all the more anxious by the extra security measures for her son. When the car-bomb blew up Chinnici and many people speculated that Falcone would be next, her condition suddenly worsened and she weakened day by day.

Falcone 'suffered but he couldn't stop: by then he'd entered a tunnel from which he'd never come out,' his sister Maria said. Their mother died two months after Chinnici. As Falcone and his sister stood in front of her body, their eyes met. 'He was telling me with his eyes that all this was inevitable, that he hadn't chosen it. He asked me to think of death as something that was possible. That his life too hung by a thread,' Maria said.

Falcone himself made light of the risks he was running. He insisted: 'I'm not Robin Hood. I'm not a kamikaze pilot; I'm not a Trappist monk. I'm just working for the state in enemy territory.' On one occasion, enemy territory included the Palermo jail. As he was preparing to question a prisoner there, another inmate suddenly appeared at the door of the interview room, brandishing a gun. Just in time, Falcone managed to slam the door shut and flee to another room. Wrong-footed, the gunman pretended to take another prosecutor hostage and demanded to be moved to another jail.

Only two weeks after eliminating Chinnici, Riina told his soldier Giovanni Brusca to prepare another car-bomb, this time for Falcone. Brusca tried to keep watch outside Falcone's home but following the Chinnici bombing, police were stopping anyone parking outside the homes of anti-mafia prosecutors and senior officials. So Brusca stationed himself at the law courts and noticed that every morning a van left a bar opposite the building to bring fresh coffee and *cornetti* pastries to the prosecutors who had just arrived for work. Brusca thought of using an identical van packed with explosives, but he gave up on the idea as he couldn't see how he could make his get-away before the bomb exploded.

Brusca reported back to Riina, who told him: 'OK, let's leave it for now. We'll talk about it again some other time.'

Buscetta had prepared himself for the moment when he heard the key turn in the lock of the door of his prison cell in São Paulo, Brazil, on 7 July 1984. As the guard swung the door open and told Buscetta to come with him, the prisoner swiftly stuck a hand in his trouser pocket and grabbed a small piece of paper which had been folded flat. He knew that Brazil had agreed to his extradition and he had no intention of giving his enemies, the Corleonesi, a chance to slaughter him once the empire of 'the Boss of Two Worlds' had shrunk to an Italian prison cell where he would rule over nothing. Inmates at the Palermo jail had recently stabbed a friend of his 58 times. He unfolded the paper and swallowed the powder it contained.

'What have you just swallowed?' the guard asked.

'Bicarbonate, because I'm suffering from heartburn,' Buscetta replied.

The boss was lying. He had decided to commit suicide and the package contained not bicarbonate but strychnine; he had smuggled the poison, which he used to get rid of rats on his estate, into jail with him when he had been arrested in São Paulo the previous October.

Over the previous few days he had tried to prepare his wife Cristina for his death, saying to her: 'Wouldn't it be wonderful if I died? For you and the children.'

'Don't talk rubbish,' Cristina retorted angrily.

'It's not rubbish, I'm being serious. People cry a bit when someone dies, then they resign themselves, and everyone starts their life anew. But as long as I exist, I know you, you'll follow me, even in Italy; and I don't want you to suffer any more humiliations. When I go there, don't come with me, and don't write to me; otherwise I'll send your letters back.' He insisted that his death would be a great liberation for the family; she and the children would no longer be forced to move from one country to another, always pointed out as the family of the mafioso Tommaso Buscetta.

Shortly after leaving his cell, Buscetta suffered convulsions and was taken to hospital where he sank into a coma. Cristina wasn't allowed to see him; prosecutors accused her of supplying the poison he had swallowed. She was dangerous, they said, and would seek to finish him off if she got close enough.

After four days in hospital, however, he was pronounced well enough to travel. He still had water in his lungs, his heartbeat was irregular and he had great difficulty speaking. Granted permission, with their children, to say goodbye to him on the tarmac, Cristina found him so pale and lethargic she thought the police had drugged him as a parting gift. She was in tears as she embraced her husband, who was wrapped in blankets and flanked by a doctor. She too was certain that the mafia would eliminate him in whichever Italian jail he was taken to.

As the jumbo jet flew across the Atlantic, Buscetta lay across several seats in the second row in business class, gasping for breath; he wheezed so badly it sounded like a death-rattle. His doctor struggled to keep him alive with a canister of oxygen and with injections to steady his heart. Buscetta rallied at one point and found the strength to ask to speak with the police officer escorting him back to Italy.

The escort, Italian deputy police chief Gianni De Gennaro, put down the whisky he had been drinking as he waited for dinner and walked up to the boss. Buscetta said something but so faintly that De Gennaro had to bend down with his ear close to the mafioso's lips to make out what he was saying.

Buscetta whispered: 'When we arrive, there are a couple of things I'd like to say to you and Judge Falcone . . .'

De Gennaro was so stunned he forgot he had not prayed in 25 years. 'Our Lady, let him live. Jesus Christ, I beg you, don't let this son of a bitch die now,' he prayed silently.

With the plane still over the Atlantic, the canister the doctor had been using ran out of oxygen. The doctor borrowed one from the cockpit, and when that ran out too the plane made an emergency landing in Milan to pick up new ones before taking off again. When the plane landed at Rome's Fiumicino airport –

with Buscetta still alive – De Gennaro immediately called Falcone in Palermo.

'I have Buscetta here with me. He wants to collaborate,' De Gennaro said.

'I'll be in Rome tomorrow,' Falcone said, as unflappable as ever. He smiled as he put the phone down and thought to himself: 'De Gennaro's drunk.'

The 'couple of things' Buscetta mentioned turned out to be the greatest blow against the Corleonesi so far.

When Buscetta started to testify before Falcone, he looked the judge straight in the eyes and announced to the latter's amazement: 'I am not your enemy.' But, he explained, he was not a *pentito* (repentant); he was not seeking forgiveness. 'I want to tell you what I know about that cancer which is the mafia, so that the generations to come can live in a more dignified and humane way,' he said.

Before continuing, Buscetta told Falcone: 'I must warn you, Judge. After these interviews with me you will become a celebrity. But they will seek to destroy you, both physically and professionally. And they will do the same to me. Don't forget that an account opened with Cosa Nostra can never be closed. Do you still wish to interview me?'

Falcone did indeed and, to ensure maximum secrecy, he took down Buscetta's testimony himself, writing everything down by hand. Over the 45 consecutive days they spent together, the judge managed to win the star witness's absolute trust, partly thanks to Falcone's childhood spent in the heart of Palermo – 'you have to learn to live and think like the mafiosi,' Falcone remarked later. He described the mafia as 'nothing more than a distortion, an exaggeration, an extreme and aberrant version of the traditional Sicilian way of life'.

Buscetta echoed: 'We're both Palermitans. A turn of phrase, a glance, or a reference to a place or an event was enough for us to understand each other.' It also helped that Falcone understood the torment Buscetta was going through in defying the brotherhood and never tricked or lied to him. Falcone said of his questioning of supergrasses: 'I knew how hard they found it to talk about themselves, to tell of crimes without knowing what the consequences of confessing might be for them.'

Buscetta's testimony was so wide-ranging it gave the state unrivalled insight. Before Buscetta, Falcone admitted, investigators had only a superficial knowledge of the mafia; they didn't even know members called it Cosa Nostra. 'With him we began to look inside it . . . He gave us the essential keys to the interpretation of the mafia, a language, a code,' Falcone said.

Starting from the early 1960s, Buscetta revealed the organisation's pyramid structure, the names of Cupola members, of clan territories, bosses and soldiers as well as the brotherhood's codes, rituals, crimes and outside accomplices. He was far from impartial; he spoke at length of the crimes committed by the Corleonesi but said little about his friends in the losing faction. The Corleonesi had become the dominant faction, he explained. 'Riina and Provenzano . . . enjoy equal power, except that Riina is much more intelligent than Provenzano and therefore has greater weight,' he said.

Buscetta branded Riina 'the most evil man in the history of Cosa Nostra'. It was Riina's climb to power, he claimed, that polluted the mafia's dignity and honour with a cocktail of gratuitous and devious violence, hatred and treason. Buscetta wanted to collaborate with the state to open a breach in the wall of secrecy that protected the Corleonesi. 'Villainous men murdered my sons and exterminated my friends and relatives, violating one of the most ancient rules of the human race, respected in the Cosa Nostra of old: the rule that the sins of the fathers must not be visited on their children.' Leggio and Riina had violated the rules of the state, of the mafia, and of the Old and New Testament.

As Buscetta himself put it, he had turned from a potential assassin into an accuser, thirsty not for blood but for justice. He claimed he no longer hated either Riina or Leggio. 'If I had the power to decide what to do with them, if I had them here in front of me, I wouldn't hurt even a single hair on their heads. I would look at them and think of my sons . . . I would ask God to forgive their murderers. Because Riina and the others will have to answer before Him for what they have done to my loved ones.'

Death would be too easy, too good for them. 'The death sentence isn't enough. For someone who's guilty, it's a liberation. I know prison well and I know what it means to spend years behind bars suffering humiliation after humiliation every day . . . If you have always commanded, if you have been powerful, very powerful, to the point of dictating life or death for others, prison life is the worst possible punishment,' he said.

There was one subject, however, on which Buscetta's lips stayed sealed. Asked about relations between bosses and politicians, he replied he would talk about them 'only if and when the time is right'. When Falcone pressed him, Buscetta answered: 'Let's establish who must die first: you or me.' Almost a decade was to pass before he agreed to say anything on the subject.

There is no doubt Buscetta airbrushed much of his own criminal career; he admitted to killing 'several people' but couldn't remember their names. Later, he told his biographer: 'It's so easy to press the trigger and see the other fall. And immediately you have a sense of liberation. I did what I had to do the best way I could.' He insisted to Falcone that he had never trafficked in drugs. But his oldest son Benedetto testified that his father was 'a big man in the narcotics traffic'. He was also excessively nostalgic about the 'dignity and honour', as he put it, of the mafia before the Corleonesi rose to power; the truth is that it has always been based on violence and fear.

Buscetta's testimony – what he had announced as simply 'a couple of things' he wanted to say – filled 329 pages of Falcone's handwriting. Aware of the brief revelations the boss Di Cristina had made seven years earlier, Falcone reflected that if only the state had acted on the information given by Di Cristina and gone after the Corleonesi he had accused at the time, the clan would probably not have become as dangerous as it was now.

After Buscetta finished testifying, Falcone asked De Gennaro to check on 3,600 different points Buscetta had made, prompting the police officer to joke to the supergrass: 'Maybe I made the biggest mistake of my life in asking Jesus Christ to let you live.'

Then Falcone signed 366 arrest warrants, making accusations which involved 300 crimes and shed light on 121 murders. Proof, had the Corleonesi needed it, that Falcone would stop at nothing.

The Maxi-Trial

In the summer of 1985, the Corleonesi sent an 18-strong death squad led by 'Little Shoe' Greco to ambush Ninni Cassarà, the deputy-head of Palermo's flying squad, as he arrived at the block of flats where he lived. A no-nonsense investigator like his friend Falcone, Cassarà had been transferred from Trapani in western Sicily after leading an unauthorised raid on an exclusive club where notables and aristocrats gambled and played poker – he blotted his copy-book by detaining the dignitaries' bejewelled wives at police headquarters. In Palermo, he managed to persuade several mafiosi to talk to him; the result was a report showing the extent of the Corleonesi's domination.

As soon as Cassarà and two bodyguards got out of the armour-plated car outside his home, the hit squad fired Kalashnikovs from a block of flats opposite; more than 200 bullets were fired. Cassarà's wife, who had been looking out for him on her balcony, saw him killed. One bodyguard also died and another was seriously injured. When Falcone, who had often joked with Cassarà about the risk they ran of getting killed, walked up to the open mahogany coffin and saw his friend's body lying inside, his face turned white as a sheet. 'This time it's no joke. I've lost a friend,' Falcone murmured.

Cassarà was 'Little Shoe' Greco's last victim. Riina had rewarded the soldier who had risen to become his chief assassin, claiming a hundred or so lives including that of General Dalla Chiesa, with membership of the Cupola but he now worried that Greco had become too powerful. Young soldiers especially idolised him, queueing to meet him when he received visitors once a week. Riina began to think that Greco might be thinking of adding him to his long list of corpses and told only three other bosses of his decision to eliminate him. 'They were the only ones in the know because if Greco had got wind of it they would have all had to go and hide, because that guy was capable of walking into a military barracks and shooting all the soldiers in it,' an informer explained.

Riina ordered Greco's closest friend Giuseppe Lucchese to carry out the death sentence. Lucchese was understandably worried about what would happen if he failed to carry out the job swiftly enough, but managed to kill Greco with a single bullet in the back of the neck as, dressed only in pyjama trousers, he made coffee for his friend. Riina insisted on seeing the body before it was dissolved in acid; satisfied, he appointed Lucchese to fill Greco's shoes as clan head.

A few days later, Riina approached the boss Cancemi, who was another close friend of Greco's. 'You know we've found the medicine for madmen?' Riina asked him.

Cancemi had no idea what Riina was talking about. He replied warily: 'That's good news.'

Riina announced: 'We've killed "Little Shoe"; he'd become crazy. I don't think that displeases you, does it?'

Cancemi felt his knees trembling. 'No, and in any case whatever you do is fine by me,' he had the quickness of mind to reply.

Greco was the first of several younger mafiosi Riina eliminated after they had distinguished themselves in his service. The godfather simply wanted to make sure they would not use their skills against him. 'Riina was cold and calculating,' the supergrass Mutolo testified. 'Instead of eliminating only those who really had tried to kill him, he used the pretext of an endless plot to bump off all those who could obstruct his programme of absolute supremacy.'

A little more than a week after Cassarà's murder, Falcone again felt the mafia's shadow hanging over him. Alarmed by a death threat from the brotherhood, bodyguards escorted Falcone, his childhood friend and colleague Judge Paolo Borsellino, and their families to the prison island of Asinara off Sardinia, where they could be more closely guarded. They stayed for two weeks, Falcone spending most of the time drafting the indictment for what was to become known as the 'maxi-trial' – the direct result of Buscetta's marathon testimony. When they got home they received a bill for all their meals on the island.

The indictment – it runs to a total of 8,067 pages – begins with the confident words: 'This is the trial of the mafia organisation called "Cosa Nostra" . . . which, with violence and intimidation, has sowed, and continues to sow, death and terror.' It was in part based on the so-called Buscetta theory, which blamed all the members of the Cupola for many murders of prominent figures – the 'distinguished corpses' – simply because they took an active part in it at the time of the killings. Out of all the Corleonesi, the indictment gave pride of place to Leggio, mentioning Riina many times but Provenzano only briefly – the latter had managed to escape attention.

Such was the size of the trial that critics branded it a 'judicial monster' in which none of the accused would be given a fair trial. When Falcone insisted on a giant courtroom being built in a wing of the Palermo jail so that the trial could physically take place, he met with a string of objections from officialdom. It was only thanks to a friend at the justice ministry that the new courtroom was built, capable of resisting bazooka fire or a missile attack and linked to the prison by an underground tunnel. The courtroom was so vast it contained 30 steel cages for the accused and could seat several hundred lawyers.

With Riina and Provenzano both on the run, it was left chiefly to the 61-year-old Leggio to represent the Corleonesi at the trial, which began in February 1986 with 3,000 armed troops deployed outside the courtroom. He sat alone in cage number 23, dressed elegantly in a dark suit with striped tie and pocket handkerchief. He would reach into the inside pocket of his jacket and pull out a giant cigar as thick as two fingers, which he played with, twirled and sniffed for hours but never lit. Other mafiosi smiled at each other; they knew he had cigars brought to his cell but never smoked them. The cigars were only props in Leggio's imitation of Marlon Brando's Don Vito Corleone in the film *The Godfather*, and were for the benefit of the television cameras.

When his turn came to speak, Leggio claimed to have no idea what the mafia was. 'I've never done anything in my life that I reproach myself with. I've never made a single enemy. I've always been a calm man,' he said. He had no patience with Buscetta: 'He should wash his mouth out with vinegar before he talks about the Corleonesi,' Leggio said. Buscetta ignored him and testified for an entire week, sitting in a bulletproof glass booth facing the judge, his back to the cages holding Leggio and the other accused.

The most virulent dispute saw Buscetta trade insults with Giuseppe Calò, whom Buscetta recruited and who had risen to head their Palermo clan. Calò, an ally of the Corleonesi, accused his former friend of being vain – 'he's always had this idea of himself as some kind of superman,' he said – and a womaniser. Buscetta also treated his family badly, he claimed. '[Buscetta's brother] came to see me in Rome . . . and told me with tears in his eyes: "Look what Masino has done, he's gone again, leaving me with one son in prison and the other on drugs,"' Calò said.

Buscetta fired back: 'The only true thing he has said in this court is that he and my brother were very close friends. What he's forgetting, in this moment, is that he sat at the table, together with the rest of the commission, when they decided the death of my brother and his son.' Buscetta turned to stare at Calò. 'Hypocrite . . . You had my entire family murdered: my brother-in-law, my sons, my son-in-law, my cousins. Why didn't you have me killed?'

'Don't worry,' Calò replied.

As the trial went on, Leggio took up painting in his cell at the suggestion of Gaspare Mutolo, a heroin trafficker and amateur artist known as 'Mister Champagne' for his taste in Ferraris and Armani suits. Leggio started painting not because he suddenly discovered a passion for art, but because he wanted to give the right impression, according to his tutor Mutolo. 'Leggio realised immediately that with painting he could make people think he was reformed, that he was a sensitive soul and no longer dangerous,' Mutolo said. To make sure people got the point, Leggio also wrote poetry and read Dickens and books of philosophy.

Leggio painted landscape after landscape, including the twisted streets of Corleone and views of the hills around the town at sunset. After three months of lessons, the prison governor was delighted, boasting that his establishment set even the most hardened criminals on the straight and narrow. Leggio's lawyers said he was inspired by Vincent Van Gogh. But Mutolo was far from proud of his pupil; in his eyes Leggio had yet to understand how to use colours and at best he produced scribbles, twisted houses and flowers without petals.

That spring, Falcone, who had divorced his first wife of 14 years, took a rare and short break to marry Francesca Morvillo, an appeals court judge who like him had a broken marriage behind her. To keep the ceremony a secret, Falcone did a normal morning's work at the law courts. That afternoon – the only time he went without bodyguards – Falcone drove himself to the city hall for the ceremony, in which only four people participated apart from the wedding couple: the mayor who married them, two friends who served as witnesses and the bride's mother, who insisted on attending. Although Francesca wanted children, Falcone refused. 'I don't want you to give birth to orphans,' he told her.

During the maxi-trial, the Corleonesi did not hesitate to threaten Falcone to his face. When he questioned 'the Pope' Greco, Riina's stooge, the urbane Greco first listed several senior judges who were friends of his and whom he had received at his home. Comparing the judge to the Argentine soccer star Diego Maradona, he said: 'Judge Falcone, you are truly skilled. You are the Maradona of judges; one has to trip you up to get the ball off you.' Falcone ignored the threat.

While Leggio played with a cigar in court and a paintbrush in his cell, Riina worked behind the scenes to ensure the maxi-trial's verdict would be favourable to the Corleonesi and to other families – as godfather, it was Riina's responsibility to stand up for all the mafiosi in the dock, not just the members of his clan. In an attempt to sway the court, Riina turned to the political establishment. Riina had no political allegiances of his own – 'The one who gives me bread, I call him Daddy,' he said.

The Christian Democrats had long been traditional allies but over recent months Riina had grown increasingly suspicious of them as he was convinced they were doing nothing to help ensure acquittals at the maxi-trial. In the spring of 1987, Riina presided over a summit in a Palermo apartment. He surprised bosses by decreeing that the mafia would now support the Socialist party of Bettino Craxi, who had harshly criticised magistrates for going too far in their probes into political corruption. Riina then read out a list of favours he expected to be granted by Claudio Martelli, the Socialist justice minister, which included softening laws on the seizure of bosses' assets.

Provenzano at first disagreed with Riina; he saw no point in turning his back on the Christian Democrats. After talking it over with Riina, however, Provenzano took a typically Solomonic decision: he wouldn't oppose the change but he would at the same time maintain his own links to Christian Democrat politicians. As Riina liked to repeat: 'Provenzano and I may have our differences, but we don't get up from the table before we've reached an agreement.' Thanks to mafia support, which included campaign funds contributed by prisoners including Leggio, the Socialists saw their vote in Palermo jump at the next elections in 1987 from 9.8 per cent to 16.4 per cent.

At the spring summit, the bosses were more united on another measure – death sentences for Judges Falcone and Borsellino and for the Palermo mayor Leoluca Orlando, who was waging an outspoken campaign against the mafia. From now on, a henchman of Riina's explained later, 'any opportunity would be the right one to kill them. There wasn't even any need to discuss it again. Falcone and Borsellino, with their determination, were real pains in the neck; their work was followed very closely by public opinion.

And Orlando talked too much, he'd become a symbol. All three of them must die.'

Concerned at the crackdown that killing someone like Falcone could provoke, Provenzano suggested leaning on politicians to have Falcone transferred to Rome.

But Riina replied: 'No, I have to kill him in Sicily.'

'The Pope' Greco, who had lived up to his nickname by reading the Bible in his cage at the maxi-trial, read out a threatening prayer in a loud voice just as judges and jury left to decide their verdict after 22 months of hearings: 'Let your conscience guide you. I wish you peace and tranquillity . . . I hope that peace may be with you for the rest of your lives.' Greco was charged with 78 murders.

After 36 days of deliberations, during which the presiding judge Alfonso Giordano grew a beard, dozens of lawyers representing mafiosi stood for hours as he read out the verdict. Riina, Provenzano and many of their allies including Greco were among 19 mafiosi given life sentences. Leggio, however, was acquitted, the court refusing to believe that he could have ordered murders after he was jailed in 1974. In total, the court handed out sentences sending 338 mafiosi to prison for 2,665 years.

Leggio remained in jail as he had old sentences to serve, but, helped by an art merchant, he consoled himself by holding an exhibition of his paintings; they were all signed by Leggio but according to Mutolo, more than half of them were actually painted by him, not Leggio.

For the duration of the maxi-trial the mafia, anxious not to make things worse for the accused, had banned any killings. The ban ended on the day the verdict was read out; the first victim, who had just been acquitted for 'lack of evidence', was shot two hours after his release as he walked into his home carrying cakes and champagne to celebrate his freedom.

Falcone may have managed to send dozens of mafiosi to jail, but for Riina it was still business as usual – or at least that was the image he tried to project. Settling down with his family in a new villa in Palermo, Riina passed himself off as a businessman. When on mafia business he used a driver, while on family outings he drove himself, always with a false driving licence. His villa, the work of a trusted architect, boasted two features he always insisted upon: a safe hidden behind a painting, and an underground, damp-free room for Ninetta to store her furs.

At the Cupola's summits, Riina would preside from a large armchair 'as big as the Pope's', according to one mafioso. He would rant and rave if it wasn't ready for him. Ever suspicious, Riina once started a meeting of the Cupola with the demand: 'If any of you has a weapon with them, please put it on the table.' Riina, of course, left his own short-barrelled, .38-calibre gun right where it was, in the leather shoulder bag he always carried.

No boss ever contradicted Riina. 'He was the one who set the agenda and we followed. Even if we didn't agree with him, it wasn't easy to go and say to someone else: "The man's mad. What's he playing at?" Because if he told Riina, two minutes later you were dead,' another boss recalled. Riina was suspicious of everyone, even of Provenzano; worrying about the latter's increasing influence in Bagheria, Riina sent a henchman to check on his every movement, noting the time whenever he left his hideout.

Word of the Corleonesi's rise to supremacy crossed the Atlantic. At New York's Café Giardino, much appreciated for its refreshing granites, the owner Giuseppe Gambino, a Sicilian-American mafioso, confided one muggy August afternoon to a friend who had just arrived from Palermo: 'You can't move so much as a finger without the people in Corleone giving you the OK first.'

'They run the show; everything comes from Corleone,' the visitor confirmed. The remarks were picked up by an FBI bug.

That December, as the maxi-trial ended, the Corleonesi sealed their dominant position in the Italian cocaine market by obtaining a pledge from the cartel of drug-traffickers in Medellin in Colombia, run by Pablo Escobar, to deal exclusively with the Madonia clan, who were allies of Riina. The following month, the merchant ship *Big John* sailed from the island of Aruba off the Venezuelan coast, officially carrying bird-droppings, guano and manure. On board were 1,300 pounds of cocaine, a first shipment costing £3 million, from which the Corleonesi planned to make a profit of £16 million.

The Corleonesi were handling wealth they could only dream of when they had been boys working the fields near their home town. It was only in the mid-1980s that official agencies first tried to evaluate the size of Italy's illegal economy, much of it dominated by the mafia. In 1985, its value was put at £26 billion, an eighth of the country's Gross Domestic Product at the time. The national turnover from drugs alone was put at about £7 billion.

Riina never forgot his intention to have Falcone eliminated. He considered and then abandoned several plans; they ranged from using a bazooka against the armour-plated cars the judge always used to ambushing him in the municipal swimming-pool where he often went. In 1988, when the judge was in the running to become Palermo's chief prosecutor, the godfather sent an envoy to Ignazio Salvo, a powerful Sicilian tax-collector.

Salvo reassured him. 'We've still got a few friends; we can still arrange things. Falcone will never become chief prosecutor,' he told the envoy. Christian Democrat politicians in Rome would see to it that Falcone was rejected. 'Tell Riina there's no longer any need to kill Falcone, because they'll destroy his credibility,' Salvo added.

When the envoy reported back to Riina, the godfather exploded: 'Are they trying to pull a fast one on me? I'll kill Falcone all the same. The politicians are looking after their own interests and they're leaving us out in the cold, to perish as if we were cannon-fodder. I've got to kill them all. The time has come to kill them.'

The Sicilian mafia was not alone in pressing for Falcone's death. The American mafia also clamoured for his murder, urging the Sicilian bosses at one meeting not to lose any more time. Falcone worked too closely for its liking with the US attorney Rudolph Giuliani, a partnership which had led to arrests on both sides of the Atlantic.

Despite his outstanding career, Falcone was passed over for the job of chief prosecutor amid a flurry of personal attacks from envious superiors, colleagues and politicians from both Left and Right. More than ever, the Palace of Justice that housed the law courts merited its nickname of 'Palace of Poisons'; it was a hot-house for gossip and slander. Critics accused the judge of being arrogant and power-hungry, he had 'intimate' relationships with defectors and was failing to prosecute politicians allegedly denounced by Buscetta. In fact, Buscetta had refused to testify on political links, telling Falcone he did not believe the state genuinely intended to combat the fraternity.

Falcone brushed off such accusations saying they were perhaps the best proof of his independence. 'I'm a judge, I'm not in the business of seeking people's approval. When you arrest someone, especially a so-called white-collar criminal, you know you're not going to please everyone. But a judge must focus on the crime, nothing else.' But his failure to be promoted to chief prosecutor, together with the unfounded accusations, left him increasingly isolated and vulnerable.

The following year, on a summer morning, Falcone was shaving in a seaside villa he and his wife Francesca rented at Mondello near Palermo when one of his bodyguards suddenly walked into the bathroom and told him: 'We have to leave right away. I've found a bomb.' A diver's bag, wetsuit, flippers and a diving mask had been found on some rocks 20 yards from the villa. The bag was filled with 58 sticks of dynamite and two battery-operated detonators; it could be set off by remote control or by anyone picking it up.

The next day, Riina told a soldier: 'It's a pity it didn't work out, because the timing was right' – Falcone's isolation was increasing as anonymous letters from a source dubbed 'the Crow' sought to spread slander about the judge. Falcone was even accused of using the supergrass Contorno in a plot to eliminate a dozen Corleonesi.

Falcone's wife was so shocked by the assassination attempt that she lost her voice for two days. Fearing increasingly for

Francesca's safety, Falcone tried to distance himself from her to protect her. He refused to let her spend the night in their flat, worrying that the mafia might try to murder him as they slept; it was safer for her to leave every evening and go to her parents' home, he argued. Falcone also toyed with the idea of staging a false separation. The judge's sister Maria, who often went to have dinner at his home, had never seen him as tense as in the days that followed the attempt on his life.

At his wife's request, Falcone's sister gently reprimanded him over dinner: 'But Giovanni, you can't expect Francesca to go home every evening.'

'You don't understand, I must be lucid, I must be always on the alert; I can't be worrying about Francesca's safety. Sometimes I don't sleep at night, I stay in an armchair because they' – the men behind the murder attempt – 'must know that I won't move from here, that I'm not afraid.'

Falcone then added: 'You don't understand. From now on I'm a walking corpse.'

To a friend he confided that he preferred to sleep on the floor; the discomfort meant he slept less deeply and as a result would be quicker to defend himself if attacked.

Unforeseen by the Corleonesi, the empire they had been so busy forging was now beginning to show signs of strain: Buscetta's testimony had led not only to the maxi-trial, it had also prompted other mafiosi to take the brave step of defying the law of silence and turning state's evidence. They had no illusions about the price they might have to pay for their betrayal. They too described themselves as dead men walking. 'By taking this step we've condemned ourselves to death. Any minute a rifle shot can hit you in the shoulders and you're dead,' an informer explained.

The first to follow in Buscetta's footsteps was Contorno, whom the Corleonesi had tried but failed to kill. After Buscetta turned state's evidence, investigators called on Contorno at his prison in Tuscany and asked him to follow Buscetta's example; until then, Contorno had given very little information to the police.

Now the investigators wanted him to reveal all he knew and to comment on Buscetta's testimony.

Contorno asked for permission to meet Buscetta before reaching a decision; he wanted not only to verify for himself that Buscetta had indeed broken the law of silence, but also to ask his advice. When he was taken to Buscetta's secret refuge and found himself in front of 'the Boss of Two Worlds', he dropped to his knees as if paying homage to a king. Buscetta leaned down and ruffled Contorno's hair. 'Cosa Nostra is finished now. You can talk,' Buscetta said. Contorno made his confession to Falcone, telling him: 'I intend to collaborate with the justice system telling everything I know about Cosa Nostra ... because I realise that it is nothing but a band of cowards and murderers.' Contorno's testimony led to 127 arrest warrants.

At a meeting of the Cupola, an incensed Riina complained at length about the 'traitors' Buscetta and Contorno, saying the mafia must do all it could to put a stop to supergrasses and must kill all their relatives. 'When their sons reach the age of 18 years and one day, they must be killed,' Riina decreed. 'Some names in particular, and all their relatives, must be wiped from the face of the earth.' To punish Contorno, an astonishing 35 of his relatives were killed.

But still more mafiosi came forward to talk. Among them was the quiet, reserved Francesco Marino Mannoia, known as 'Mozzarella' because of his pale complexion due to a life spent refining heroin. A former lieutenant of Riina's vanquished enemy 'the Prince' Bontate, his life had been spared by the Corleonesi thanks to his reputation as a talented chemist. Obeying an order from the mafia, he had been forced to marry a boss's daughter rather than the woman he loved and who was carrying his child. The rest of his family were no strangers to the organisation. His brother Agostino was himself a drugs and arms trafficker, and his mother, sister and aunt had all helped to hide Agostino's heroin and guns when necessary.

When word spread that Marino Mannoia was considering defecting, his relatives began receiving death threats. Agostino was the first to be killed: his car, riddled with bullets, was found but his body had vanished. When police questioned Agostino's mother, she repeated a couple of times, 'I don't know anything,' before adding only: 'If he comes back, he comes back. If not, we just put up with it.' Like the rest of the family, she knew that the mafia spared relatives who distanced themselves from traitors and her refusal to cooperate may have been an attempt to save her own skin.

But Marino Mannoia's mother herself received death threats, as did his sister and aunt. The three women refused the protection offered by the state – Marino Mannoia had begun to testify to Judge Falcone by then – and simply moved from Palermo to Bagheria. His sister let it be known that she never wanted to hear his name again. This did not satisfy the Cupola, which despatched a soldier to follow them and found out not only that the three women were still in contact with Marino Mannoia, but also that they were about to sell their properties in Sicily before joining him at his secret refuge.

The mafia delivered an exemplary punishment to persuade Marino Mannoia not to betray it and to discourage anyone else from talking. Shortly after sunset one winter evening in 1989, as his mother, sister and aunt left their home by car, a death squad in three cars, who had kept in touch with each other with two-way radios, shot at them with a rifle and three revolvers; the gunmen virtually ripped a back door from its hinges in order to fire inside. The fraternity eliminated all three women in one blow, as it feared, in the words of one of the killers, 'uncontrolled reactions by possible survivors'.

Never before in the mafia's history had three women been slaughtered in such a way. For Buscetta, the murders went beyond even what the Nazis had been capable of: 'Even though my relatives were killed too, I was shocked when I found out. I would expect them to kill Marino Mannoia's father, but those women, no.'

Despite the danger of retaliation, dozens and then hundreds of other mafiosi revealed what they knew over the next decade, their testimony ripping to shreds the lies that had protected the secret society for so long, starting with the biggest of them all – that the mafia simply didn't exist.

'A Question of Courtesy' – Riina Fights to Keep his Promises

The verdicts of the maxi-trial gave Riina one of his biggest headaches yet: the fate of so many jailed mafiosi. As Buscetta explained, the mafia did not fear the state. Its real concern was respecting the promises of protection it had made to imprisoned members: 'The man of honour has always gone to jail certain that his family will not starve; he's sure that those who are outside will do all they can to get him out. The failure to respect these commitments is very serious.'

What mattered to Riina was to ensure that the Supreme Court in Rome, when it reviewed the maxi-trial verdicts, overturned as many jail sentences as possible and crushed once and for all the Buscetta theory that all the members of the Cupola were responsible for many mafia murders. Riina put pressure on the Christian Democrat Salvo Lima, the ex-mayor of Palermo who was now a member of the European parliament. Riina bluntly told Lima, who had promised a favourable outcome: 'Either you keep your word or we kill you and your family.'

Riina assured mafiosi that pressure from friendly politicians on the Supreme Court would make it overturn any guilty verdicts. Riina felt certain that the case would fall into the hands of Judge Corrado Carnevale, a Sicilian whom mafiosi saw as 'manageable' and their guarantor in Rome. The judge was 'a brand name, a guarantee; a man of huge intelligence, whom we all admired', one supergrass testified. 'When someone said "There's Carnevale", the immediate reply was "Praise the Lord".' Carnevale, labelled 'Sentence-killer' by the newspapers, had overturned some 500 verdicts in his career. Accused of helping the mafia, he was, however, acquitted by the Supreme Court.

It was at this time that Riina also sought to forge links with a businessman who was to become prime minister, Silvio Berlusconi – Italy's richest man with a fortune of £5.6 billion. According to the boss Cancemi, the godfather summoned him and ordered him to find the Palermo mafioso Vittorio Mangano, who had worked in Berlusconi's 145-room, eighteenth-century villa at Arcore near Milan as a bailiff, stableman and bodyguard. The property boasted a library of 10,000 antique volumes and a price-less art collection. Cancemi testified later: 'Vittorio Mangano told me he was the boss of this estate. One day he hitched up his trousers and he has a wad of 100,000 lire banknotes in his socks with an elastic band around them. He told me this was money from drug trafficking and a few kidnappings.'

The message Riina sent to Mangano through Cancemi, according to the latter's testimony, was blunt. Cancemi was to tell Mangano that it was Riina who controlled Berlusconi and Marcello Dell'Utri, a Palermitan businessman close to Berlusconi. Riina added: 'Tell him to step aside, otherwise I will remember he gave a gun to Stefano Bontate' – a reference to Mangano's present of a gun with exploding bullets that he had given Riina's late enemy. 'It's in the interest of Cosa Nostra,' Riina explained.

Cancemi obeyed and passed the message on to Mangano. 'You've got to do me this favour. Don't ask questions,' he said.

Mangano, however, protested: 'But why? I've had it in hand for a life-time, it's a lifetime that I've done everything I wanted there.'

'Do me this favour. When that one (Riina) tells me it's for the good of Cosa Nostra, what am I supposed to say to him? I can't say anything, he's sealed my mouth shut,' Cancemi said.

A crestfallen Mangano dropped his gaze. 'If you tell me we must do it, then let's do it.'

Berlusconi's group and Dell'Utri, Cancemi testified, sent Riina the sum of £53,000 every year – Cancemi called it 'a contribution' – through intermediaries; he said that he had seen the money handed to a boss. Riina then allegedly distributed it among clans.

Criminals raised the pressure on Berlusconi in 1988. As Berlusconi confided to a friend in a bugged telephone call: 'I'm in a pretty big mess. I've got to send my children away, they're leaving now to go abroad because they want extortion money from me in an ugly way . . . You know, they told me that if by a certain date I don't do something, they'll give me my son's head and display his body in the cathedral square . . . That's not a very charming thing to be told and so I've decided: I'll send them to America and that'll be the end of it.'

Berlusconi, who is not a defendant but a witness in an ongoing trial focusing on Dell'Utri, has denied knowing anything about Mangano's mafia links when he hired him and said that he sacked him as soon as he learnt of them; Berlusconi has also denied claims that he or Fininvest had dealings with Riina or any mafiosi. Dell'Utri has also said he knew nothing of Mangano's mafia ties at first and got rid of him when he did learn about them.

From 1990 onwards, Riina is believed to have settled with his family in a four-bedroom, two-floor villa in Palermo set in a park of pines, palms and age-old trees. Part of a complex of 15 villas behind high walls, hedges and an automatic green gate, Riina's home was the one set furthest away from the main road, at the end of a private drive that wound its way through the complex. The villa, its walls decorated with wood pannelling and material of various shades of pink, was equipped with a lift and a swimming-pool; on cool evenings, the family could sit out on a veranda.

Registered under false names, Riina's two sons and two daughters went to school, escorted by an associate with a clean criminal record to avoid arousing suspicion if they were stopped by police. The godfather's wife Ninetta lived a closeted life in the villa and the strain imposed on family relations was intense. In an outburst picked up by a police bug, Ninetta's mother railed at her children's fate: 'Calogero died in a shoot-out. Another son was poisoned. The third is either in jail or on the run. I can never see my beloved daughter Ninetta. What do I get out of this life? The mafia has ruined my family. Salvatore Riina, it's all your fault!'

The same bug recorded the anger of Ninetta's two spinster sisters when they learnt that Riina had reprimanded her for standing on the villa's balcony. 'Who does he think he is? Our poor sister can't even get a breath of fresh air. It's not as if she's a prisoner,' one sister protested.

Marriage to the godfather had its compensations, however. A jeweller received a visit from Ninetta, who brought him a holdall crammed with valuable necklaces, bracelets and watches to store in his safe. Riina also called on the jeweller, entrusting him with a massive crucifix of solid gold studded with diamonds, as well as golden ingots, diamonds, rings with the letter 'R' engraved on them and several costly watches. When the jeweller was arrested and turned state's evidence, the valuables were seized by police and valued at £710,000.

The snake-pit atmosphere of Palermo's law courts, where critics sarcastically called Falcone 'the legend' or 'the best of us', proved too much for him. In the spring of 1991, exasperated by the growing paralysis of investigations in Palermo and evidence that he was no longer free to pursue his own enquiries with his usual thoroughness, Falcone accepted the offer of a senior post at the justice ministry in Rome. As the new director of penal affairs there, he would no longer lead investigations himself, but he hoped to set up a framework which would benefit prosecutors investigating organised crime across Italy.

The Rome offer was like a liberation to him. As Falcone, dressed in a grey tracksuit emblazoned with the letters 'FBI' which American friends had given him, packed his files in his Palermo office, he confided: 'There's nothing left for me to do in this city. It's impossible to work here: one step forward and three steps back, that's the way the fight against the mafia goes.'

He was under no illusion that moving to the capital would put him beyond the mafia's reach. 'Sure, they haven't killed me yet,' he said, 'but the show's not over yet. My account with Cosa Nostra is still open. And I know that I will only close it with my death, natural or otherwise.'

Shortly before he was due to leave Sicily, Falcone lunched with his friend Judge Pietro Grasso and three journalists in a restaurant near Catania's harbour; he had testified that morning at a trial. As his bodyguards kept an eye on the room from a nearby table, he spoke with optimism of what he planned to achieve in Rome. He lost his temper only once, when he was asked about a whispering campaign that accused him of letting Sicily down in fleeing the island because the failed assassination attempt at his seaside home had scared him.

For once the usually reserved Falcone, who hated talking about himself, burst out: 'What do these people think? Do they think I'm trying to save my life? I'm not scared of dying. I'm a Sicilian, I am.' He grabbed hold of one of his jacket buttons between thumb and index finger and pulled on it hard. 'Yes, I'm a Sicilian and for me life is worth less than this button.' As ever, Falcone joked about death, mocking the fatalism so typical of Sicilians – there's nothing you can do about death so you might as well accept it.

Once he had settled in Rome in a drab flat at police head-quarters near the Quirinale Palace, the former summer residence of popes, friends were struck by how much happier he was; they hadn't seen him so relaxed in years. Every morning when he called his secretary, he would ask: 'Hello, has Kim Basinger called for me?'

But even in Rome, the personal attacks against Falcone didn't stop. In the months following his arrival, he worked hard to set up the DIA, an anti-mafia agency that would coordinate all investigations nationally. But fellow-judges accused him of creating a body tailor-made for himself, and urged him not to apply for its leadership, simply because he was working for a Socialist justice minister and this, they argued, meant he was no longer politically impartial. Falcone was also working on a new law offering defectors benefits in jail and protection for them

and their families if they went into hiding, and helping to institute tough new prison regimes for mafiosi.

He felt safer in Rome than in Palermo, so much so that he
began taking risks; he went to a couple of classical music concerts
and even gave his bodyguards the slip one evening when he
borrowed a battered old Fiat car to go out for a meal with a
friend.

'Where's the escort?' the friend asked him when they met.

'No escort, I'm a free man this evening,' Falcone replied.

'Have you gone mad?' the friend asked, incredulous.

'Believe me, this is the best defence. Who do you think will
recognise me inside such a wreck? Everyone expects to see armour-
plated cars in front of me and behind me. Naturally, I would
never do such a thing in Palermo,' Falcone said.

One morning in the spring of 1991, Falcone allowed himself
another 'transgression' he would never have attempted in Palermo;
he walked out of the justice ministry near the River Tiber accompanied only by a colleague and went to a bar for a coffee. It was
only after they had returned to the ministry that Falcone told his
colleague that in the bar he had spotted the mafioso Giuseppe
Madonia, whom he recognised as one of the killers of the *carabiniere* police captain Emanuele Basile. The officer had been shot
dead while holding his five-year-old daughter in his arms, his wife
at his side. Falcone called the police, who rushed to the bar, but
Madonia had disappeared. Eventually, Falcone persuaded himself
the incident was a coincidence and refused to let it worry him.

In fact, Riina had ordered Madonia and other mafiosi to shadow
Falcone. They were watching his comings and goings at the
justice ministry and had noted that he often went to a restaurant on the island in the middle of the River Tiber – both were
considered as possible places for his planned murder. 'We were
thinking all the time about how to kill Giovanni Falcone; it was
almost as if it had become a race among us to see who would
get there first. Everyone tried to do his bit and help out,' a supergrass said.

★

In an interview with the author eight months into his Rome post, Falcone showed himself to be, as much as ever, a dedicated 'servant of the state'. Outside his office, an armed bodyguard lounged in an armchair. Visitors had to go through two bullet-proof doors to reach the room where Falcone's collection of miniature china and crystal geese sat at odds with the insignia given to him by the police forces of five continents hanging on the walls.

Courteous and clearly a man in a hurry – he had no time to waste, speaking quickly and to the point – Falcone was at pains to stress that he was only doing his job in battling the organisation which had sent him death threats for the past quarter of a century. 'What drives me? Just the knowledge that everyone must do their duty. *Basta* (Enough).' He did not hide his irritation at questions about his personal commitment. 'We'll talk only about the mafia. Not about me. I don't have anything to do with it,' he said in typically sardonic style. 'It seems really odd to me that such questions can be asked of an employee of the state ... A phenomenon like the mafia isn't resolved by heroism – only by hard, tiring, humble day-to-day work.' For him, this was the key to fighting the secret society. 'What we need is an acceptable standard of commitment against the mafia – a standard for people to do their duty by and then there won't be the need for so-called "heroes".'

Falcone spoke of his concern that following the fall of the Berlin Wall two years earlier, the brotherhood could seek to recycle its dirty money in the then Soviet Union or in other East European countries. 'There are big problems to tackle ... It's one of the many problems [East European countries] must deal with,' he said. 'We need international collaboration to get more efficient results.'

Asked whether Italy would ever defeat the mafia, he replied: 'It's a human phenomenon. And like all human phenomena, it has a beginning, it has a zenith and it has an end.' But he didn't say when he thought that end might come.

★

In an attempt to torpedo the Supreme Court's study of the maxi-trial verdict, Riina eliminated Judge Antonio Scopelliti, due to act as prosecutor, in August 1991. Scopelliti, who had taken thick files of the maxi-trial with him on holiday at his childhood home on the Calabrian coast, had never asked for bodyguards and had not been assigned any. His only protection was two local police officers who out of affection for the judge escorted him to the seaside whenever they had some spare time. He was killed as he drove home from the beach. The 'Ndrangheta, the Calabrian mafia, carried out the murder as a favour to Riina. 'It's a question of courtesy,' an informer said.

Far from torpedoing the case, the murder only bought Riina some extra time, as a new prosecutor was soon appointed. A frustrated Riina crafted an ambitious strategy which came to be known as 'the strategy of terror'. Traditional allies within the state were no longer delivering, he argued at a series of meetings in late 1991, and so now the fraternity must 'wage war to make peace'; it must launch a series of attacks against the state – a wave of murders and bombings of selected targets. It must use violence and then negotiate from a position of strength. The strategy, Riina pledged, would not only save the mafia from attempts to destroy it, such as the maxi-trial, but would also give it more power than it had ever possessed.

At one summit, Riina complained about politicians who could not be trusted, saying: 'I've had it up to here with politicians. Don't come and ask me for an explanation if some politicians get killed.' He announced the creation of a new party, formed by freemasons and professionals close to the mafia; the aim was to break up Italy into three independent states, with one ruling over all of the south including Sicily. That way, Riina said, 'Cosa Nostra will itself become a state.'

In an unusual move, the Corleonesi tested the waters before launching their new strategy. Provenzano gathered bosses around a long table in a house on the slopes of Mount Etna and ordered them to carry out an unusual opinion poll; they should contact friendly politicians, freemasons and businessmen, brief them about

Riina's plan and ask them what they thought. The survey's results were what the Corleonesi wanted to hear: those polled said they wouldn't stand in the way.

Such consultations were a rare step for the Corleonesi. There was no canvassing when expelled mafiosi set up a federation called the *stidda* (star) in south-east Sicily and rebelled against the mafia in the late 1980s, demanding more control over their own territory. Provenzano instantly launched a slaughter which saw some 300 people die in the province of Agrigento alone in the space of three years. Many of them were teenagers known as 'baby-killers' whom the rebels had recruited on the cheap.

In early 1992, Riina put his plan to assassinate Falcone on hold for a few weeks as he awaited the Supreme Court's decision on the maxi-trial verdicts, concerned that jailed mafiosi would blame the murder for any unfavourable ruling.

Like Riina, Falcone was also concerned about the fate of the maxi-trial – but for very different reasons. Falcone worried that time was running out. The slow pace of Italian justice would lead to many mafiosi being released if the time limit set on their case expired. He also feared that if the case was handed to the 'sentence-killer' Judge Carnevale, his work of many years would be wrecked and the mafiosi would walk free. Thanks to his position at the justice ministry, Falcone managed to ensure that judges like Carnevale would from now on take it in turns to preside over cases brought before the Supreme Court. The new rule ensured that the maxi-trial did not go to Carnevale, but to another presiding judge.

The Supreme Court delivered its verdict in January 1992: it upheld the Buscetta theory, decreeing the Cupola bosses responsible for all the most serious murders, and confirmed a host of life sentences. The verdict was the biggest setback so far to the mafia and a huge blow to Riina's prestige. The godfather now 'has the death-rattle' in his throat, Buscetta commented. 'And "Shorty" (Riina) will turn nasty, very nasty now.' Another super-grass said of Riina at the time: 'An animal, when he is injured, does more harm than when he's well.'

For Falcone, the ruling marked the triumph of his career. The stunned judge confided: 'My country doesn't understand what's happened. This is a historic event: this event has shattered the myth of the mafia's impunity.' Falcone finally broke the decades-old rule that trials should almost invariably end in acquittals for mafiosi on the grounds of insufficient evidence. For years the secret society had emerged from these trials with its prestige and power increased.

That evening, Falcone bought a bottle of champagne and celebrated with some colleagues at the justice ministry. 'But it wasn't a light-hearted evening,' one colleague recalled. 'We knew something big had happened and that, somehow, we would have to pay.'

5
Mafia Terrorism

1992–1996

Giovanni Brusca is 'Operational'

Giovanni Brusca, whom Riina picked to plan Falcone's murder, had long lived in the mafia's shadow. His grandfather had protected the bandit Salvatore Giuliano, and the brotherhood had recruited his father. Brusca first set foot in a prison at the age of five, when his father was in jail. With the complicity of several guards, his mother smuggled the boy in with the laundry so that his father could see him. Brusca hated going to school and his mother would beat him daily to make him go, with extra beatings on special feast days to make him go to church. He stopped attending school at the age of ten, but his mother did manage to make an altar boy of him, although only for a brief period.

From the age of 12, Brusca's father made him responsible for taking supplies of food and clothes to fugitives, among them Provenzano and Bagarella, who were hiding near his home in San Giuseppe Jato, a town between Palermo and Corleone. As a teenager, he often helped his father oil his rifles and pistols, which he kept buried in the fields. At 18, overweight and with sloping shoulders, he committed his first murder; he had no idea why the victim had to be killed, but he did the job nonetheless. Brusca and two others fired a barrage of bullets at the victim as he drove past, but managed only to wound him seriously before he fled; he died months later in hospital.

A year later, Brusca ambushed a thief who had challenged the mafia's authority, as he came out of a cinema, and fired into the crowd with a double-barrelled gun, hitting only the designated victim. Brusca then rushed home, hid his gun, changed his clothes and returned to the spot. From then on, he often went back to the scene of his crimes, to enjoy the buzz of the crowd and the police activity. 'I've always been very cold before, during and after the crime,' he wrote in his memoirs. 'I might sometimes be reluctant to become "operative". But once I'd decided, all the worries, the fears and the doubts disappeared.'

When Brusca entered the mafia at the age of 19 in 1976, Riina himself presided over the initiation ritual, earmarking him as being from now on not only part of the Corleonesi faction but also one of Riina's personal henchmen. Brusca's father, who named Riina as regent of the local clan when he was arrested, advised his son. 'Make sure you and Riina always see eye-to-eye. Always keep him informed about what you're doing. What he does is OK by me. Don't move a finger unless Riina knows about it,' the boss told his son. Riina and Brusca, who rose to become a member of the Cupola, became so close they came to understand each other virtually without speaking. 'We didn't need long speeches. We only met for a few minutes . . . What mattered was when Riina said: "That one has to be killed,"' Brusca explained.

In his memoirs, Brusca made no secret of how little taking human life troubled him. 'I've tortured people to make them talk; I've strangled both those who confessed and those who remained silent; I've dissolved bodies in acid; I've roasted corpses on big grills; I've buried the remains after digging graves with an earth-mover. Some supergrasses say today they feel disgust for what they did. I can speak for myself: I've never been upset by these things.'

Only rarely did his victims confess under torture; an interrogation session lasted half an hour at most. 'We'd hit the guy on the legs with a hammer, saying to him: "Talk or we'll break them . . ." We might pull his ear with pliers, but only to hurt him and to make him understand that we were serious.' This usually achieved nothing. 'At that point the guy knew perfectly well that we'd kill him. The condemned showed superhuman strength. We realised that and we'd say the fateful word: "*Niscemuninne*" (Let's get out of it).' The torturers would then strangle the victim.

Brusca didn't even need to be told who his victims were. A boss near Agrigento once asked him 'as a favour' to kill anyone he saw on a given tractor, at a given time and in a given spot in the countryside near the city. 'I found three and I killed three,' Brusca stated simply. He followed a bizarre rule-book. He once recalled hurrying to carry out a murder even though one of the four-man team of killers was missing. He had been in a hurry, he explained, because the victim was getting married three days later. 'We could hardly make his woman a widow,' Brusca said.

When he had to move around, Brusca would travel escorted by mafiosi hiding in a van and armed with Kalashnikov rifles. If a police patrol stopped the van and opened the back door for a routine check, his bodyguards were under orders to shoot immediately.

Brusca first heard about the plan to assassinate Falcone in February 1992, at a meeting with Riina and four other bosses in a Palermo villa. They all considered Falcone a dangerous enemy and now that he was a candidate for the job of Italy's new national anti-mafia prosecutor they feared he would cause yet more problems.

When Riina spoke of Falcone's elimination, the boss Raffaele Ganci turned to him and said: 'This time we get down to the job properly and we stop only when we've finished it.'

The bosses didn't just want Falcone killed. They also wanted to punish the former Palermo mayor Salvo Lima as a 'traitor' because he had failed to help in the maxi-trial; both Falcone and Lima should be killed immediately, they agreed. The bosses then took it in turns to suggest other victims, chiefly senior prosecutors and police officers.

But Falcone was the one who mattered most to Riina. The bosses discussed what they saw as Falcone's weak point – his set routine. Every weekend, they explained to Brusca, the judge flew from Rome to Palermo, always driving down the motorway from the airport to reach his home. They told Brusca they had already measured the speed at which Falcone's convoy usually travelled

– 90 m.p.h. on average – and planned to blow it up on the motorway.

Riina asked Brusca: 'Can we get the explosives?'

Brusca, who had helped blow up Judge Chinnici, Falcone's superior, with a car-bomb nine years earlier, replied immediately: 'No problem.'

'And a remote control?' Riina said.

Brusca repeated: 'No problem.'

Lima was the first Riina dealt with, less than a month later. On 12 March Lima, now a member of the European parliament, left his home in Mondello, Palermo's seaside resort, to go to a hotel where he was due to discuss arrangements for a dinner in honour of ex-prime minister Giulio Andreotti. The 64-year-old Lima, whose career in politics had stretched over the past half a century, sat in the passenger seat of a car driven by a friend, a history professor. Another friend rode in the back.

Shortly after Lima left his home, two gunmen riding a powerful Honda motorbike and wearing helmets roared up to the car and opened fire as they passed by. The first bullet hit the tyre of a front wheel and sent the car skidding onto the pavement. More shots were fired, hitting the windscreen and the right front headlight. The motorcycle stopped a short distance from the car and turned.

'They're coming back! *Madonna santa* (Holy Virgin)! They're coming back!' Lima shouted.

One bullet just missed the history professor and hit Lima in the chest. The wounded politician managed to open the door and get out of the car. But Lima's elegant coat got stuck in the door and he had to tear it off before he could start running up the street.

Lima stopped at the entrance to a villa but he could not open the gate and was left stranded. The motorbike caught up with him. One of the gunmen delivered the *coup de grace* with a bullet fired from some 20 inches away; it entered through the back of his neck and exited through his forehead. He fell a few yards from the car, near a rubbish bin behind which his friends had found refuge. Later, firemen used a hose to wash his blood off the street.

Early the next month, Provenzano's beloved Saveria suddenly reappeared in Corleone after having vanished for 19 years. Their two sons had completed their studies – under false names – at schools and private institutions in Palermo and nearby Monreale where they learnt English, French and German.

An elegant Saveria, dressed in a sober grey jacket and skirt, walked into the barracks of the *carabinieri* police on the main piazza with her two sons and asked to see a senior officer. She announced: 'I'm Bernardo Provenzano's partner. I want to live in peace in Bernardo's town and give my sons a quiet life.' People in the town thought Saveria had returned because Provenzano had died. The real reason for their return was Riina's intention to murder Judge Falcone; Provenzano wanted to ensure that his family would not be affected by the police crackdown he knew would follow such a killing.

As far as Brusca could see, Provenzano took no part in the planning for Falcone's assassination. Riina, however, met Brusca every two weeks to discuss it. Brusca put Provenzano's absence down to his habit of making others do the dirty work in order to remain 'clean' himself. It was decided that only bosses would take part in the execution of the plan. This was a question of prestige; traditionally, only clan heads turned leading figures into 'distinguished corpses'.

The original plan was to blow up a bridge over the motorway from Palermo's airport to the city with more than 2,000 pounds of explosives as Falcone's convoy passed underneath. But Brusca, who inspected the bridge, thought the plan was too difficult to carry out. He also vetoed another idea, that of packing explosives into a pedestrian passage running under the motorway; he argued that the impact of the explosion would be weakened by the blast emerging from both exits.

Brusca instead picked a metal drain pipe only 20 inches in diameter which ran under the motorway near the exit for the town of Capaci. 'It was perfect, tight and small. We knew what we were doing,' Brusca commented later with more than a little self-satisfaction. 'We'd taken into account the fact that some "civilians" might pass by. But it was one possibility in a thousand and we hoped that no one would flank Falcone's car.'

To obtain the explosives he needed, Brusca turned to a relative who worked in a quarry, while a boss close to Riina supplied the rest. From a mafioso nicknamed 'the Engineer' because of his technical know-how, Brusca obtained remote controls, the kind used by children to fly model aeroplanes. Brusca tested them in open country, using old-fashioned flash bulbs to simulate explosions. When a flick on the remote control set off the flash bulb, the test was a success.

Brusca now had to practise with a car travelling at the speed of Falcone's convoy, to ensure the bomb would explode at precisely the moment the judge's car passed by. Brusca needed to work out how much time the signal from the remote control took to reach the receiving unit, which then triggered a thin blade that shifted one-and-a-half inches to blow up the bomb.

Surveillance had now established that Falcone's white Croma turbo travelled down the motorway at an average speed of 85 m.p.h. On a quiet country road north of Corleone, Brusca and his accomplices carried out tests with a powerful Lancia Delta. Brusca established that in the time it took for his flick of the remote control to set off the flash bulbs, the car travelling at about 85 m.p.h. covered 23 to 33 feet. Brusca carried out more tests at the spot designated for the murder to ensure his timing was right. He used a fridge which had been abandoned on the edge of the motorway some 65 feet from the drain pipe as a marker. He decided that when Falcone's car passed the fridge, he would flick the switch.

In mid-April, Brusca was ready to test the explosives. He and his accomplices filled three-foot-high tubes each 20 inches in diameter, like the drain pipe under the motorway, with 24 pounds of explosives. They dug a ditch with a mechanical digger, placed the tubes at the bottom of it, then covered them with 140 cubic feet of concrete. The next day, when the concrete had dried, Brusca blew up the explosives.

The impact was devastating. After filling in the crater, Brusca reported back to Riina that he was now 'operational'.

At sunset on a late April evening, Brusca and eight other mafiosi met by the motorway to put the explosives in place. Surveillance had established that Falcone's car always travelled in the fast lane and Brusca decided to place the explosives only under the two lanes on the airport–Palermo side of the motorway. After measuring the width of the motorway with a rope, Brusca walked up to the mouth of the 20-inch wide drain pipe and started to crawl inside to take a close look. But he was tired after all the preparations he had made in the previous days and felt unable to breathe in the tiny, claustrophobic space. 'If I go inside this I'll die,' he thought to himself before crawling quickly out again. An accomplice tried to enter the pipe, but he too felt faint and had to give up. However, Nino Gioè, a boss in his mid-40s cheerfully crawled in and shouted: 'I could go for a *passeggiata* (walk) with my girlfriend in here, there's no problem!'

Despite his claustrophobia, Brusca was determined that he should be the one to place the first of the 13 metal drums into which he and his team had packed some 770 pounds of explosives. Twelve of the drums weighed 55 pounds each and the thirteenth 77 pounds; they made a hole in the biggest one to make room for the detonator. To avoid leaving any fingerprints, Brusca put on a pair of leather bricklayer's gloves. He placed the drum on a skateboard and started to push the skateboard ahead of him, struggling to worm forwards on his belly. He found the task hugely difficult and felt 'like a dog with my hands stretched out ahead and my face touching the earth'. Slowly, he managed to propel the first drum under the middle of the motorway, using a small tube that ran inside the drain pipe to measure the right distance. Gioè and an accomplice then took it in turns to place another two drums. Just getting the first three drums into position took them several hours and they still had another ten to do.

Two other mafiosi who had been acting as armed lookouts suddenly signalled that everyone should hide immediately. From behind trees and bushes, Brusca and his men saw two police officers stop their patrol car on the edge of the motorway and go and relieve themselves. In the middle of the night, the officers left without spotting the mafiosi or the drums of explosives.

The pause prompted Brusca to think of a new idea. He asked Gioè: 'Why don't we lie down on the skateboard on our stomachs? Let's go inside feet first, we can push the drums with our feet. We'll tie a rope to our chest, when I yank it that will mean it's time for you to pull me out.'

The new method was much faster and it took only an hour-and-a-half to place the other ten drums, with the wire from the detonator left hidden among weeds placed around the mouth of the drain pipe. Brusca and his men finished the job at 4 a.m. and drove home. Brusca, in a car with a couple of others, recalled: 'We didn't chat or make any wisecracks on the drive. We talked little, we were too tense, concentrating on the job, careful not to get anything wrong. Like military types. I was calm, couldn't have been calmer.'

The next day, they started to watch the motorway. The vantage-point Brusca had chosen was on a hilltop more than 400 yards away, by an almond tree in blossom. Brusca cut off a branch from another tree to give him a clear view of a stretch of motorway. The bosses relieved each other in shifts, watching every week from Thursday afternoon to Saturday, sitting on a stool and using a telescope. The system wasn't perfect: Brusca found out later that his men had missed Falcone twice during the month of May. On one occasion, Falcone had driven past with his friend and colleague Judge Borsellino late at night, after Brusca's team had gone home.

'If we'd known, we'd have killed two birds with one stone. *Pazienza* (Patience),' Brusca reflected.

For three weekends Brusca and his men kept watch, waiting.

★

On 22 May 1992, a Friday, Falcone spent part of the evening at his office in the justice ministry, meticulously putting his affairs in order and feeding some documents he no longer needed into a shredder. A colleague Falcone had befriended noted that the judge, whose desk had always been a jumble of bulging files, had suddenly started keeping it obsessively tidy. This change may have had something to do with a virulent campaign against Falcone's candidacy to serve as the national anti-mafia prosecutor which deeply irritated the judge.

The next afternoon, Falcone and his wife Francesca flew from Rome to Palermo on a secret, unscheduled flight. From Punta Raisi airport, their armour-plated car driven by Falcone in the middle of a convoy of three, they then headed for Palermo along the motorway that runs beside the coast.

When Brusca flicked the switch of the remote control, a geophysical observatory in Agrigento on the other side of Sicily which monitored earthquakes registered the resulting blast at 5.56 p.m. and 48 seconds. Although he was some distance away, Brusca saw clearly flames and clouds of dense smoke billow up from the motorway. It was only afterwards that he heard the drums exploding one after the other in quick succession – he described it as 'ba-ba-bang', 'ba-ba-bang' – together with the pounding sound of pieces of tarmac raining down and the shrill of burglar alarms from nearby villas set off by the blast. For just a moment, Brusca felt shock at what he had done. 'What's happening? What the hell have I done?' he exclaimed. When the smoke cleared, he saw that the flashing blue light of one escort car was still turning on its roof.

All three bodyguards in the first car in the convoy, which was catapulted into an olive grove more than 60 yards away, died instantly, their faces so damaged as to be unrecognisable. Three other bodyguards who had been riding in the last car were injured but got out of the wreck as quickly as possible, their guns at the ready; their first thought was that they would now be shot and killed.

But no shot came and the bodyguards saw Falcone's car, its front section missing, perched on the edge of a crater 45 feet wide and 11 feet deep. It had crashed into a wall of tarmac thrown up by the explosion and was covered by rubble. They rushed up to the judge's wrecked car and saw that its three occupants – Falcone in the driver's seat, Francesca sitting next to him and the driver Costanza in the back – were badly injured. Falcone's head moved back and forth, his face a mask of blood. Francesca had fainted, her eyes still open and gazing upwards.

One of the bodyguards walked up to the judge's bulletproof window, which had survived the blast, and called out to him by his first name: 'Giovanni, Giovanni.'

From behind the window, and trapped inside the wreckage, Falcone turned his head. The judge was still conscious but his gaze, the bodyguard said later, had become 'empty, lifeless'.

It was only when the fire brigade arrived that rescuers managed to lift him out. As firemen struggled to extract the other victims, they heard Falcone, who apparently realised what had happened, say: 'If I stay alive, this time I'll make them pay . . . '

At Palermo's main hospital, doctors struggled for half an hour to resuscitate the 53-year-old Falcone but he died of severe internal haemorrhages, just over an hour after the explosion, in the arms of his friend Judge Borsellino, who had raced to be at his side. The 46-year-old Francesca was still alive when she reached the hospital; she repeatedly asked for news of her husband and urged doctors to take care of him. In a twist of fate which highlights how the mafia permeates every aspect of life in Sicily, Professor Andrea Vassallo, the first doctor to treat Francesca, had previously been sent to trial by Falcone as a friend of the Corleonesi. A supergrass had alleged that Vassallo didn't hesitate to treat mafiosi and the doctor was sentenced to five years in jail. He and his colleagues did all they could to save Francesca but she too died of her injuries a short while after her husband. The driver Costanza survived; later, he attributed this to Falcone taking his place in the driver's seat. If Falcone had been sitting in the back, he said, the judge would have survived.

Brusca and Gioé drove from the vantage-point back to Palermo. 'We were satisfied at the result we'd obtained, even though we still didn't know what had happened exactly. We drove calmly, but at the time we were stunned, because we'd raised Hell,' Brusca related. On the motorway, they passed police cars and ambulances, sirens wailing, heading to the scene of the explosion. Brusca saw some police road-blocks when he entered Palermo but no one stopped him.

The bosses had agreed to meet at the villa where three months earlier Falcone's assassination had been planned. When Brusca arrived, he learnt from the television that the judge was fighting for his life in hospital. The mafiosi's faces fell. 'Holy shit, how's it possible?' the boss Cancemi exclaimed. 'That cuckold, if he survives, he'll break our balls, he'll destroy us!'

'That cuckold, if he doesn't die he'll make life hell for us,' Brusca said.

Twenty minutes later, a news flash ran along the bottom of the television screen: 'Giovanni Falcone is dead.'

Cancemi jumped up from his chair. 'That cuckold wanted to ruin everyone!' he shouted, spitting at the set as if he had Falcone in front of him. Brusca stared at Cancemi in disbelief as he kept spitting and shouting, 'That cuckold, that cuckold! At last!' Brusca thought that Cancemi had gone mad; his frenzy was unworthy of a man and of a figure of Falcone's stature, he reflected.

Cancemi slipped his hand into his trouser pocket, gave a few banknotes to a young soldier who had been watching the news with them and told him to go and buy a bottle of champagne. When he returned, the bosses toasted Falcone's death.

The mafia rejoiced even in prisons. 'When the news bulletin came, there was an explosion of celebration, people clapped . . . in the cells, we toasted each other and drank,' a supergrass who was in jail at the time said later.

A year earlier, Falcone had ended his memoirs with a tribute to the 'distinguished corpses' claimed by the mafia and the words: 'One usually dies because one is alone, or because one has got into something over one's head. One often dies because one does not have the right alliances, because one is not given support. In Sicily the mafia kills the servants of the state that the state has not been able to protect.'

After Falcone died, Borsellino and his escort drove straight to the crater on the motorway. Dazed, he held a handkerchief to his mouth and nose as the stench of smoke, diesel oil and cordite stung his eyes. He climbed over the twisted, incadescent remains of a car engine and stood staring silently at the wreck of Falcone's car.

As Borsellino headed back to his office in the deserted law courts, where lights burnt only in the offices of the anti-mafia prosecutors, he thought to himself: 'This is only the beginning.' He had many times told his student daughter Lucia: 'Giovanni is my shield against Cosa Nostra. They'll kill him first, then they'll kill me.'

'I'm Racing Against Time' – Judge Borsellino

At the funeral for Falcone, his wife and the three bodyguards in Palermo's Church of San Domenico where great Sicilians are buried, a tiny, 23-year-old woman dressed in black walked up to the altar and began to speak in a frail voice. Rosaria, widow of the bodyguard Vito Schifani, demanded justice 'in the name of all those who have given their lives for the state'. Her voice then rose to a shout as she addressed the killers directly, her appeal echoing down the aisles of the vast church:

> Men of the mafia, I know you are here . . . I forgive you but you must go down on your knees. If you have the courage to change . . . but they don't want to change, they don't change . . . If you have the courage to radically change your designs, be Christians once again.

A few days later, Riina summoned the bosses who had executed the killings to a celebratory meeting. The godfather was euphoric, delightedly relaying what he knew of the state's reaction. 'They're going crazy,' he told them. 'They didn't expect it. They've been forced to ask for help from the American secret services.' Cancemi later testified that, oozing self-confidence, Riina claimed he had the tycoon-turned-politician Berlusconi and his Sicilian associate Dell'Utri under complete control: 'I'm putting everything on the line, we can sleep easy. I've got Dell'Utri and Berlusconi in hand and that's a good thing for all of Cosa Nostra.' Berlusconi and Dell'Utri have denied any contact with Riina.

Riina was more determined than ever to press ahead with his strategy of terror; his next target would be Judge Borsellino. But this strategy was beginning to create dissent. The boss Gioè had taken part in Falcone's murder but believed Riina was leading them all into a dead end. He confided to a friend. 'What can we do? Either we get a life sentence, or the Corleonesi shoot us. Or we slip a rope around our necks and we kill ourselves,' he said.

Ganci, who had also helped kill Falcone, was the only boss who dared to take Riina aside and express his misgivings directly to the godfather. Riina cut him short, saying: 'Stop. The responsibility is mine, it has to be done as quickly as possible.' As he walked away, Ganci unburdened himself to another boss, muttering: 'This one wants to burn us all up.'

For Riina, it was now time to press what he firmly believed was his advantage. As he had explained a few months earlier, he must 'wage war to make peace' with the state; now was the time to negotiate. To political contacts who remain mysterious, Riina presented a long list of demands, which included a drastic review of the maxi-trial verdict – he wanted all life sentences cancelled – abolition of the law offering protection to supergrasses, a reform of the law on seizing mafia assets and new measures to make it easier for convicts to obtain house arrest or be detained in hospital.

At a June summit, during which he read his list aloud, Riina reported in a calm, confident tone that his negotiations were going well. To ensure the demands were met, he said, the mafia must turn its back on the politicians then in power and instead back Berlusconi and Dell'Utri who, once in power, would help the organisation. 'We have to cultivate them, we have to assist them today and even more tomorrow,' he concluded, saying this was for the good of Cosa Nostra. Berlusconi and Dell'Utri have denied any contact with the fraternity, let alone doing its bidding.

The godfather had a personal objective. According to Brusca, he had his heart set on returning to Corleone as a free man; the only sentence which Riina had and which had been confirmed by Italy's highest court, was the one given to him at the maxi-trial. If he could have that verdict overturned, Riina reasoned, he could put a stop to his life on the run – the godfather was apparently blind to the fact that a court would sooner or later convict him of more recent crimes. But by late June Riina's confidence had vanished. He told Brusca that a contact – he didn't give the name – had rejected the list out of hand, protesting: 'You're crazy. We can't negotiate on this basis.'

In a sign of Riina's increasing desperation, his brother-in-law Leoluca Bagarella publicly petitioned the Italian government the following month – the first time the mafia had done so. A prisoner, Bagarella read out what he called 'a petition' during a court hearing. Announcing that he was speaking in the name of prisoners held in strict isolation – most of them were convicted mafia killers – Bagarella demanded an easing of their prison regime. The prisoners would eat less, spend less time in the open air and beat their crockery against the metal bars of their windows until the powers that be dealt with their grievances, Bagarella warned. The protest spread quickly to other jails across Italy, with several bosses making public appeals – a sign that their prison regime was anything but 'strict'. In one statement, the convicts expressed their concern that their demands might 'frighten, condition or represent a threatening voice' for members of parliament working on a reform of their prison conditions – a typical mafia threat. The protest died out without achieving anything.

Riina wasn't the only one trying to negotiate. The *carabiniere* colonel Mario Mori contacted Ciancimino, the ex-mayor of Palermo close to the Corleonesi, to seek help in the search for fugitives. At a fourth meeting, Ciancimino, who was living in Rome, announced that 'they' – by whom he apparently meant Riina and other bosses – were willing to negotiate through him and that the talks must take place abroad. Ciancimino then asked abruptly: 'What are you offering?'

Caught off guard, Mori replied: 'Here's what we offer: the various Riinas, Provenzanos and their friends give themselves up and the state will treat them and their families well.'

Ciancimino exploded. He slapped his hands down on his knees then jumped up from his armchair and burst out: 'You want me dead, or rather you want to die too! I can't say that kind of thing to anyone.' Ciancimino showed Mori the door and told him the negotiations were over.

Facing both failure and humiliation, Riina decided to wage war once again.

For 57 days after the assassination of his friend Falcone, Judge Borsellino lived with death at his side. Aware that he was the obvious next target, he worked day and night to advise prosecutors investigating Falcone's murder; he flew to Germany on the trail of hitmen and to Rome to question a new defector. A colleague said of Borsellino at the time: 'There was an air of terrifying sadness about him. Many of us noted that he seemed to have death in his eyes.' The judge told his wife: 'I'm racing against time. I feel I can see clearly what the mafia is up to. I've got so much work to do, I've got so much work to do . . .'

Borsellino took some comfort, however, from a rare show of popular outrage at his colleague's assassination; Palermitans hung white sheets from their windows with slogans against the mafia scrawled on them and more than 100,000 people demonstrated in the streets of the city. In a popular tribute, flowers, photographs and messages were left under a magnolia tree outside Falcone's home. A group of schoolchildren left the note: 'There are a million things to say to you, but the first we can think of is: "Thank-you".' More than ever Sicilians gave the lie to Don Fabrizio Salina's fatalistic view in the novel *The Leopard*: 'Sleep, my dear Chevalley, sleep is what the Sicilians want, and they will always hate those who seek to awake them.'

That summer Borsellino won the trust of the underboss Leonardo Messina, a new witness from San Cataldo in central Sicily. A miner's son, arrested as he planned to carry out a murder during a religious procession, Messina described the mafia as his nursery; his grandfather had been a boss and his family were members through seven generations. He called the rise of the Corleonesi 'a tragedy without end' and testified:

They created tragedy in all the families. They took power by slowly, slowly killing everyone . . . often using us to do the job . . . We were as if infatuated with them because we thought that by getting rid of the old bosses we would become the new bosses. Some people killed their brother, others their cousin and so on, because they thought they would take their places. Instead, slowly, the Corleonesi gained control of the whole system.

Questioning another supergrass, Vincenzo Calcara from Palermo, brought Borsellino face to face with a mafioso who had been ordered to murder him. Calcara told the judge: 'We were to shoot you with a rifle equipped with a telescopic sight – a real professional job. They had chosen me as the killer. They even gave me the weapon. I would only have had to press the trigger . . . If the attempt failed, there were plans for a car-bomb.'

In early July, a little more than two months after the loss of Falcone, Borsellino fell into the habit of embracing colleagues and even the porter at his block of flats – a show of affection that surprised them all as he had never done so before. One of his bodyguards, surprised by how strained he looked, asked him what was the matter. Borsellino replied: 'I'm worried. I'm worried for you boys because I know that the TNT has come for me and I don't want to drag you in.'

On the afternoon of 19 July 1992, an exhausted Borsellino slept for a couple of hours, watched the Tour de France cycling race on television and then called his mother. 'I'm coming to see you,' he told her.

At about 5 p.m., when the car carrying Borsellino and his two escort cars braked sharply to a halt outside his mother's home, a car-bomb blew up. The explosion killed Borsellino, severing his right arm. It also killed five bodyguards, wounded 18 people and damaged the block as high as the eleventh floor. It took the police a whole week to remove human remains found in the street.

At the funeral for the bodyguards in Palermo's cathedral – Borsellino's widow refused to accept a state funeral and instead held a private service from which politicians were banned – furious police bodyguards and other officers surged forward to shout 'Justice! Justice!' at the Italian president, prime minister and government ministers attending the ceremony. Their uniformed colleagues had to struggle to keep them at a safe distance from the state's representatives. The aisles echoed with shouts of 'Jackals', 'Assassins' and 'Resign'. The leaders of the state, pale with fright, had to be hustled outside to safety as mourners pressed towards them.

For the first time since the war, the state responded with more than a brief, pointless knee-jerk reaction to the murder of its 'servants'. First, the government despatched 7,000 troops to Sicily to free up policemen for investigative work. Then the Rome parliament approved a package of emergency measures which Borsellino and Falcone had lobbied for without success. The law gave police new powers to carry out house searches without warrants, infiltrate clans in undercover 'sting' operations and bug private phone calls and conversations. The law also introduced a six-year jail sentence for politicians caught paying for votes from the mafia. Soon afterwards, the state gave itself the means to coordinate the fight against the fraternity across Italy with two new bodies – the DIA (Italy's FBI) for the police and an anti-mafia prosecutor coordinating 26 sections in different cities – a job which should have been Falcone's.

The Corleonesi had brought the state to its knees; Riina seemed to be closer than ever to bending it to his will and pressed on with his strategy. One evening that autumn, Brusca and two other mafiosi hid in the gardens of the villa where the influential tax-collector Ignazio Salvo lived, while he entertained a guest for dinner. The dinner over, the gunmen shot Salvo dead as he and his wife accompanied their guest to the front gate. Salvo, in Riina's eyes, had failed to defend the mafia's interests with politicians.

After Salvo's murder, Riina sent a message to Brusca: 'We need another blow. Who've you got to hand?' Brusca suggested the senior prosecutor Judge Pietro Grasso. Brusca wanted to blow up the home of Grasso's mother-in-law in Monreale, which the judge often visited, but he had to give up on the idea because the wavelengths of a bank's alarm system interfered with his remote control.

Riina didn't stop at ordering the murder of outsiders. The godfather discussed a plan to use a car-bomb to kill a mafioso who was notorious for carrying up to three guns on him at all times. When Brusca asked Riina for the green light to carry out the murder, Riina replied: 'No problem, go ahead.'

'But it's risky, we might kill some children,' another boss said.

Riina shrugged: 'So what? So many children die in Sarajevo and nobody worries about it.' Despite Riina's comment, no such attack was carried out.

Instead, the boss Vincenzo Milazzo, who had dared to speak badly of Riina and the Corleonesi, was shot dead as he stepped out of his car. After burying him in a field, the killers searched for his girlfriend, who was pregnant at the time; they believed she knew everything about him and were worried that she would talk to one of her relatives, an intelligence officer. She was strangled to death and buried alongside the father of her unborn child.

Riina appeared to be more powerful than ever. His authority had been recognised as far away as Colombia by the drug-trafficker Orlando Cediel Ospina Vargas, described by investigators as the biggest cocaine distributor in the world for Colombia's drug cartels. As he negotiated supplying a vast drugs and money-laundering ring spanning 15 countries, a police bug recorded him saying: 'It's time we did things seriously. I'll expand exports, I'll send all the cocaine that's needed, but then we need an organisation able to manage the distribution and I want nothing to do with dilettanti; I want people who know the job, people who can be trusted.' He insisted: 'I want to do business only with Riina's Corleonesi; they must be the guarantors of the affair.'

The negotiations had gone well, the Corleonesi assuring the drug-trafficker that they could handle and launder any sum, however large. The Corleonesi won a pledge from the Colombian cartels to give them a monopoly over the distribution of cocaine all over Europe, to be bought through the Bonnano family in New York. Cocaine was shipped from Colombia to Italy, the Netherlands and Spain, concealed among cargoes of frozen fish, bananas, flowers and leather goods. The cocaine was paid for through 15 front companies, including a wine export company based in Corleone, and through bank accounts in America, Switzerland and Austria. A police operation codenamed 'Green Ice', the name given to laundered and frozen dollars, dismantled the ring in late 1992 with 201 arrests in Italy, Spain, Britain, America and Costa Rica. In a lock-up garage in central London, police found a 22-cubic-metre pile of banknotes worth £2 million.

Reaching out from Corleone, the mafia's tentacles could not have spread wider.

The Clan's First Traitors

Watching Falcone's funeral on television in jail, the Palermo soldier Giuseppe Marchese was moved to tears by the appeal of the bodyguard's widow Rosaria Schifani in church – 'Men of the mafia, I know you are here . . . I forgive you but you must go down on your knees.' To avoid being seen weeping by other prisoners, Marchese locked himself in a bathroom where he cried silently. Less than two months later, Marchese turned state's evidence.

Marchese's betrayal was a heavy blow for the Corleonesi – not so much because of what he had to say, but because of who he was. Marchese had been recruited by Riina himself and was the first member of the Corleonesi clan to become a supergrass. He had been Riina's driver and was even related to him through his wife Ninetta: he was the brother-in-law of Bagarella, Ninetta's brother. Until Marchese talked, the Corleonesi could pride themselves on being the most secretive, watertight clan of all; no outsider ever infiltrated it and no insider ever betrayed it. The collaboration of a member of Riina's inner circle should have led to an immediate death sentence for Marchese's family. But as his sister was married to Bagarella, she was spared by Riina.

The assassinations of Falcone and Borsellino prompted many other mafiosi to talk. By January 1993, 270 had broken the law of silence, taking advantage of a new, American-style protection scheme which Judge Falcone had helped introduce. The state pledged to give informers false names and false identity papers, even forging school certificates and university diplomas if necessary. Subsidies would help the turncoat and his family leave their homes and start a new life elsewhere in Italy or abroad.

Never before had the mafia suffered such a challenge to its authority and now mass desertion threatened. It could no longer guarantee a future, let alone immunity, to many of its members and so many broke ranks, taking advantage of judicial benefits and reduced jail sentences. The avalanche of defectors fed off itself: the testimony of a mafioso would trigger arrests and several of those arrested would testify in turn, prompting yet more arrests and more mafiosi to talk, the cycle repeating itself again and again. Many Italians began to believe that, at last, the mafia could be defeated.

As the number of informers increased, Riina became more careful. Summits became few and far between, with the godfather preferring to meet bosses on their own to ensure secrecy. At one rare meeting of family heads dedicated to supergrasses, Riina did not beat about the bush. 'The evil is these supergrasses, because if it wasn't for them, even if the whole world united against us it would be no skin off our noses. So we have to kill them all . . . starting with children six years old. That way we'll give these supergrasses a good lesson!'

Riina's intended 'lesson' shocked Cancemi, a heroin trafficker, so much that he began to contemplate giving himself up to the police and turning state's evidence. Cancemi had two children and six grandchildren. 'Children have always been my life,' he said later.

The mafioso who was to bring down Riina single-handedly and without firing a shot, the olive-skinned shepherd's son Baldassare Di Maggio, was only 26 when the Corleone boss took him under his wing. Di Maggio's first test, in 1981, was to murder a truck driver. He had no idea why the man had been condemned but knew better than to ask the reason – 'Don't ask too many questions,' was the first advice his mafioso father had given him. Di Maggio passed the test and was rewarded with an invitation to dinner from Riina; Di Maggio was from the town of San Giuseppe Jato, whose clan, led by the Bruscas, was among the closest to the Corleonesi.

In a villa on a hillside near the town, among olive groves, vine-yards and orchards where tomatoes and peppers grew, Di Maggio dined on pizzas and roast chicken served by Riina's wife Ninetta.

After the meal, as Ninetta cleared the table, Riina turned to Giovanni Brusca and asked about Di Maggio. 'How did the soldier behave?' Riina said.

'Well,' Brusca replied.

'If everyone had solid balls like you lads, we'd have Sicily wrapped around our little finger,' Riina decreed.

Four months later Di Maggio, an apprentice car mechanic, joined the mafia. Self-confident and strong-willed, he rose quickly and when the clan's elderly leader Bernardo Brusca and his son Giovanni were jailed in the mid-1980s, Di Maggio was chosen as acting head. He became a loyal henchman to Riina, serving as his driver and bodyguard, as well as strangling victims on the godfather's orders and dissolving their bodies in acid. He traf-ficked in drugs, blew up the villas of anyone who stood in the mafia's way, took hefty commission from public works contracts and bought Kalashnikovs, bazookas and explosives. Soon, Di Maggio was rich enough to plan what he stressed to his archi-tect must be a 'Hollywood-style' villa, with columns, a giant swimming pool and valuable paintings on the walls.

Giovanni Brusca was released in 1991 and Di Maggio had little choice but to submit and take a more minor role. This was not the only source of frustration for Di Maggio. He was married and had two young children, but he had fallen in love with Elisabetta Scalici, an entrepreneur's daughter. Their relationship was gossiped about in town and mafiosi saw it as a violation of the 'code of honour'. Di Maggio was so set on Elisabetta that he ignored his own parents when they urged him to end the affair. They asked the town's patriarch, Bernardo Brusca, to help their son 'come to his senses', but this too failed to sway Di Maggio.

When Elisabetta became pregnant, Di Maggio decided their life would become unbearable if they remained in Sicily. Di Maggio gave up on the Hollywood-style villa, which remained just a dream, and the lovers emigrated to Canada. But Di Maggio failed to find a good job and Elisabetta missed Sicily and her family. They came back after only a few months. Di Maggio had abandoned his clan and had some explaining to do. He went to see Riina, who greeted him with a kiss on both cheeks. A humble, respectful Di Maggio asked for forgiveness and permission to rejoin the clan. Riina let him talk and then reprimanded him severely: the mafia had its own laws, the godfather said. Di Maggio was married with two children, how could he not only start an affair but make his mistress pregnant too? Di Maggio would never become a boss – not in a thousand years!

Di Maggio realised Riina's words spelt death for him if he remained in Sicily; the news that he wanted a bigger role for himself in the clan would spread, and someone would sooner or later try to eliminate him. He was also worried by the kiss Riina had given him – many times he had seen Riina embrace designated victims and lull them into a false sense of security before eliminating them. Di Maggio fled to northern Italy where Elisabetta gave birth to a baby boy. Di Maggio feared for his life and took to wearing a bulletproof vest.

The *carabinieri* police were the first to reach Di Maggio. When they searched his flat at the request of their Sicilian colleagues, they found a gun and a hundred or so bullets. But Di Maggio seized the chance to seek revenge on the godfather.

Di Maggio stunned his captors by announcing: 'I can show you how to capture Riina.'

'Who was the Judas?' – Riina's Fall

The thin, wiry Captain Sergio de Caprio, or *Ultimo* (Last) as he preferred to be called, was an anomaly in a para-military force like the *carabinieri* police. The cigar-smoking Captain De Caprio wore his long hair in a pony-tail, and preferred to dress in jeans and a worn leather jacket rather than wear uniform. Born in Tuscany – his father was also an officer – De Caprio had started his career hunting fugitives down in Milan. At the head of a team nicknamed 'the Dirty Dozen', he had chosen the codename 'Last' because, he explained, he had been the last to join the team. His men said that, when on duty, he was always the last to go home. The captain saw his job as a kind of guerrilla warfare; he and his team were 'warriors' or 'guerrillas' and he draped an enormous red flag stamped with the face of Che Guevara over his desk.

De Caprio's guiding rule was that to catch a fugitive, you must live anonymously and blend into your neighbourhood. Assigned to hunt bosses, he and his 15-strong team settled in Palermo in the summer of 1992; they assumed false names and stayed in hotels or rented flats instead of living in the force's barracks. Among themselves, his men used codenames like 'Serpico', 'the Viking' or 'the Shadow'. That August, De Caprio had the idea of placing bugs in the butcher's shop owned by the boss Raffaele Ganci – unknown to the captain, Ganci was the one who had spotted Falcone's car leaving his block of flats before he was murdered. The bugs allowed De Caprio to start uncovering Riina's protection network.

When the boss Di Maggio began to testify to De Caprio's

colleagues in northern Italy, he asked for pen and paper and drew two maps showing the areas of Palermo in which he believed Riina might be living, not knowing the godfather's precise address. He then explained that Riina was very close to the Sansone brothers, two big Palermo builders, and that one of them sometimes served as Riina's driver.

Flown to Palermo aboard a secret flight, the supergrass was debriefed by Captain De Caprio. From 8 p.m. onwards on the night of 14 January 1993, the informer sat patiently watching hour after hour of videos filmed by De Caprio from a van parked in front of a green gate leading to the residential complex on Via Bernini in north-west Palermo, whose residents included the Sansone brothers. As one video after another was played, De Caprio, watching for a reaction, pulled on cigar after cigar. Shortly after midnight an exhausted Di Maggio, his eyes red with strain, jumped up in his chair. The video he was watching showed a woman getting into a car.

'Stop, stop. That's Ninetta,' the defector said. He had recognised Riina's wife.

'Are you sure?' De Caprio asked.

'Absolutely, Captain. I've seen her dozens of times over the years. I even drove her to church in my car,' Di Maggio replied.

At 6.30 a.m. the next morning, De Caprio and his men deployed in the streets around the entrance to the residential complex. The captain, who had shaken off the sleepless night with a capuccino in a bar, waited in an unmarked car. Di Maggio was also watching the gate, hidden in a van.

More than two hours later, the captain said to a colleague: 'Now I've had enough, he's got to come out.'

A minute afterwards, at 8.52 a.m., a small Citroen car stopped outside the gate. As the driver waited for the gate to open, the supergrass recognised him. 'That's Salvatore ... um ... I don't remember his surname. But Riina often used him as his driver,' he said.

The car entered the complex, the gate swinging shut behind it. Three minutes later, the gate swung open again. Sitting next to the driver was a stocky figure with a swollen face and heavy jowels.

'It's Riina, it's Riina! Grab him!' Di Maggio whispered.

Alerted instantly via radio, the captain warned all his men. 'It's him. It's up to us now, brothers,' he said.

The Citroen covered half a mile before it reached a red traffic light and stopped.

'Attack positions,' Captain De Caprio ordered on his radio.

De Caprio's unmarked car pulled up on the driver's side of the Citroen, so close the two almost touched. Through his open window, he asked to see the two men's papers.

'Why?' the driver asked.

'What's the problem?' Riina echoed.

Wary in case the two men were playing for time in the hope that Riina's henchmen might pass by and attack him, De Caprio shouted: '*Basta* (Enough), get out!'

De Caprio ran up to the front passenger door, grabbed Riina by the throat and, threatening him with his gun, made him stretch out face-down on the tarmac while his men hurled themselves out of three other unmarked cars and rushed to pull Riina's driver out.

'Get your head down!' De Caprio shouted at Riina as he pulled his arms behind his back and checked he wasn't carrying a weapon. De Caprio never bothered to carry handcuffs – he simply didn't like using them – so he used his scarf to tie Riina's hands behind his back. 'You're Salvatore Riina,' De Caprio said, although still unsure.

'You're making a mistake,' Riina replied.

'You're Salvatore Riina,' De Caprio repeated.

'I don't know who this Riina is,' Riina said.

As he spoke, Riina stared fixedly at De Caprio with his small, dark eyes. De Caprio noticed there were swollen bags under them. Suddenly he felt certain this was the godfather. 'It's over. We've won,' he thought.

Riina produced an identity card made out in a false name describing him as a shepherd.

The piece of paper didn't fool De Caprio. 'It's him, brothers,' he said into his radio.

He bundled Riina into the back of his car. De Caprio wrapped a scarf around the godfather's neck and held him with his face pressed to the back of the seat in front of him. The captain held the scarf so tight that Riina could barely breathe and started coughing. De Caprio reflected that his grandfather used to cough often, so it didn't bother him that Riina was coughing.

The captain saw his quarry was terrified – Riina's face was pale and his eyes wet. The officer found himself feeling sorry for the godfather. Then he realised that Riina was scared because he had no idea who had seized him and was probably thinking he was about to be executed. This irritated De Caprio, because he believed that a boss, let alone a godfather, must never be afraid.

'But who are you?' Riina asked.

For a moment, De Caprio toyed with the idea of keeping Riina in the dark or making him believe that he had been seized by rivals. 'We're *carabinieri* officers. You're under arrest,' De Caprio said. He then asked his prey what his name was. Riina refused to reply.

Riina was still pale and his eyes damp when he was driven into barracks opposite Palermo's Norman Palace. He was made to sit in front of a photograph of General Dalla Chiesa hanging on the wall. It was only then that Riina admitted who he was. 'Yes, it's me. Call my lawyer,' he said, sitting stock still on the chair.

It was the end of 23 years, six months and eight days on the run. For most of that time, the state had made little or no effort to find him.

In his rust-coloured checked jacket, brown corduroy trousers, green polo shirt and matching cashmere scarf, and expensive, British-made shoes, Riina looked to one prosecutor who approached him like a quiet, harmless country gentleman. He was polite and respectful towards his captors, in the best tradition of captured bosses. But apparent calm was belied by brief moments when Riina's eyes flashed with anger. And whenever a senior officer introduced himself to him, the godfather stared intensely into his face and said: 'Excuse me, what did you say your name was?' Later, Riina asked other officers: 'Who was the Judas? Who sold me?'

In his pockets they found £300 in cash, a photograph of his wife Ninetta and their four children standing around a birthday cake and an old coin he carried as a good luck charm. In his black shoulder bag was another £1,450, also in cash, a Casio calculator, three notebooks with brief notes such as 'Finished 16 apartments' – a packet of Tiparillo cigars and some medicine for headaches and indigestion. Riina also carried an image of Saint Joseph, with whom he probably identified, not as the patron saint of artisans but, as in popular culture, the father of the family – in this case, the mafia.

Immediately after the arrest, prosecutors asked for a search of the residential complex Riina had emerged from, but De Caprio blocked this. The mafia didn't know that the complex was known to authorities, he argued, and surveillance would catch anyone who came to fetch Riina's family. Besides, no boss would store incriminating documents at home, the captain insisted. His idea was to let the Sansone brothers, Riina's close allies, believe that no one knew where the godfather lived, hoping they would then lead him to other mafiosi. The prosecutors agreed and shelved the idea of a search, on condition that the complex be kept under 'absolute and constant' surveillance.

But on the afternoon of Riina's arrest, the surveillance was halted without the prosecutors' knowledge while De Caprio's men combed through company registers to find out what they could about the Sansones. The captain believed a spy-van parked for days at a time at that spot, in an area monitored by the mafia, would soon have attracted attention. 'After a bit, someone would have knocked on the door to say: "Officer, you must be tired. Would you like a coffee?"' De Caprio argued.

This left the field clear for mafiosi to retrieve Riina's family. Two mafiosi picked up Ninetta and their four children while several others, well-armed, watched over the street outside the residential complex. The mafiosi drove the family, escorted by another car, to the railway station. True to type, Ninetta said nothing during the trip, in a car crammed with six people and bulging suitcases – not even 'thank-you', one member of her escort noted acidly, adding: 'For *the* family of Corleone, nothing was too much to expect and its members didn't feel the need to thank those who had risked their lives for them.' Dragging their suitcases, the family walked into the railway station, waited a short time, then walked out again to take a taxi to Corleone. The aim, should they be spotted, was to give the impression that they had just got off a train from northern Italy.

Two days later Riina's two sons walked into the Corleone cemetery carrying flowers. They ignored the many tombs of the victims claimed by their father's clan and instead knelt before the tomb of their grandfather, who had been killed by the explosion of a German cannon shell half a century earlier.

Shortly after her arrival, Ninetta called at the *carabinieri* police station in Corleone. 'I've always been with my husband and my children these past years. I educated them myself. I've come back because this is where they should grow up,' she announced. In fact, her children did go to school, according to a supergrass.

When an officer tried to ask her about Riina's crimes, she replied: 'My husband isn't the person you describe. He's an exquisite man. I wish all men could be like him, an exemplary father. He's too good, he's a victim of circumstances.' Then, in a comment which hinted at Riina's fury with the supergrasses, she said: 'The supergrasses are having it all their way now and the state is just allowing itself to be manipulated by them.' A few weeks later, chased by television crews as she arrived with her children at a Rome prison to visit Riina, she complained: 'I'm a mother, a mother like all the others. I'm not a circus bear or a beast to chase after. I'm tired of running away.'

With Riina's Palermo villa still watched over only by mafiosi, the boss Angelo La Barbera was instructed to 'remove everything that can be removed'. No trace of the Riina family was to remain. La Barbera and other mafiosi turned into dogsbodies for the day, hoovering everywhere and repainting the walls to cover up any fingerprints. Fearing that a large truck driving through the villa's gates would draw unwelcome attention, they used only a couple of cars, taking away chiefly silverware and paintings. As for the rest, a supergrass said – 'furnishings, household linen, clothes, everything there was' – they simply made a great pile in the garden and set fire to it. Ninetta's luxurious furs and the dowry linen her mother had embroidered for her were burnt to cinders. When he heard what La Barbera had done, Ninetta's brother Bagarella complained darkly: 'He even burnt souvenirs which had sentimental value. He deserves to be killed.'

It was only 18 days after Riina's arrest that the villa was finally searched. All they found was a photograph of his children. A public scandal over the failure to search it earlier prompted prosecutors to accuse De Caprio and his superior Colonel Mori of helping the mafia; they were later acquitted.

At his first court appearance, Riina appeared relaxed and smiling and denied having anything to do with the mafia. He told the court that he worked on building sites, earning only £170 a week on which he struggled to feed his wife and four children. 'I'm a worker, Your Honour, not the man who's described in the newspapers and on the television,' he said. Riina ridiculed the Italian state's efforts to find him for 23 years: 'Nobody ever looked for me. I went to work in the morning. Nobody ever stopped me. I took the train to Trapani (in western Sicily). I took the bus. Nobody ever said anything to me.'

He was virulent in his condemnation of informers: 'I'm the lightning rod for these people . . . they all accuse me, because each one earns more by talking about Salvatore Riina: the state pays these gentlemen.'

'You know Cosa Nostra . . .' the judge attempted.

'Through the television,' Riina shot back.

What of the defector Mutolo's accusation that Riina was the true head of the Cupola, the judge asked?

'That's all lies. Mutolo's the man who, each time he is arrested, they catch him red-handed busy dealing in drugs; he's always dealing in drugs. He's a wonderful grocer, that's what Mutolo is. He can say all he wants, but none of it is true.'

'Marchese also describes you as boss . . .'

Riina interrupted: 'Why does he describe me like that? Because Marchese, who was given a life sentence, is of course a free man now. It's obvious making these statements is worthwhile. I want to state that I haven't committed any murders, that I didn't give orders to kill anyone's relatives, because no one has done me any harm . . . You have to look elsewhere, you have to search high up, you mustn't pay attention to me, Salvatore Riina, a poor peasant.'

Asked again about the mafia, Riina replied: 'I'm not part of the mafia. I don't know what it is. I read about it in the newspapers.'

In the two years that followed the arrest of the 'poor peasant', as Riina called himself, police seized from him villas, farmhouses, apartments, offices, shops, depots, garages, trucks, cars, land and shares worth a total of £160 million. Many of the shares were in companies owned jointly with Provenzano, in sectors as varied as health supplies, textiles, wine, agriculture, urban and industrial waste disposal and television advertising and production. What was confiscated represented only a tiny fraction of Riina's fortune. Police estimated Riina to be worth up to £1.3 billion and that most of it had been spirited abroad.

Riina's capture was a pleasant surprise to the *carabiniere* Captain Francesco Iaccono, the murdered General Dalla Chiesa's successor, stationed in Corleone. He was amazed to see local people coming up to him to apologise. 'They feel guilty for not having shown themselves our friends in public before. All sorts of people – peasants, bar-owners, professionals – come and shake our hands on the piazza quite openly now,' he said.

But Corleone didn't rejoice unanimously at Riina's arrest. Many worried whether the *pax mafiosa* (the mafia-imposed peace) would continue to hold and whether the streets would remain free of crime. Corleone's monthly newspaper *Città Nuove* (New Towns), which campaigned bravely against the mafia, ran an editorial under the headline 'Hopes and Fears':

> Once more we have seen two Corleones, the democratic and civilised one which has rejoiced and that which is subservient or an accomplice to the mafia . . . We are with the first . . . The 'silence' of so many old people who have lived with the mafia for years and who remember with terror the dozens of people killed in the 1960s is understandable. We understand the concerns of so many housewives, brought up in the mafioso sub-culture, who confusedly ask themselves: 'Who will protect us now?' We answer only that the democratic institutions of the state and our clear consciences must protect us.

Riina's family soon got itself noticed in Corleone. The eldest son Giovanni, heavily built like his father, liked to throw his considerable weight around, telling anyone who upset him: 'Don't you know who I am? I'm the son of Salvatore Riina.' One evening he turned up at a nightclub with a group of friends and insisted they all be allowed in free of charge. The argument went on and on until Provenzano's son Angelo, who was also present, walked up and told him: 'Look, I'm paying, so you have to pay too.' Giovanni backed down and paid.

In 1994, Riina's sons were rumoured to have smashed a plaque honouring the judges Falcone and Borsellino in the main piazza of the town. The mayor, Pippo Cipriani, reacted quickly and replaced the plaque within just a few hours. It was Cipriani who had renamed the square as a tribute to the murdered judges earlier that year, after his election at the head of a leftist coalition. The election, in the town known as the mafia's capital, was a political revolution. Born and raised a few streets away from the Bagarellas, Riina's in-laws, Cipriani chose the renaming of the square as his first official act. At the inauguration ceremony, he announced that from then on the town hall would make sure it was represented as a civil plaintiff in all trials involving mafiosi from Corleone.

Cipriani, with the anti-mafia association Libera, went on to host one of the town's most moving challenges to the secret society. As police marksmen carrying pump-action shotguns equipped with telescopic sights stood guard on nearby rooftops, Palermo's chief anti-mafia prosecutor Giancaro Caselli, Libera's head Father Luigi Ciotti, Borsellino's sister and the mother of a bodyguard killed with the senior police officer Ninni Cassarà read out in a relay in the main piazza the names of 394 innocent victims killed by organised crime in Italy in the previous 50 years. It took more than three hours to read out all the names.

Prayers, Politics and the Battle for Riina's Succession

Riina's arrest caused 'complete confusion', according to the boss Brusca. Clan chiefs who suddenly found themselves leaderless stopped consulting anyone else. 'There wasn't the unity there used to be, because the father of the family, the boss of bosses, didn't exist any more,' he said.

The battle for Riina's succession saw two rivals emerge, both of them Corleonesi – Provenzano, Riina's life-long partner, and Leduca Bagarella, the brother of Riina's wife Ninetta. Provenzano made little secret of his eagerness to succeed Riina. Shortly after Riina's arrest, he sent a message to bosses: 'As long as there's still a Corleonese free, everything will continue as before.' Provenzano quickly got himself elected head of the Corleonesi, but at a price: he had to promise that before contacting the heads of other clans, he would always consult Bagarella.

Bagarella lost no time in spreading slander against his opponent, confiding to several bosses that he believed Provenzano had betrayed Riina. After all, Bagarella added, who else stood to benefit as much from Riina's capture? The whispering campaign reached Provenzano himself and he asked his right-hand man Giuffrè: 'Do you believe this too?' Giuffrè of course replied that no, he didn't believe it.

The rivalry between Provenzano and Bagarella became a clash over the mafia's future. Bagarella wanted to continue Riina's campaign of terror, convinced that only violence obtained results, while Provenzano wanted to take a low profile. Giuffrè was struck by how Provenzano turned his back on violence and on the terror attacks he had previously supported, now believing that they backfired. 'We had to make Cosa Nostra invisible to give us time to get reorganised in peace and quiet,' Giuffrè explained. Provenzano made no secret of his new conviction, so much so that he created what became known as a 'pacifist' faction, which included several bosses from Palermo and other cities who were worried by the police repression that had followed Falcone's assassination.

'This was a recycled Provenzano; he used to be warlike and now he adopted the holy air of a cardinal,' Giuffrè said. Giving the go-ahead for a murder was now apparently a source of great suffering for Provenzano; as he gave his consent he would spread his arms wide and lift his eyes towards Heaven as if to say 'if it cannot be avoided, let God's will be done'. Provenzano even changed the way he talked; he no longer said, 'We'll do this', preferring instead a more cautious 'In my opinion . . . but what do you think?' Provenzano had turned into 'a maestro of good manners, a diplomat'.

Provenzano, however, showed no hesitation in dropping such 'good manners' when he was particularly set on taking yet another life – including that of Captain De Caprio, who had arrested Riina. Provenzano wanted to torture him to find out who had betrayed Riina. He explained: 'There's the possibility of taking this Captain De Caprio alive and you know why I want to take him alive. If it fails, we kill him . . .'

His audience fell silent. One boss broke the silence: 'But do we really have to wage war on the state?'

The boss Cancemi said nothing but made an eloquent gesture familiar to any Italian – he joined his palms in front of his chest as if in prayer and moved them up and down, signalling: 'Why should we bother?' The rebellious gesture was noted by Provenzano. Soon afterwards a friend of Cancemi's warned him to be on his guard and not accept any appointment with Provenzano. Three weeks later, Provenzano sent word that he wanted to see Cancemi at 6 a.m. the next morning; Cancemi went straight to the police, escaping certain death and becoming the first member of the Cupola to turn state's evidence. He later gave up the wealth he had accumulated, worth £33 million. The plan to seize De Caprio came to nothing.

Bagarella, Provenzano's rival, wanting to go much further and much faster, took matters into his own hands. A month after Riina's arrest, Bagarella met three allies who decided to launch attacks outside Sicily; they aimed to exploit an unwritten rule which gives mafiosi freedom to operate as they like away from the island. Their first target was Maurizio Costanzo, a plump chat-show host who had dared to say, when one boss was held under arrest in hospital, that he hoped the boss would get a tumour. The comment was enough to prompt the Cupola to condemn Costanzo to death, but the murder had been delayed to allow for the killing of Falcone.

Then, after Riina's arrest, Costanzo commented on his show: 'If I was in the habit of drinking, this evening I'd get drunk I'm so happy.' No fewer than three clan heads were watching: Bagarella, Brusca and Gioè. They could wait no longer. Gioè came up with several ideas which were all approved. Each was designed to spread alarm, with advance warning given to the authorities every time. One was to place a bomb inside the Leaning Tower of Pisa; another to plant packs of poisoned snacks in supermarkets; and a third to scatter syringes infected with the HIV virus on the beach in the popular Adriatic Coast resort of Rimini. The bosses believed these would all strengthen their hand and force the state to bow to their demands.

However, the arrest of Gioè shortly after the meeting meant all the plans were shelved, save for the attempt on Costanzo. A car-bomb exploded in a Rome street one evening as Costanzo and his girlfriend were being driven past. The explosion damaged his car, but failed to harm him or his companion.

The Bagarella faction remained set on unleashing more attacks and this time consulted more widely. Ever cautious, Provenzano asked for time to think things out, then gave his backing to new terrorist-style attacks, but only outside Sicily. The authorities, he argued, would think they were the work of terrorists like the Red Brigades and this would ease the police pressure on the mafia.

★

The mafia entrusted the selection of targets for a wave of bombings to Matteo Messina Denaro, a boss in his thirties whom they considered as their in-house art expert and who once boasted: 'With the people I've killed, I could create a cemetery.'

From Trapani in western Sicily, Messina Denaro was the son of a patriarch so respected that New York's Bonanno clan sent its recruits to him for training. A drug-trafficker, Messina Denaro loved luxury and was fond of Versace clothes, silk scarves, Rolex watches and Cristal champagne. In the evenings, he would roar off in his armour-plated Porsche to a seaside resort with his latest girlfriend. Reading a cartoon gave him the idea of equipping the Porsche with two machine-guns that would pop out of the boot, but he never did put this wish into practice.

A letter he wrote to a girlfriend called Sonia gave a glimpse of how he saw life in the mafia: 'I've got to go, I can't explain to you the reasons for my decision. Right now fate is against me, I'm fighting for a cause which can't be understood. But one day it will be revealed who was on the side of reason.' The letter was found by police in a hideout he had abandoned.

Women apparently appreciated Messina Denaro. Another girlfriend, Maria, sent a note to him: 'Please don't say no. I really want to give you a present. You know, I read in a magazine about videogames that the *Donkey Kong III* cassette has come out and I can't wait for it to be in the shops so I can buy it for you. You're the most beautiful thing there is.'

Messina Denaro made his selection of targets and reported back. The attacks were scheduled for late May.

Strung out among pine and olive trees on a ridge facing the Mediterranean near Agrigento are ancient Greek temples honouring Jupiter and other gods. In early May 1993 a crowd of 100,000 faithful gathered in front of them to hear Pope John Paul II, who was visiting Sicily.

Clutching a crucifix and raising his index finger towards Heaven, the Pope spoke directly to the men of the mafia in a hard, emotional voice: 'Mafiosi, be converted. One day the judgement of God will come and you will have to pay for your wrongdoing ... In the name of this Christ resurrected, of this Christ who is life and truth, I say to those in charge: be converted, for the love of God ... And to you, brothers, I say: Evil will not triumph.'

The paved courtyard of the majestic Uffizi Gallery in the heart of Florence's historic centre, thronged by day with tourists queueing to see the masterpieces by Leonardo da Vinci and other masters housed inside, was virtually deserted on the night of 27 May 1993 when, shortly after 1 a.m., a car-bomb exploded in a nearby street.

The blast toppled a stone tower, the Torre dei Pulci, punched through the windows of the Uffizi Gallery just behind it and swept down the marble corridors, knocking busts of ancient Roman emperors from their pedestals and tearing into the fragile canvas of paintings. The falling tower crushed to death the Academy's keeper, his wife and their two daughters. A fire started in a nearby house, in which another man died; 35 people were injured.

In the Uffizi Gallery, the blast destroyed three paintings by two seventeenth-century disciples of Caravaggio, damaged 173 others including works by Titian, Velasquez and Rubens, and also damaged 42 ancient busts and 16 large statues, decapitating the famous Discus Thrower. The blast was so powerful it raised and shifted the dome of the Church of Santo Stefano and Cecilia near the picturesque Ponte Vecchio bridge over the River Arno,

That July a bomb exploded in Milan, killing five people, followed by two more blasts in Rome – all within a few minutes of each other at about 11 p.m. The first bomb in the Italian capital, outside the Basilica of St John, seriously wounded a security guard and pulverised frescoes; the second, outside the Church of San Giorgio al Velabro, sent the portico, the huge main door and several walls crashing down.

Three days later, the mafia sent an anonymous letter to two newspapers: 'All that has happened is only a beginning. After these latest bombs, we inform the nation that the next ones will explode only during the day and in public places, because they will be exclusively aimed at taking human lives. PS: We guarantee there will be hundreds of them.'

That summer, Bagarella complained to the Brancaccio clan on Palermo's outskirts about Father Giuseppe Puglisi, a priest who campaigned against the mafia especially among children and teenagers. In one homily, Puglisi had condemned mafiosi as 'beasts' and 'animals', challenging them to meet him in a local piazza. 'Let us talk together. I would like to meet you and understand why you stand in the way of those who try to help your children and teach them lawfulness and mutual respect,' Puglisi said. The clan had him eliminated. One of the hitmen testified later that the priest had smiled at them and said 'I was expecting this' just before they shot him in the back of the neck. It was the first time the mafia had killed a priest who had fought it.

As under Riina's rule, the mafia switched from violence against the state to negotiation with the state and back again. Riina had left many problems unsolved – there was still no ruling that life sentences be overturned; mafiosi were still held under a prison regime of strict isolation; and there was still what the fraternity saw as over-generous treatment of supergrasses.

Bagarella tried to dust down a mafia blueprint which dated back to the end of the Second World War – a vision of Sicily as the 51st member of the United States of America, which would mean the island being governed from Washington. The city would be the most distant capital from which Sicily had been ruled in the past 2,000 years, leaving mafiosi a free hand to do as they pleased. But when Bagarella sent an envoy across the Atlantic to meet the influential Italo-American boss Saro Naomi and ask him whether the United States would be interested in having Sicily as the 51st federal state, Naomi burst out laughing. Bagarella's venture into politics limited itself to founding, with the approval of the jailed Riina, a movement called Free Sicily; its aim was to recruit members supposedly to promote the idea of an independent 'Sicily for Sicilians', and act as a lobby to push for reforms that the brotherhood wanted.

Provenzano gave only lukewarm support to the movement because he believed that an independent Sicily would take many years to achieve. Instead, he concentrated on the tried and tested strategy of seeking political contacts who, once they had been helped through elections, would push through the laws the mafia demanded. His lieutenant Giuffrè explained: 'The mafia doesn't give nothing for nothing; it has to gain something. So I give something to you, politician, and you give something to me, mafioso. I give you power, I send you to Rome; you must guarantee me immunity, favours, profits. Until we're completely even.'

According to Giuffrè, Provenzano followed Riina in attempting to negotiate with the media mogul Berlusconi in the summer of 1993 as he prepared to create a new, conservative political party – Forza Italia. For months, Provenzano consulted bosses to find out about Berlusconi and establish whether the new party and Berlusconi's close associate Dell'Utri in particular could be trusted.

That summer, in a fax to his newspaper *Il Giornale*, Berlusconi dictated the line it should follow on judicial issues. The text included criticism of investigators who, on the basis of 'mostly unreliable statements by obliging supergrasses who want to obtain benefits', accused a suspect of mafia association, depriving him of his personal freedom. For prosecutors, Berlusconi could only be referring to mafiosi and his fax corroborated Giuffrè's testimony. Berlusconi denies this.

The boss Mangano, who almost two decades earlier had worked for Berlusconi at his villa, allegedly flew regularly from Sicily to Milan to meet the tycoon's close associate Dell'Utri over the next two years. According to a defector, Dell'Utri promised Mangano that the new party, if it won power, would pass a series of laws favourable to the mafia, including an easing of the strict prison regime. But Dell'Utri insisted: 'You've got to stay calm, you've got to stay calm. *Basta* (Enough) noise, *basta* violence. We need peace and quiet to get things done.' Dell'Utri says there is no truth in such accounts.

Finally, Provenzano made known his plan. 'All right, we back

Forza Italia,' he announced at a summit. The mafia was in good hands, he added, before listing the reforms he had demanded: measures to discourage supergrasses, limited seizures of mafiosi's property, lighter sentences, a scaling down of police investigations and the cancellation of previous convictions.

But Provenzano warned that the road ahead would be long and difficult. 'We'll need ten years to sort everything out . . . We need a period of serenity and tranquillity. We need time both to heal and reorganise Cosa Nostra and to find other political backers who are valid and efficient.' If the violence continued, he said, the police, prosecutors and public opinion would all continue to watch, control and judge the organisation and this would make life harder for 'the friends of the friends' who were supposed to help it. Mafiosi, including Provenzano's foe Bagarella, welcomed his move and started to work for the Forza Italia party.

For all its influence, there is no suggestion that the mafia has the power to swing a general election. Elected prime minister in 1994, Berlusconi played down its significance; what worried him was its impact on what the world thought of Italy: 'What is the mafia anyway? A ten-thousandth, a millionth. How many mafiosi Italians are there compared to 57 million citizens? And we don't want a hundred or so people to give a negative image all over the world.'

Provenzano's plea for 'serenity and tranquillity' was welcomed by clan chiefs who had objected to the assassinations of Falcone, Borsellino and Father Puglisi. The boss Pietro Aglieri, devoted to Provenzano and the most intellectual of mafia fugitives – he was passionate about philosophy and theology – secretly met Father Giacomo Ribaudo, a Palermo priest. Aglieri, who prayed often in front of an altar in his hideout, told the priest that many mafiosi were thinking about Pope John Paul II's appeal for them to convert, and added that several were ready to give themselves up. They wanted 'to start a new life', Aglieri said. The mafiosi were willing to confess to their own crimes, but they wanted to ensure they would not be asked to accuse their companions. The idea led nowhere, however, and was quietly dropped.

Provenzano's political stand was the first time he had come out into the open and taken personal responsibility for an issue of the highest importance to the mafia. Riina's partner was beginning to act like a godfather himself.

Luciano Leggio, patriarch of the Corleonesi, died in prison in Sardinia in November 1993 at the age of 68 after suffering from breathing difficulties, tuberculosis of the spine with lesions to the vertebrae, and serious atrophy of the bladder. When his body was flown back to Corleone, local authorities refused to grant permission for a public funeral. Instead, Father Girolamo Leggio, the dead boss's first cousin, conducted a service in the Church of Santa Rosalia. The coffin was then driven to the cemetery and buried near the tombs where 29 years earlier he had hidden his guns.

Neither Leggio's name nor his photograph featured on the tomb, as if in death he was still in hiding. Surrounding him were the remains of many of his victims.

The Kidnapping of Giuseppe Di Matteo, Age 12

Set on sticking to Riina's strategy of terror and exasperated by the rising number of informers, the Bagarella faction resolved to deliver an exemplary punishment to a supergrass to discourage any potential traitors. The blow, Bagarella hoped, would demonstrate the mafia's invincibility. In a lime depot on the outskirts of Misilmeri east of Palermo, Bagarella and three other bosses – Brusca, Messina Denaro and Giuseppe Graviano – debated about who to single out for this punishment.

One boss suggested targeting the families of two defectors from the Corleonesi clan but Bagarella vetoed the idea. He argued that the families had broken off all relations with them, so kidnapping or shooting relatives would have no effect. The true reason for Bagarella's opposition, however, was that he was related to both of them.

The bosses focused on two other defectors, both of them from Brusca's clan. The first, Di Maggio, whose evidence had led to Riina's arrest, was quickly ruled out as nothing could be done; his relatives, who were watched by Brusca, apparently had no contact with him. The second, Mario Di Matteo, looked more promising.

A soldier known as 'Half Nose' because of the slightly deformed shape of his nose, Di Matteo had carried out kidnappings, murders – he helped to prepare Falcone's assassination – and other crimes. Arrested in June 1993 and accused of murder, he had begun to talk in October. The first to shed light on the planning of Falcone's murder, he named more than half a dozen bosses, including Riina, Bagarella and Brusca. 'With his testimony he sent us all to Hell,' Brusca said. There was good reason to fear Di Matteo would cause yet more damage: as a soldier under Brusca, he knew several of his hideouts and might lead police to him.

The meeting agreed on Di Matteo as the chosen victim. Brusca had no doubt what he would like to do to him. 'I hated Di Matteo,' he said later. 'I'd have willingly killed him with my own hands.' But the supergrass was under police protection in a secret location well away from Sicily and out of his reach.

Another idea was suggested. One boss had a vague memory that the child of an informer in Naples had once been kidnapped; why not do the same thing and kidnap Di Matteo's son, the 12-year-old Giuseppe?

Messina Denaro and Graviano argued that the boy should be kidnapped and got rid of instantly. 'We take him and we kill him immediately,' Messina Denaro said; 'that way we don't have to worry about anything else. It'll be a warning to the others.'

Brusca had lived with the Di Matteos, hiding in their home the previous year. He had often played with the young Giuseppe. But he instantly backed the idea of kidnapping him. Brusca argued that they should hold on to the hostage rather than kill him immediately – not out of pity for Giuseppe, but because he believed that this could force Di Matteo to go back on his evidence. Brusca had met the supergrass Marino Mannoia in jail and knew that killing an informer's relatives, as had been done with Marino Mannoia, simply did not pay. All it achieved was to make outsiders realise that his testimony was genuine and to make him even more determined.

Brusca was convinced that a way of making Di Matteo retract his testimony could be found; Di Matteo could easily argue his confession had been obtained by torture. In fact, the law of the time meant that even if Di Matteo did recant, his testimony would have remained valid in court. But the bosses had no idea that kidnapping Giuseppe was a pointless crime from the very start.

★

Based on Di Matteo's testimony, prosecutors issued arrest warrants for 18 bosses and soldiers in November 1993. Twelve days later, on 23 November, at 4.45 p.m., the supergrass's son Giuseppe started his scooter outside the riding school where his parents kept a horse his family had bought for him. A bright, lively and sensitive boy, Giuseppe was passionate about his horse, spent long hours exercising it at the school and travelled all over Sicily to take part in competitions.

Six men dressed as policemen from a special anti-mafia unit, with guns at their hips, walked up to Giuseppe. Nearby were two cars, one of which had a blue flashlight on its roof. The men told him he must come with them as they would take him to his father.

'Are you Di Matteo's son? Look, we're from the protection service. We have to take you to your father,' one of the men said to Giuseppe.

'My father! Of course I'll come!' Giuseppe exclaimed in delighted surprise.

The boy chatted calmly with his escort. He had no idea of his fate; the men were not policemen but mafiosi who had disguised themselves with wigs and false moustaches. The men took him to a house where they locked him up in a small room. Still unsuspecting, he talked to the guards who were on shifts keeping him company. These men wore balaclavas; when Giuseppe asked why, they told him this was for their protection as their task was to protect supergrasses. One of them asked him what he thought of his father's decision to reveal what he knew. Giuseppe replied that his father had made the right choice.

That evening the kidnappers tied Giuseppe up and left him alone in the cold, dark room. The boy began to cry for the first time since his abduction; he must have realised by then that he wasn't under the protection of the police, but was in danger.

'Giuseppe wasn't tied up so as to hurt him,' Brusca, chosen to oversee the kidnapping, claimed later. 'He was tied up to ensure he couldn't move, couldn't escape; that is to make him harmless; I repeat, not to hurt him.'

★

Giuseppe's mother Francesca, a strong-willed woman who worked for the local health authority, waited in vain for her son to come home. On the afternoon he went missing, she telephoned and then rushed to several hospitals, afraid he had been hurt in a road accident. There was no trace of him.

Shortly after 9 p.m., someone slipped a note – a piece of paper folded in half and stapled – under the door of Giuseppe's paternal grandfather, who doted on him. 'The boy is with us,' the note read. 'Your son must keep quiet about it. Don't tell the police if you care about your grandson's life.' The note insisted that the supergrass must 'stop talking'.

Di Matteo was told of the kidnapping by his wife five days later when they met in Rome where he was staying in a safe-house, his police bodyguards watching over him. The couple's relationship was tense. She had complained openly that Di Matteo's decision to talk put her life in danger, but refused to join him on the witness protection programme. He accused her and the rest of his family of abandoning him at a very difficult time. Relations between the two were so bad that when she told him about the kidnapping, Di Matteo thought at first that she was lying; he thought it was a ploy to stop him talking. She managed to convince him she was telling the truth and the couple agreed to obey the kidnappers' order not to tell the police – and not even the bodyguards just a few yards away from them.

There was no more news of the boy until 1 December, when two Polaroid photographs of Giuseppe, who was frowning and holding a newspaper dated two days earlier, were slipped under the grandfather's door. On one of the photographs, Giuseppe had written: 'I'm not worried and I'm well.' A separate, anony-mous note read: 'As you can see he's alive and kicking, but you haven't yet done what we asked, so it's in your interest to get on with it immediately because otherwise you can give up hope. Stop his mouth.' The latter was a reference to Di Matteo.

The mother thought of turning to Brusca for help. He knew Giuseppe well, he was a friend of her husband – surely he would be willing to help, she reasoned. But she was told that Brusca could no longer be found and her attempts to get messages to him apparently failed. She supposed that her son was being held by another clan. She never suspected Brusca of playing a role in the kidnapping, believing he wasn't 'so nasty as to be able to kidnap the boy, whom he knew'.

One afternoon in early December, Di Matteo vanished from his safehouse to search for information about his son himself and find out the price for his freedom. Thirty-six hours later he was back in his refuge, where his wife visited him. The couple argued furiously and, in tears, she begged him to stop testifying. 'You must think of your son,' she pleaded. She mentioned three times a hearing due later that month, at which Di Matteo was to testify about Judge Borsellino's murder.

At the hearing, Di Matteo refused to talk. On 14 December, he reported Giuseppe's disappearance – three weeks after the boy had vanished. But when police asked to see the first note sent by the kidnappers, his mother said the grandfather had burnt it in a fit of rage.

Giuseppe quickly realised that he had been kidnapped and that it was because of his father's testimony. The boy argued with his guards that he could not be blamed for his father's actions, but they paid no attention.

Brusca ordered all those who approached him to wear balaclavas. 'We don't know whether the boy will go back alive,' he explained. The balaclavas were also aimed at keeping the guards' identities secret from each other in case one of them should ever inform. Brusca himself didn't bother to wear one; he didn't show himself to Giuseppe and all the guards knew the kidnapping was his responsibility.

Brusca showed little interest in the hostage's plight. It was enough for him to be told that the guards, as he said later, 'kept Giuseppe in good conditions, made sure he didn't lack anything, and didn't wall him up alive'.

A few weeks after his abduction, Brusca drove Giuseppe in a station-wagon – the boy was made to lie in the boot, his hands and feet tied together – to a new hideout, a farm off the Palermo–Catania motorway. In a 15-foot-square room on the ground floor, Giuseppe was attached with a rope his captors called 'the noose' to an iron ring sunk into the wall. The room's steel door, which had been made specially, could be opened only from the outside and had a small opening through which food was passed. He was never allowed out of the room, except to go to the lavatory. The jailers took to calling him 'the little dog' or 'the bastard's son'.

One of the kidnappers, Michele Traina, filmed the hostage regularly. Brusca was particularly proud of Traina, an ex-thief who although not a mafioso 'has the law of silence in his veins', according to the boss. Told that he might one day be freed and return home to his parents, Giuseppe obeyed his captors and willingly agreed to be photographed and filmed and to write letters to his family; they were all sent to his relatives and were the only way he could communicate with them.

Brusca chose Giuseppe's grandfather, a farmer, as his negotiation partner for good reason: 'I knew he would have given his soul for the boy,' Brusca said. As the kidnapping stretched over several days, then weeks, then months, Brusca became the father of a baby son by his girlfriend. Fatherhood did nothing to soften his treatment of Giuseppe.

At dusk one evening the grandfather was approached on his farm by a stranger, a young man who told him he must go and speak with his son. 'Tell your son that if you want to save the boy he must withdraw everything he's said,' the stranger said. A month later, again at dusk, the stranger made another visit. He showed Giuseppe's grandfather a note in the boy's handwriting: 'Grandfather, help me, go and see my father and talk to him. Convince him he must save me.' The stranger told the grandfather to 'stop your son's mouth'.

As Brusca had predicted, the grandfather did all he could to persuade his son to withdraw all of his testimony, something Di Matteo refused to do. The grandfather even bit Di Matteo's ear in a fit of fury. Brusca told the old man afterwards: 'You must have a word in your son's ear, not eat it.' In desperation, Giuseppe's grandfather sent word that he was willing to take his place if this could save the boy. 'Kill me, not my son or my grandson,' he said in a message to the kidnappers. The offer was rejected.

Through a friendly mafioso, he appealed to Provenzano. Learning that Bagarella was behind the kidnapping, Provenzano, the anger in his voice barely suppressed, asked him to consider releasing the boy.

Bagarella retorted: 'We've thought it all out. Let Di Matteo do his duty towards his son and we'll be at his disposal.'

But Bagarella hadn't 'thought it all out'. At his home, a seventh-floor flat in central Palermo, his wife Vincenzina, Riina's sister, reprimanded him again and again about the kidnapping, which she heard about on the television news. She wanted a child and refused to accept his assurances that the boy would come to no harm. 'How can you expect God to send us a child if you do these things?' she asked him.

Bagarella and Vincenzina had been engaged for 15 years before they married, during which time he was arrested several times, several uncles and cousins of hers were killed and two of her brothers were sentenced to life in jail. Marriage brought her little happiness as she became increasingly depressed by the terror campaign Bagarella and the Corleonesi were waging against the state; her brother's decision to defect also weighed heavily on her. When she failed to conceive, she saw it as divine retribution for Giuseppe's kidnapping.

Vincenzina hanged herself in May 1994. It is not known whether she committed suicide alone or whether she asked Bagarella to help her die. He spirited her out of their apartment with the help of three friends, taking the lift when no one was around. He then drove her body away in a car and buried it in an unmarked grave. He kept the location secret.

Di Matteo showed no sign of wanting to 'do his duty' as the kidnappers demanded. His son remained a prisoner. In the spring of 1994, as the weather became warmer, Giuseppe was allowed an occasional shower. No one bothered to cut his hair and it grew long and straggly. In the early summer, as the olive harvest approached, the owner of the farm worried that the peasants he would hire to do the work might discover Giuseppe's prison, so he was moved to another hideout.

From then on, Giuseppe was moved again and again, sometimes only spending two weeks in the same place. Each time he made the journey in a car boot, tied up and with a hood over his head, a separate car travelling ahead in case of a police road-block. One prison was a bathroom in a villa near a pizzeria outside Castellamare del Golfo in western Sicily – the window was sealed and the door replaced by one made of steel. One of his captors later described why he thought this was a good location for the boy: 'He could have a shower because he was locked in the bathroom, so he could do whatever he wanted. He could go to the toilet . . . as far as hygiene is concerned, I mean.' Giuseppe had no one to talk to. The kidnappers communicated with him only through handwritten notes, afraid he might recognise their voices if he were ever freed.

At the end of that summer, Bagarella promised two other bosses that Giuseppe would come to no harm – as long as he was still a minor. Bagarella told them: 'Not even a hair on the head of this boy must be touched. If I don't kill his father, we'll see what we should do about the boy when he's 18 to 20 years old. Not even a hair must be touched because we're not barbarians, it's the others who are barbarians . . .'

Shortly before Christmas, Giuseppe was moved again. The brick-layer Giuseppe Monticciolo, who was being tested as a possible mafia recruit and known as 'the German' because of the precise way he carried out orders, tied up Giuseppe's wrists and fore-arms with sellotape – his hands behind his back – put a hood over his head and lifted him into the boot of a car. During the night-time journey to the new prison, Giuseppe cried because the sellotape cut into his flesh; he shouted out that the tape was pointless, given that he was locked up in the boot and could not flee. But it was only when the kidnappers arrived at the new hideout that they took off the tape.

Giuseppe was escorted into a house and locked up in a small, bare and windowless room with just a mattress on the floor. The door had a spy-hole in it but a rag was hung over it to stop him seeing out. Monticciolo tied Giuseppe with a rope to a hook in the wall. 'He's a lively boy who's already a mafioso, he won't waste the slightest chance to escape,' Brusca had warned the guard. As he watched Giuseppe, Monticciolo thought how right Brusca was:

> I'd never seen someone so dignified as that emaciated boy after so many deprivations . . . What I saw before me, tied up and covered up, was a mafioso in the most 'noble' sense that I attributed to that word at the time. Without a complaint and without deigning to talk to us or ask us any questions, he let himself be locked up in his cell without protest. And he sat down immediately on his bed, forgetting our presence a moment later. He didn't move even one muscle when I suddenly opened the spy-hole to check on him.

The boy was stunned when, not long after the door was locked, the guard Traina asked if he wanted a pizza and what kind he would like – it was the first time a kidnapper had spoken to him, never mind to ask such a thing.

'What do you mean, are you kidding?' Giuseppe said, adding immediately afterwards: 'Any pizza's fine.'

The next morning, Brusca's brother Enzo caught sight of Giuseppe. 'His clothes weren't very decent and his long hair looked awful,' he said later. He bought some clothes for the boy and cut his hair – Giuseppe's first haircut in a year. The shorn hair was then burnt to avoid leaving any trace behind.

Over the months that followed, Brusca kept up the pressure on Giuseppe's family, sending video tapes to show, as he claimed, that 'the boy wants for nothing'.

But Di Matteo, far from going back on his testimony, wanted

to take the law into his own hands and fight back. Brusca learnt that the supergrass had repeatedly given his police bodyguards the slip and travelled to Sicily to seek his friends' help in launching an offensive against him. Two other informers, Brusca learnt, were also plotting against him.

'I was starting to lose my lucidity. I had the state against me, the supergrasses were organising themselves against me behind the state's back, and Bagarella and Messina Denaro had left me all the burden of the kidnapping,' Brusca said.

All Bagarella did was ask Brusca repeatedly as the months passed: 'What's the news?'

'We're hoping we'll get good results,' Brusca replied.

'But why don't you put an end to it?' Bagarella said – he meant killing the boy.

'No, I don't feel ready to take that step yet,' Brusca stalled.

After two more moves, Giuseppe was taken in August 1995 to a house near Brusca's fiefdom of San Giuseppe Jato, where a specially built bunker awaited him. Arriving at night as usual, the boy was led to a walk-in cupboard. Using a remote control, his kidnappers activated a hydraulic lift which lowered part of the floor down to the cellar, which had been dug out under the house with spades and shovels. There were two rooms measuring 16 by 32 feet, each with a lavatory. The two windows were sealed off and the bunker was equipped with a rudimentary ventilation system to compensate for the lack of fresh air.

The kidnappers walked Giuseppe through the first room and into the second, which was to be his cell. It had a bed with a metal frame, whose four legs were cemented into the floor. The door, which had a small opening, closed on the boy. No sound filtered into the room.

Giuseppe was left alone for most of the day and no one both-ered to guard him at night. Brusca ordered Vincenzo Chiodo, his chief jailer: 'You mustn't open the door, ever. Even if you see he's dying, don't ever open the door on your own.' Chiodo, who wore an overall and a balaclava to prevent Giuseppe recognising him, at first told the boy to face the wall when he passed food to him through the opening in the door, which had a small shelf on the inside.

After a few days, Giuseppe tried to talk to Chiodo. 'Compared to where I was before, you're much more . . . It's obvious you have a family of your own,' the boy said.

Chiodo's only reply was to ban Giuseppe from talking to him.

The bunker was damp, so much so that Giuseppe's blanket became covered in mould and his captors replaced it. They also gave him a small camp stove, which he used to warm milk. Occasionally, he was granted permission to change his underwear. He kept his bunker as clean as he could, putting his rubbish in bags which he passed through the door to his jailer.

The kidnappers never gave up trying to make Di Matteo withdraw his testimony. More photographs of Giuseppe were sent to his grandfather. In one letter, the boy was made to ask his grandfather to kill his uncles as the price for his liberation. Later, he asked one of his guards whether this had been done.

'Yes,' the guard lied.

Hampered by lack of cooperation from Giuseppe's family, the police found it impossible to track him down. Vigilante security guards did catch the jailer Chiodo as he prepared to set fire to someone's property; but he was detained only briefly. The police searched his home soon afterwards, but his role in the kidnapping was not discovered.

A worried Chiodo told Brusca's brother Enzo of the two incidents. Enzo told him: 'Be careful, because they're sure to be watching you now. Be careful; remember the responsibility weighing on your shoulders, because if they discover the boy or something else there'll be more uproar than after the Falcone murder.'

Chiodo asked Enzo repeatedly whether the hostage would be freed or not, but every time the reply was that only Brusca could take that decision. Later, Chiodo found out that Giuseppe had recognised both the Brusca brothers; he had called them by their first names and asked them to take their balaclavas off. For the kidnappers, this meant it would be almost impossible for Giuseppe to be freed. The boy had virtually signed his own death warrant.

Over a meal in early January 1996, two of the kidnappers joked about killing Giuseppe, mainly to scare a third, who protested: 'No, it's not right. You've got to be kidding. Let me eat.'

Guarding Giuseppe became such a burden for 'the German' Monticciolo that he pressed Brusca to eliminate the boy. At lunchtime on 11 January 1996, Monticciolo spoke at length to Brusca about the problems and risks involved in looking after Giuseppe; he was worried that the police might follow him, he said.

'Let's get out of it, let's get out of it,' Monticciolo said, using the mafia phrase which meant committing a murder.

'We'll see. Let's be careful, but getting out of it isn't possible any more,' Brusca replied.

Monticciolo insisted, saying that keeping Giuseppe alive had become too dangerous. The town of San Giuseppe Jato near the bunker was full of police patrols; it was high time they got rid of the hostage. Brusca retorted that the kidnapping must continue; he still hoped to make Di Matteo withdraw his testimony.

As the two men talked, the main evening news bulletin started on the television. The news reader said that Brusca had been given a life sentence for the murder of the tax-collector Ignazio Salvo. The silence in the room became 'deathly quiet', Monticciolo recalled later, adding: 'In a fraction of a second, I saw in front of my eyes mountains of corpses which were slowly dissolving in sulphuric acid.'

As a detailed account of the verdict followed, the boss became violently red in the face but he spoke calmly: 'That cuckold Di Matteo will understand what he gained by having me condemned to life in jail. I don't want any trace to be left of this bastard's son.'

'What?' Monticciolo said mechanically.

'Get rid of that little dog, immediately,' Brusca said.

'But . . .'

'Kill that bastard's son,' Brusca said simply. He stared hard at Monticciolo. 'If you're not capable of doing it, I'll come and do it myself.' Knowing Brusca, Monticciolo took this to mean that Brusca would have killed the hostage first and then him and the other jailers. Brusca added: 'I don't want even his bones to be found and I want it done this very evening.'

At the house where Giuseppe was hidden, Brusca's brother Enzo announced to the jailer Chiodo: 'We have to kill him.'

Chiodo didn't bat an eyelid. 'Who has to do it?' he asked.

'You do it, my son,' Enzo said. 'That way you'll become a real man of honour.'

This would be his first killing but Chiodo didn't hesitate. His experience so far was limited to helping make bodies 'vanish', but he had learnt the lesson Enzo had drilled into him many times: 'Never, ever get cold feet.' Chiodo didn't even stop to think that Giuseppe was just a boy; nor did he think of what his own children might think of him. 'It wasn't as if you could say no at a time like that,' Chiodo explained later. 'I was a soldier, I executed orders.'

The three kidnappers began by fetching two ten-gallon containers of acid which Brusca kept at a nearby house, and an empty 44-gallon drum. They placed rags on the floor before dragging the biggest of the drums into the house as quietly as possible to avoid being overheard by Giuseppe or anyone passing outside. Then, using rags to muffle the noise as much as he could, Chiodo cut the lid off the top of the drum with a mallet and chisel.

Shortly after he completed the task, Monticciolo returned with two 20-litre plastic containers filled with acid.

The kidnappers, still as silently as possible, then carried the drum and the containers of acid into the walk-in cupboard and took them down in the lift. They placed the drum and the containers by the door to Giuseppe's cell.

Enzo and Chiodo, wearing balaclavas, handed a sheet of paper to Giuseppe through the opening in the door. 'Write anything you want to say to your family – persuade them!' the jailers said.

Chiodo ordered Giuseppe to write to his grandfather, telling him that everyone had abandoned him and that he had tried to commit suicide, but had been saved.

Chiodo told Giuseppe he would be back soon to fetch the letter and went back up in the lift to the kitchen on the floor above. Chiodo grilled some meat for the kidnappers' dinner and the three of them enjoyed a relaxed meal.

The meal over, Enzo Brusca walked outside to cut a piece of rope and tied a knot in it to form a noose.

The kidnappers then took the lift down to the bunker. Chiodo ordered Giuseppe to pass his letter to him through the opening in the door and then told the boy he and his two friends were about to enter his cell.

'Stand with your face to the wall!' Chiodo shouted.

Giuseppe, perhaps thinking this was a routine check of the windows – the jailors regularly verified whether he had tried to force them open – did as he was told and stood by his bed in a corner.

Chiodo slipped a balaclava over his head, wary that the boy would be alarmed if he saw all three jailers not bothering to hide their faces. Chiodo then made to open the steel door but the bunker was so damp the door had become almost rusty, and Chiodo had to strain against it.

He walked into the cell, followed by the other two. Monticciolo had seen Giuseppe so rarely he was struck by how feeble he was. He had never been outside for a walk during the whole of the two years and three months he had spent as a hostage. The only time he had breathed fresh air had been through a hood as he was moved from one prison to another, tied up and locked in a car boot. He was so weak that he remained completely passive throughout what followed.

Chiodo ordered him to stand facing the wall with his arms raised, and held the noose ready while his accomplices each seized the boy by a shoulder.

'Are you taking me home?' Giuseppe asked.

Coming up behind him, Chiodo slipped the noose around his neck and pulled on it so sharply that the boy lost his balance and fell backwards. The jailers quickly stretched Giuseppe out on his back, his arms folded across his chest. Enzo brought the full weight of his body to rest on Giuseppe's arms, crushing him.

As Monticciolo approached to place himself on Giuseppe's legs, he said to the boy: 'I'm sorry but your father's behaving like a cuckold.'

Enzo too apologised to his victim: 'I would have looked after you like the apple of my eye if your father hadn't been a cuckold. I'm sorry . . .'

The jailers found there was hardly any need to hold Giuseppe down while Chiodo strangled him. He didn't resist; his only reaction was to gaze around the cell before a single, slow spasm shook his body. 'He no longer had the strength to breathe, he was sinking slowly, slowly,' Monticciolo said later.

The killers waited for Chiodo to finish his job. Enzo placed his head against Giuseppe's chest several times to check if he was dead and each time the boss heard the heartbeat become more and more faint.

Chiodo felt himself weakening; his legs started to shake – it was, after all, his first killing. He asked Monticciolo to take over. As he walked out of the cell, he saw Monticciolo pull hard on the rope, stamping heavily on the noose to make it even tighter round Giuseppe's neck.

Chiodo took a few gulps of fresh air outside and then took the lift back down to the bunker. 'Give me the rope back,' he said to Monticciolo, who was still pulling on it.

'It's OK, forget it,' Monticciolo replied.

Enzo Brusca testified later: 'At the end I saw two tears come out of Giuseppe's eyes. It seemed as if it took an eternity for him to die. I don't know, maybe it was a few minutes, but I don't know how many minutes it lasted . . . Anyway, it was all over.'

The jailers checked thoroughly that Giuseppe was dead; they had to be absolutely certain because if his body was still prone to spasms it might splash them with acid once they had submerged it. It didn't take long to make sure the body was lifeless.

Chiodo testified: 'The boy didn't understand anything, because he wasn't expecting it, he wasn't expecting anything and then, by that time, the boy no longer had the reaction of a normal boy, he seemed soft. Even if he wasn't short of food, he wasn't short of anything, but . . . I don't know, the lack of freedom, let's say the boy was very soft, he was tender, he looked as if he was made of butter.'

Chiodo added he was certain that death had been a liberation for Giuseppe 'given what the boy had been through . . . what he went through in there, even if he was treated well by me, because he lived in those conditions, locked up in there, not knowing whether it was a sunny day, whether the sun existed, what the sky might be like'.

The jailers left the body where it was and went into the next room to pour the acid, slowly and carefully, into the drum. The small room stank with the vapours from the acid. That task completed, they returned to the cell and stripped the body naked. Chiodo then grabbed hold of it by the legs, while Enzo and Monticciolo each took an arm. They carried it to the drum and gingerly lowered it into the liquid. Once the body was submerged, they took the lift to the floor above, leaving an opening in the floor of the walk-in cupboard to let the fumes escape.

They walked out of the house into the open air. Enzo and Monticciolo each embraced Chiodo and kissed him on the cheeks. They congratulated him on a job well done. To Chiodo, it felt as if they were wishing him a merry Christmas. Still on edge, he soothed his nerves by smoking a couple of cigarettes and chatting to his accomplices.

After a while, Enzo turned to Chiodo: 'Go and see how things are going, check whether the acid's working or not.'

Ever the good soldier, Chiodo did as he was told. He took a stick with him and, braving the stench of the acid that had eaten away at the corpse and made the air in the bunker impossible to breathe, he looked into the drum. Stirring the acid with his stick, all he saw that remained of the body was an arm and part of the back. Chiodo did not stay to take a second look; anxious to escape the vapours, he quickly returned to the others.

The next morning, he went down to the bunker to again check the liquid in the drum. It had turned a dark colour. Giuseppe's body was completely liquified. The only trace of his death which remained was the noose, which the acid had failed to destroy. With a tin can, Chiodo painstakingly scooped the acid out of the barrel and poured it into the containers, emptying them in the field above, which would later be ploughed.

When Chiodo showed Enzo the noose, the latter said with a smile: 'The acid hasn't done anything to the rope, keep it as a trophy!'

But Chiodo burnt it instead, along with all other traces of Giuseppe's kidnapping: his clothes, the mattress and the drum itself, to ensure no acid would be found on it. With an axe, Chiodo hacked to pieces the metal frame on which the mattress had rested.

For Brusca, Giuseppe's kidnapping and murder was the first sign of the Corleonesi's decline: 'It was the first symptom that we were losing control of the situation and that, in the attempt to get back in control, we became locked in a spiral and never got out.'

In his memoirs, Brusca admitted that he did not hesitate to order the death of a 14-year-old boy, a crime which achieved nothing, as his father never did withdraw his confession. 'I became "the monster" for having committed that crime. Perhaps I wouldn't have become that if I'd killed only Judge Falcone and his wife. I'm perfectly aware that an act of that kind cannot be forgiven nor forgotten,' Brusca wrote.

He refused to ask for forgiveness for Giuseppe's murder. He wrote: 'Does repenting for such actions mean anything? I don't know. Does asking for forgiveness mean anything? I don't know ... Is there any point in feeling ashamed when you've ordered the death of a boy who could have been your son? I don't know.'

All he could do now was to reveal in as much detail as possible 'the background to that tragedy. More than that is not humanly possible.'

Testifying before the prosecutor Judge Alfonso Sabella after he turned state's evidence following his arrest, Brusca said he had acted 'on an impulse' in condemning Giuseppe to death. 'If I'd had a moment to think about it, more calmly, it's possible he might still be alive.'

Judge Sabella pointed out that several bosses had argued that Giuseppe should be eliminated, so how could Brusca have decided 'on an impulse'?

Brusca replied: 'Judge Sabella, anything I say to you today would make me look like a hypocrite. Believe it or not, I can say that before God I've thought about it, I've had misgivings . . . At the same time, I want to add that I get hugely annoyed, it bothers me, when other men of honour justify their collaboration with the state by blaming the killing of Giuseppe Di Matteo. Those who name him have committed crimes too, some bigger and some smaller than those I committed.'

For all Brusca's protestations, the truth was that even if Di Matteo had retracted his testimony, his son's life would not have been spared. The mafia was thirsty for vendetta, and as Brusca admitted there was never more than 'one hope in a million' that the boy would be released.

To a shocked Judge Sabella, Brusca repeatedly insisted that he had not murdered a child: 'Giuseppe was 12 when he was kidnapped, but he was 14 when he died. He wasn't a *bambino* (child) any more.'

None of the other kidnappers ever expressed any real regret for what they had done. They all insisted they had 'treated Giuseppe well'. Chiodo, who also defected, claimed that he had treated him 'very humanely' but saw no contradiction in admitting the kidnapping had been 'a non-stop nightmare' for the boy. It was only after he turned informer that Chiodo apologised to his own children for not stopping to think of them when he agreed to kill the hostage.

The defector Di Matteo lost a son but none of his mafioso mentality. He blamed his relatives for Giuseppe's death. They should have threatened Brusca's family immediately after he had turned state's evidence, he said. 'As soon as I started to collaborate, someone should have gone to Brusca's mother and warned her: an eye for an eye, a tooth for a tooth. We didn't do it and the one who paid for that was the most innocent of us all.'

A judge severely criticised the Di Matteo family's attitude towards the kidnapping as 'static, fatalistic, fence-sitting . . . the expression of a backward-looking, mistrustful environment impregnated with a mafioso subculture'. The family failed to give to the police the messages and videotapes they received and failed to supply clues which could have helped investigators save Giuseppe. 'Instead, mafia justice, which they appealed to, showed its most insensible and ferocious face,' the judge said.

As Brusca concluded in his memoirs, referring to a photograph that was widely published in Italian newspapers after Giuseppe's murder: 'I understand perfectly well that, even in 50 years' time, the photograph of that kid on horseback who died in that way will symbolise Cosa Nostra much more efficiently than a hundred books.'

6
The Mafia Turns 'Silent'

1995–2002

'Enough Massacres; Enough Murders' – Provenzano's Rule

In his attempt to win control of the mafia, Bagarella sought to exploit his family tie to Riina, his brother-in-law, by taking Riina's eldest son under his wing. Giovanni Riina closely resembled his father, who had taught him target shooting when he was still a child.

In early 1995, when Giovanni was 19, Bagarella persuaded his nephew that he was being followed by two men from Corleone who were planning to kidnap him, and sent him to map out the routines of his supposed kidnappers. Bagarella made clear he would take on the problem himself. 'I want to deal with this lot; I've got a few friends in Corleone,' Bagarella told Giovanni.

When all was ready, Giovanni gave just one blunt order: 'Break their balls.'

One late afternoon in January 1995, a death squad which included 'the German' Monticciolo, one of Giuseppe Di Matteo's kidnappers, and the mafioso Leonardo Vitale, set out for the clothes shop where their victim worked. Monticciolo later told the story:

There was so little traffic in Corleone that we had no difficulty getting to the shop. We got out of the car and, like normal clients who had left things a bit late, we walked into the shop shortly before sunset. Lots of other customers were there buying things. Like every time that I had a precise objective, they looked blurred to me – the way people say an eagle sees when he dives down on his prey. Shifting a couple of obstacles out of my way, I started to shoot at him from less than a metre away, followed immediately by Vitale. That rosary of death seemed to be without end, but I was counting. Indifferent to the panic and the shouts that I could hear around me, I continued to shoot, walking close to him. A handful of centimetres from the head of that being who a few moments earlier was still a man, I fired two shots into the head at close range, to give him the *coup de grace* and then slowly I turned to get away. I'd carried out the order I'd been given.

The shopkeeper's sister and her husband were murdered a month later, shot as they drove through Corleone; their three-year-old son, who had been sleeping on the back seat, survived unharmed. Celebrating the murders, Bagarella told Monticciolo: 'I'm sure that this time, they've understood who's in charge in Corleone.' Once again, the Corleonesi had killed in their home town, brazenly showing their faces as they did so because they were confident that the law of silence would continue to hold. No witness would dare to accuse them.

There is no doubt that the idea of kidnapping Giovanni had never even crossed the mind of the victims; Monticciolo speculated that the real reason for the murders was simply that the shopkeeper and his sister were cousins of the supergrass Contorno.

That summer, Bagarella asked Giovanni, still a teenager, to come and see a murder carried out. The intended victim had been sentenced to death because he wanted to avenge his slain father and also because he refused to share his crime profits with bosses. Giovanni did much more than just stand by and watch. According to informers, he first kicked the victim, then placed a noose around his neck and pulled. The man's body was dissolved in acid. Giovanni's fellow-killers judged it a promising beginning; he showed initiative, kept his calm and didn't avert his gaze when he strangled his victim. They congratulated him on his performance; he'd done 'very well indeed', one mafioso said. A proud Giovanni boasted about his first killing to a friend.

When Monticciolo met Giovanni shortly afterwards, the latter rushed up and told him excitedly, before he even had time to get out of his car: 'I strangled him myself, with my own hands, while Uncle (Bagarella) crushed his head under his feet. The cuckold even had the cheek to ask why we were killing him. Isn't that true, Uncle?'

'My nephew has become a man!' Bagarella exclaimed. 'He killed that dog on his own and you all saw how he did it, without trembling or hesitating.'

But Bagarella's attempt to use the Riina name as he lobbied for command came to nothing, as he was arrested two days after the murder. Two drug traffickers who knew his address had tipped off the police shortly after they were caught.

The arrest of Bagarella neatly rid Provenzano of his only rival and he was acclaimed as the new godfather. Age, disease and a lifetime on the run were beginning to take their toll on the 62-year-old Provenzano. Balding, with short, greying hair, he was a little stooped and walked with difficulty. When he went to the bathroom, he often shouted out in pain because of trouble with his prostate. A devotee of homeopathic medicine, he followed a rigid diet of mainly grilled meat, fish and vegetables.

But despite his age and health problems, Provenzano was now firmly in charge. He was strong enough to ditch Riina's terror campaign and launch a new strategy with the aim of ensuring minimum risk and maximum profit for the fraternity. His *consigliere* (adviser) Lipari suggested 'an image-makeover' to Provenzano: the new godfather should 'make himself look as pure as a virgin again because the bombings and killings had left him aching all over'. Lipari argued such a transformation would preserve the godfather from arrest and would help him in his business dealings.

Lipari could speak very freely to Provenzano. A former surveyor for the motorways, who first worked for the veteran Badalamenti, he had switched to the Corleonesi and risen to oversee Provenzano's links to both businessmen and politicians. Lipari became a millionaire by registering Provenzano's wealth under his name but he grew rich on his own account too, spending his wealth on yachts and a collection of vintage cars. Provenzano and Lipari were so close that, together with their partners, they went on a short cruise sailing across the Mediterranean to the Tunisian coast – on a yacht the godfather had bought from his *consigliere*. The two men also saw *The Godfather III* together at a cinema in Palermo.

Lipari was one of several advisers outside the mafia whom Provenzano relied on: businessmen, doctors, lawyers – all professionals unknown to the police. He often kept their identities secret even from his closest lieutenants. The search for such professionals stretched as far as Brussels; in one bugged conversation, mafiosi discussed the need to recruit trusted associates there so that they could divert subsidies from the European Union.

Speaking to a small group of bosses, Provenzano explained that under his rule, the mafia would seek to become invisible over the next five to seven years. This, he said, would allow for things to calm down enough to enable it to make money and find new allies.

'We mustn't make any noise,' Provenzano kept repeating. When one boss near Palermo carried out one murder after another, getting rid of enemies on his territory, Provenzano at first gave him the vague instruction: 'Follow the rules.' When the murders continued, Provenzano summoned the boss again, this time telling him: 'Look, you have to understand that I rule with my brain.' The murders stopped. As Giuffrè explained: 'The point was not to cause a stir, so that investigators would leave us alone. We had to do things quietly.'

No killing could take place save in exceptional cases and then only with Provenzano's blessing. Fewer bodies would mean fewer stories in the press and as a result public opinion and the government would care less about the mafia. True to his nickname 'the Accountant', Provenzano would coldly decide according to a mathematical maxim whether or not to allow a murder: 'We have to evaluate how much trouble this person causes alive or dead,' he would say. If the person's death caused more trouble than if he was allowed to live, then he would be spared. If the opposite was the case, he must be eliminated. When taking such a decision, Provenzano also liked to quote another simple motto: 'Someone who betrays once can betray twice.'

Discretion must also be the rule for relations with politicians. Provenzano urged that he and the other bosses, rather than flagging their support for certain politicians as they had done in the past, should now take a step back. The sponsorship of a big name had too often become known to the politicians' rivals, who then made huge capital out of it. Far better, Provenzano recommended to general approval, to forge relations through an intermediary with a clean criminal record.

Provenzano's change of tack was typical of the mafia's nature, what Judge Falcone called 'its capacity to change yet remain true to itself . . . there is *always* a new mafia ready to replace the old'. His leadership marked a complete break with Riina's. Turning his back on his predecessor's onslaught against the state, Provenzano based his new strategy on the *pax mafiosa* of old, the peaceful co-existence with the state respected by the mentor of his youth, Corleone's Dr Navarra. Provenzano's mafia would enforce its will and accumulate wealth without littering the streets with 'distinguished corpses'.

'*Basta* (Enough) massacres; *basta* murders. We have to set up businesses. There are so many legal ways of making money,' Provenzano told young soldiers. Under his rule, bosses infiltrated firms directly, taking shares in 'clean' companies to help the mafia become invisible. Bringing in vast sums, Provenzano imposed a 2 per cent levy on all businesses; even those headed by mafiosi or close to the brotherhood.

The godfather banned the use of explosives and arson attacks to force businessmen or shopkeepers into line if they refused to pay protection money. From now on, such conflicts would be resolved by a new 'complaints desk', managed by a friendly mafioso in an anonymous block of flats. A long procession of small and big entrepreneurs called on him, invariably protesting that they had 'always been available', meaning that they had never hesitated to pay up in the past. One entrepreneur complained that he had already reached an agreement with a boss, but now he was being asked for money by another mafioso. Another protested that he was heavily in debt and pleaded for permission to suspend his payments.

The speed with which the mafia judge pronounced his verdicts – the ruling was almost always immediate – impressed the police who monitored the complaints with a hidden camera and microphone; they were used to the more snail-like pace of the Italian judiciary. But dealing quickly with so many appeals prompted one mafioso to complain like any stressed office worker: 'Why can't we just have a bit of peace? First they want this, then they want that . . . '

Provenzano amazed even bosses with the precautions he took on the run. For Brusca, Provenzano was 'caution personified'. He shunned mobile phones, which could reveal his whereabouts. Unlike other men of honour, who would sooner or later leave their safe houses and simply avoid busy streets where they might be recognised, Provenzano 'was capable of staying walled up alive for months and months. When we'd see him again he'd be as white as a sheet.' He thought nothing of spending several nights in a row in a sleeping bag if he thought it necessary. He gradually reduced the number and size of meetings he took part in, preferring to see just one boss at a time. Occasionally, he travelled in an ambulance to ensure no one saw or troubled him.

When Provenzano did have to go to an appointment in a remote area, he would get up at 3 a.m. and have his henchman Giuffrè and his driver take him to the meeting place half an hour before dawn. Provenzano and his escort would then keep watch until the time for the appointment came, ready to flee if anything unexpected happened.

Despite Provenzano's precautions, police came close to catching him in 1995 when a supergrass gave them advance notice of a meeting he was due to hold with other bosses at a farmhouse near Mezzojuso east of Corleone. The informer went to the meeting and spent ten hours with Provenzano. But the officers failed to intervene, officially because they did not have time to set up a proper security cordon. A year later the supergrass was murdered just as he was about to enter the witness protection programme.

Provenzano trained his family well. When police started following his eldest son Angelo in the hope he would lead them to the godfather, Angelo soon realised he was being watched. Unknown to the police, he took down the number plates of cars he found suspicious. With a few telephone calls, the Corleonesi discovered that the cars were registered with the interior ministry in Rome, with rental agencies, or that the registrations corresponded to cars that had long since been destroyed.

To keep in safe contact with bosses, only a couple of whom knew where he lived, Provenzano devised an efficient, private postal service. He would write a letter on an electric typewriter, using numbers from 1 – for the godfather himself – to 164 to stand for the names of bosses, *consiglieri*, soldiers and other associates. For any other names or words he wanted to conceal, he used a simple code similar to one used by the ancient Roman emperor Julius Caesar, in which the number 4 stood for the letter 'A', 5 for 'B' and so on. Once he had finished writing, he would fold the letter up again and again until it was no bigger than the tip of his thumb; he would then sellotape it together, with only the number of the person it was addressed to visible. The tiny package would then be passed from hand to hand until it reached its destination.

The godfather adopted a humble, pious tone in his letters. He almost always started by thanking God for his good health, often quoted from the Bible and ended by blessing the person he was writing to. Provenzano had become increasingly devout over the years; he read from the Bible every day, marking passages that were important to him or copying out extracts into a notebook, a kind of spiritual diary. Even in hiding, Provenzano had a priest as his spiritual father. Perhaps influenced by this cleric, Provenzano went as far as to consider the idea of creating a 'new' mafia which would embrace mostly Catholic moral and religious principles, but the idea came to nothing.

Provenzano was by no means the only mafioso who saw no conflict between his criminal career and his religion. Men of honour placed themselves under the protection of God, a figure who in their warped faith always forgave them every crime they committed; pseudo-devotion to Catholic beliefs was their way of keeping their consciences clean. One mafioso who had confessed to a hundred murders explained, when confronted by an investigator who asked him how he could reconcile his crimes with his Catholic faith: 'There's no contradiction because I've never killed for a personal motive. It's always been because bosses ordered me; I'm like a soldier who obeys orders.'

Provenzano rarely gave anyone orders, asking for some instead. 'I can't give orders to anyone and I'm looking for someone who can give them to me. What I can say is: "in your place I'd do this" but not: "you must do it",' he wrote in one letter. 'God willing, I want to be a servant; give me orders,' he said in another.

Nor did he like to take a clear-cut stand. In one letter, he commented on a boss who reported having 'a good-level political contact who could allow us to manage lots of big works'. Provenzano, his spelling and grammatical mistakes apparently a deliberate attempt to confuse anyone who intercepted his letters, wrote that he didn't know enough about the politician to make a decision on using him or not. 'Because in today's world, you can't trust anyone, they might be crooks? Could they be cops? Could they be infiltrators? And could they be naive people? And could they be great schemers?' Provenzano wrote.

The godfather never even hinted at violence. 'Common sense must prevail,' he recommended vaguely. For bosses used to Riina's dictatorship, the lack of clear guidance from Provenzano was baffling and frustrating. He sounded more like an eloquent priest than a godfather, as in this passage: 'I ask you to be calm and honest, correct and coherent; learn to put to good use the hardship you have experienced; don't disbelieve everything that people say to you, nor should you believe in everything they say; always seek to find out the truth before speaking and remember that one piece of evidence is never enough to be certain of something, in fact you need three pieces of evidence.'

Brusca Confesses

In the spring of 1996 police arrested a Palermo boss and, after decrypting the telephone numbers in his diary, established that one was Brusca's mobile phone. The next morning, Renato Cortese, a senior member of the Palermo police unit charged with hunting bosses, intercepted the calls Brusca made and tracked the mobile phone's signal down to the area around Agrigento.

A tall, soft-spoken figure with a thick beard, who smoked Tuscan cigars, the 32-year-old Cortese was a newcomer to Sicily. Born in a small coastal village in Calabria in southern Italy, he studied law in Rome and had toyed with the idea of becoming a lawyer before joining the police instead in 1992. He was training in Rome when he heard of Falcone's assassination; the killing horrified him and that summer, when he was sent to Palermo, he was elated at what he saw as his chance to help fight the mafia. Not wanting to worry his mother, Cortese told her that he would be teaching at the police training school. But as soon as he reached Palermo, he asked to join the flying squad and spent his first months patrolling the city day and night.

Two years after his arrival, Cortese was transferred to the 40-strong unit hunting bosses. Coming from southern Italy gave him a head start on his colleagues from the north; he soon became skilled at interpreting bugged conversations, even when men of honour were whispering to each other in the dialect of Palermo or of other Sicilian provinces. Cortese relished his job. Married with a son, he put up with 24-hour shifts and spending Christmas and New Year not with his family but out on the job or in his office, where he liked to work with the lights dimmed and classical music playing. He took to wearing dark glasses to hide the bags under his eyes resulting from sleepless nights.

Cortese was understandably reluctant to talk about the risks he ran. 'What can I say? I do think about the danger involved. I think about it sometimes but it doesn't change anything. The job's got to be done. And I'm still here, aren't I? I don't go around with bodyguards. This is my only escort, see?' Cortese said when asked by the author about the dangers he faced, reaching out to grab the .357 Magnum ordnance revolver he kept by the keyboard of his computer.

When Cortese caught up with Brusca, the boss had been spending the past month in a villa near Agrigento's waterfront. Both the Brusca brothers and their families lived in the house: Brusca with his girlfriend and their five-year-old son, and his brother Enzo with his wife and daughter. Incredibly, Brusca kept the boy's existence a secret from his mother, his mafioso father and the mafia; he had helped kill or seen killed too many relatives of mafiosi not to worry that talking of his son could one day put the boy's life at risk.

The murder of the teenage Giuseppe Di Matteo out of the way, Brusca was busy preparing an £800,000 shipment of cocaine, heroin and hashish to America. He often used his mobile phone because he needed to finish collecting the funds necessary to pay for the shipment. He also used it to appoint a new head for a Palermo district – he preferred not to risk a visit to the capital – and to send henchmen to smart boutiques to buy clothes from the fashion houses Versace or Valentino for himself and his girlfriend. Brusca spent lavishly on clothes and had a collection of 20 Cartier and Rolex watches.

Brusca and his clan spent liberally on weapons too. Four months earlier, a supergrass led police to the biggest arms cache ever seized from the mafia – an underground bunker near a country house. The depot contained a missile-launcher and ten missiles, a grenade-launcher, 25 Kalashnikovs, 50 rifles, 35 pistols, 50 hand-grenades, 88 pounds of explosives, 10 anti-tank bombs, 15 silencers, remote-controlled detonators, telescopic sights for precision rifles and bulletproof jackets.

To find Brusca, Cortese's officers ventured through the area where they had tracked down his mobile phone signal; they travelled in battered old cars, posing as peasants or lovers. They borrowed an ice-cream van and parked it in the street, hoping it might attract Brusca's son. They eventually found the villa where they believed Brusca was living and risked night-time patrols, driving quickly past it in the hope of catching sight of him on his terrace – they had learnt from intercepting his calls that his mobile phone worked only outside the villa. The road led to a wood where couples went courting, so they thought the risk of being noticed was acceptable.

But one night in May the whole operation was jeopardised when Brusca, who had been standing outside the villa, spotted three men – all of them officers in plain clothes – drive past. He immediately rushed inside and ordered his brother Enzo: 'Go and check who's in that car. If they're cops, shoot them.' Together with another mafioso, Enzo drove off in pursuit. The officers spotted the car following them and managed to give it the slip, hiding their car in the woods and making their way down a mountainside to their hotel, which they finally reached at four in the morning.

Shortly after 8 p.m. the next evening, Brusca was talking on his mobile phone when he saw a motorcycle carrying two men pass by. The sight made the boss suspicious again, as he had never seen that motorcycle on his street before – Brusca prided himself on his photographic memory. The motorcycle turned and approached the house, stopping outside the gate; Brusca heard what sounded like two strong explosions from its exhaust. Brusca immediately realised this was a signal of some kind. 'We've had it!' he shouted to his brother, before rushing out and throwing his mobile phone as far away as he could – his first thought was apparently to get rid of it as evidence. He ran away from the villa and into a field. He didn't get very far, as 400 policemen were surrounding the house. Knocked to the ground, he sought to shield himself as several officers lashed out at him, punching and slapping him. He felt no anger and understood their fury: he had killed Falcone and their colleagues, the judge's bodyguards.

So many blows rained down that Brusca pretended to faint and the policemen calmed down. But after he was bundled into a car, two hooded officers who sat on either side of him kept pinching him so hard they left bruises on his skin.

'You're a bastard, you killed our men . . . You must die in prison. Don't turn state's evidence or we'll kill you ourselves,' they told him.

Their superior, sitting in the front passenger seat, turned and made them stop. Throughout the drive, Brusca never said a word.

When Brusca arrived at police headquarters in Palermo, an officer put handcuffs around his wrists and threw away the key. When the time came to remove them later that evening, the fire brigade had to intervene with an electric file capable of cutting through steel, which left Brusca with two long scars on his wrists. He was nursing his injured wrists when a relative of one of Falcone's murdered bodyguards entered the room. The relative grabbed a framed photograph of Falcone and his colleague Borsellino and smashed it down on Brusca's head, the shattered glass cutting his nose.

On the morning after his arrest Brusca, again in handcuffs, was made to walk through a small crowd as police escorted him from headquarters to a car that would take him to the Palermo prison. The crowd hurled insults at him, shouting that 'the monster' had finally been arrested and applauding the police. The hostility of the crowd, Brusca said later, 'massacred me morally . . . Everything I did in Cosa Nostra was in the belief that I was helping the weak and now I was being repaid with applause for the policemen who arrested me . . . I felt as if the world was upside down.'

Brusca turned state's evidence. He confessed to committing 'more than 100 murders, but less than 200'. There were so many murders that Judge Sabella, the prosecutor who questioned him, realised it was pointless to simply ask which ones he was responsible for. Instead the judge got a list of all unsolved murders in several provinces; then Brusca worked his way down the list, stopping at the ones he was involved in.

One murder had made an impression on him – that of the couple whom Bagarella had claimed wanted to kidnap Riina's eldest son Giovanni in Corleone. Brusca couldn't forget that the couple's three-year-old son had survived the shooting. 'When he will grow up, in 15 or 20 years' time, he'll say: "I was a little boy. And you, Giovanni Brusca, killed my mother and my father. And you killed them for nothing." I can't forget it, it weighs so incredibly heavy on my conscience.'

For Brusca, the mafia's fate depended on boys like that one: 'Palermo and Sicily are full of men and women who, when they were small, saw their father killed in front of their eyes or are in any case orphans. What goes through their heads? Have they forgotten? . . . Family feuds in Sicily can last decades.'

Brusca concluded his memoirs with an unconvincing claim of repentance: 'All I have done in my life I have done with strength, conviction and pride. It's my only justification . . . I have long asked God for forgiveness. I have never asked for forgiveness from the relatives of the victims because I didn't want to revive their pain.'

After Brusca, it was the turn of another potential Corleonese heir to fall – Riina's son Giovanni. His arrest a month after Brusca's prompted his mother Ninetta to write an open letter to the Rome newspaper *La Repubblica*: 'I've decided to open my heart, which is swollen and overflowing with sadness for the arrest of my son Giovanni . . . At home we all miss him, our family situation has become Hell, we cannot accept that a boy barely 20 years old, with no previous convictions, is first arrested, then questioned for two days and then jailed,' she wrote.

Concern over her offspring's future prompted Ninetta to ask for an appointment with Cipriani, the mayor of Corleone who had taken a strong public stand against the mafia. He received her in his office in the town hall and was chilled by her steely gaze. Her quiet but determined manner, as well as all he knew about her husband, intimidated Cipriani, so much so that he felt, as he recalled later, 'as if my stomach was burning, as if I'd drunk a glass of sulphuric acid' – an appropriate image, as this was the chemical mafiosi use to dissolve the bodies of their victims.

But Cipriani had lived through so much violence in Corleone – as children he and his schoolfriends were told by anxious parents not to play outside in the evenings in case they stumbled on a murder – that he was determined to take a firm stand with his visitor. Struggling not to betray his nervousness, Cipriani greeted Ninetta politely and asked her why she had come to see him.

'I haven't come here before to talk about my children because I was sure that if I'd done so the newspapers would say I'd come to threaten you,' Ninetta began.

Her mention of a possible threat was hardly calculated to reassure Cipriani. 'This is the home of the people of this town. For the right things, it's open to all,' he replied, somehow finding the strength to add: 'Of course, for the wrong things, it isn't.'

'All I want is that my children are not discriminated against in Corleone. I want them to be free to study and find jobs like any other young men and women. I want them to have a quiet life,' Ninetta said.

'If you want your children to have a quiet life, you'll have to make a clear choice and renounce your family's past. But if you continue in the family tradition, then you'll have to pay the price,' Cipriani said.

The meeting ended without any agreement being reached. Cipriani realised afterwards that Ninetta had been careful never to mention her husband.

Giovanni Riina was given a life sentence in jail. Ninetta and the rest of the family showed their contempt for Italian justice by staying away from the courtroom; Giovanni was alone when he was sentenced. Not even his lawyers were present. After the verdict, Cipriani suggested that the children of mafiosi be taken from their parents if the latter insisted on bringing them up in the mafia tradition.

Riina's third-born son Giuseppe Salvatore, known as Salvuccio, fared little better. He started out as a businessman, overhauling a tractor-selling outlet in Corleone. But he soon got involved in a plan to steal, via the internet, several million pounds from the Bank of Sicily; however, the plan came to nothing. Devoted to his father, Salvuccio was one of the few mafiosi who still defended Riina's strategy of terror. A police bug intercepted his conversation with a friend as they drove past the spot on the motorway from Palermo to the airport where Falcone had been blown up nine years earlier.

'In May (1992) there was this massacre, in July the other one (the murder of Borsellino) and then in January they arrested my father. I don't know how things would have turned out if the state hadn't crippled him,' Salvuccio said. 'The campaign of terror should have continued,' he said, expressing only disdain for Provenzano: 'He didn't have the balls,' he said.

When a petrol pump attendant refused to serve Salvuccio, telling him that he had only a little petrol left and that he had to save it for the forces of law and order such as the police, Salvuccio retorted: 'I'm order here.'

In another bugged conversation, Salvuccio complained to his family about 'that cuckold of a mayor, I'd like to blow up his mouth every time he talks!' After more such taped insults, Cipriani was given a police escort. Arrested and charged with mafia association, extortion and money laundering, Salvuccio was sentenced to 14 years in jail, reduced to eight years on appeal. He was released in early 2008 after almost six years in prison.

The Riinas suffered yet another blow when authorities seized from them a luxurious, 30-room villa on Corleone's outskirts and turned it into an agricultural college. The garish 'Villa Riina', as it was known, boasted three floors of red and black Indian marble, a church-like rose window in the entrance hall, heavy chandeliers of Swarovski crystal, stuccoed walls, a lift and air-conditioning. Student volunteers cheerfully stripped the villa of its furniture and turned a kitchen into a chemistry laboratory.

For at least several months until late 1998, Provenzano ran the mafia from behind an ordinary, mahogany and iron desk in a small room in the Primavera (Spring) driving school in a block of flats in the centre of Palermo. Bosses, lawyers, doctors and politicians called on the godfather there, passing a poster in the reception area which read simply: 'The value of a smile'. Among those visiting the driving school were Provenzano's 'postmen', the men who carried his letters, folded into tiny packages and tied up with sellotape.

Officers led by Captain De Caprio, who had arrested Riina five years earlier, managed to place a hidden microphone in the driving school in December 1998. One conversation picked up by the bug showed that discontent over Riina's decision to launch a frontal attack against the state was still simmering on, six years after Falcone's assassination. The conversation was between the mafiosi Carmelo Amato, the manager of the school, and Giuseppe Vaglica.

'What good did Falcone's death do us? OK, people make mistakes, but wouldn't it have been better if Falcone hadn't died that way?' Vaglica asked.

'Remember that ever since the Earth was created, you don't touch the state. You don't touch the state because if it wants to, it'll crush your balls,' the manager replied.

'They're the ones who've got power,' his friend said.

'Unfortunately you've got to forget about the state, you mustn't give a damn about it. The state does what it wants,' the manager said.

Only 12 days after the microphone was planted in the school, the manager walked up to it, grabbed it and threw it away; someone had tipped him off. 'We're moving out, no one should go to the Primavera any more,' ran the message passed from boss to boss.

Dissatisfaction with Riina's terror strategy was so widespread that four bosses and one outsider – Provenzano's personal doctor

Antonio Cinà, who had long acted also as his adviser – arranged for a meeting with him to discuss its impact. They met at five o'clock one morning in a farmhouse near Mezzojuso. When they arrived, they found that the main room was a mess: piles of pasta boxes, tinned sauces, soft *caciotta* cheese, plastic plates and glasses were strewn around. The five cleared a space for themselves at the table and sat down.

The bosses told Provenzano why they were unhappy. Many politicians were still friendly, they said, but the police were cracking down hard on the fraternity. The ruling Cupola hadn't met for years; it couldn't do so because 80 per cent of its members were in jail.

'We're in a stalemate,' Provenzano's *consigliere* Lipari said bluntly.

Provenzano gave a tight smile; he too would like to see a new Cupola elected but he was in no position to rock the boat. 'What happens if I say: "Gentlemen, let's put this toy back together again?" What happens if from jail I don't receive orders to do it? Taking a decision like that would mean going against them: against Riina, against Bagarella. Because, as you know, things went the way they did . . .'

Lipari interrupted him. 'Listen, it's not as if we're two-year-olds. Don't get annoyed, but I'm going to take the liberty of saying this to you, because we know each other well. Not everything which was decided at the time can be defended; we can't agree with everything. Because in the past the right things were done and the wrong things too.'

One boss, delighted by Lipari's outburst, got up and walked up to him, pursing his lips as if he was about to kiss him. The other participants also backed him; they agreed that the terror campaign was the worst disaster to have hit the mafia and that now its members must have the right to say so aloud. Provenzano watched and listened in silence. The only remark he made was typically non-committal. 'We need time . . .' he said.

Searching for a Ghost

When the detective Cortese was offered promotion as head of the Palermo police unit hunting bosses, he accepted without hesitation despite the fact that in 1985 the Corleonesi had killed one of his predecessors, Beppe Montana, in a small fishing village outside Palermo where he was renting a summer holiday home.

As soon as he took up his new job in 1998, Cortese decided to focus on the biggest name on the wanted list: Bernardo Provenzano. Cortese had very little to go on. Until the murders of Falcone and Borsellino, no one had thought of going after Provenzano – the priority was Riina and the state didn't have the resources necessary to search for both. There were few clues as to what Provenzano looked like; the best police had was a 1959 photograph which showed him as a 26-year-old looking as if he had just walked out of a barber's shop, his hair sleek and shiny with a generous coating of brilliantine.

Cortese began his hunt by ploughing through everything supergrasses had ever said about Provenzano, as well as arrest warrants, indictments and sentences issued by Sicilian courts. Then he arranged to meet and question several defectors, either in jail or in hideouts where they lived under police protection.

Many talked of Provenzano but he remained a ghost; Cortese found it impossible to build a precise image of him. This was unlike anything Cortese had experienced; with men of honour like Brusca, he had been able to find concrete traces of their existence and their movements in Palermo and its province – they used mobile phones, they had relations with their families, they had mistresses. But with Provenzano there was nothing;

supergrasses mentioned seeing him only two or three times and even these were vague recollections. Some were even convinced Provenzano was dead.

What fascinated Cortese the most as he researched his quarry was not so much Provenzano's bloodthirstiness – there were no surprises there, given he headed the mafia – but his cunning. He was amazed by how sly, how 'diabolical' as he put it, Provenzano was. Cortese tried to always bear in mind that whenever he expected Provenzano to do one thing, the godfather would do the complete opposite.

Cortese became convinced that he must seek some clues in Corleone, the fiefdom where Provenzano's criminal career had started and which was home to both his blood family and his mafia family.

The terrain Cortese and his officers ventured into was a high-risk one. Within a few miles of the centre of Corleone, a new face could result in the alarm being raised, with the movements of 'foreigners' closely monitored. 'Corleone is the kind of place where any outsider – even if no one knows he is a cop – is seen with suspicion,' as Cortese put it. He knew it was out of the question for his men to drive around in marked police cars, or to appear in uniform. He would use the method he had perfected over the years, a mix of traditional techniques and hi-tech – old-fashioned surveillance by his men, together with hidden microphones and telephone taps.

Cortese's first target in Corleone was the home of Provenzano's companion Saveria, the mother of his two sons. Since she had returned to Corleone in 1992, as far as Cortese could find out, Saveria had received little news from Provenzano; a few letters which investigators managed to intercept indicated that Provenzano saw her and his sons only once or twice a year. She looked to Cortese like the classic mafia wife – rarely venturing out of the house, faithful to her man and completely dedicated to her family.

Cortese had a sneaking respect for Saveria. She had, after all, not only sacrificed her life for Provenzano's sake but also helped to ensure that neither of their sons had anything to do with his fraternity. Paolo, the youngest son, passed his Palermo university examinations in foreign languages with top marks and won a state scholarship to Germany to teach Italian. When the scholarship ended, he stayed in Germany and taught Italian in a school.

Angelo, the other son, began studying to be a surveyor but he had no time for university and decided to become a businessman instead. Concerned about his son's future, Provenzano sought advice from his *consigliere* Lipari, who insisted that Angelo should finish his studies. A university degree would be better for the boy than any inheritance, Lipari wrote in one letter. 'You'll understand that any business initiative will always be under strict control,' Lipari wrote. Angelo ignored this advice, cut short his studies and opened the Splendor laundry in Corleone. He soon realised this was not the business venture he had dreamt of, complaining to his father that he was barely covering his costs and sometimes even losing money.

The venture ended when authorities seized the laundry. Angelo vented his frustration. 'How can I defend myself from the accusation of having contaminated chromosomes?' he asked, denying he had ever had anything to do with the mafia. 'I condemn every form of violence . . . I've made my choice,' he said. 'Preventing me from working honestly, denying me a right that is protected by the constitution, means encouraging me to commit a crime. If I commit crimes, punish me. But why make my surname such a burden on me?' But police wrecked another of Angelo's projects when they discovered a letter to his father in which he outlined a plan to buy some land and open a holiday farm with help from European Union subsidies. Angelo found himself a job as an insurance salesman, but his employer dismissed him when this got into the newspapers; he changed jobs yet again, selling hoovers and other household appliances.

After watching over Saveria's home for several weeks, Cortese's men were able to get in to place electronic bugs inside but these failed to pick up any mention of Provenzano. In late 1999, however, Saveria and her two sons were heard discussing plans for a three-week Christmas trip to visit Provenzano's brother Simone in Willich, north-west Germany. Every time the family talked about the trip, they lowered their voices. A pasta-maker was asked to prepare fresh pasta on the eve of the trip but was told it was for a gift to a doctor. Saveria's sister, despite her poor health, baked a large number of *buccellati* cakes, a Sicilian seasonal speciality investigators knew to be among Provenzano's favourites. Saveria herself seemed to treat the trip as much more than a family visit.

Cortese became suspicious. He thought the family would actually meet Provenzano himself in Germany and transferred several of his officers to a gym near the brother's home, made available by German authorities. When the family flew to Germany, a minuscule bug stuck into the padding of a seat picked up the two sons' conversation, a plain-clothed officer in the seat behind them recording them as he pretended to listen to his iPod. They never mentioned their father. Cortese missed Christmas with his family and ended up celebrating the start of the new millennium in the gym. Saveria and her sons came and went, but the godfather stayed away.

Cortese concentrated his hunt not only on Provenzano's family, but also on those who had long been suspected of links to him. Chief among these was the *consigliere* Lipari, whom police had described as early as the mid-1980s as a long-time adviser to Provenzano. Lipari had finally been jailed, so Cortese bugged his conversations with visitors to the prison. Chatting with his family in 2000, Lipari indicated that he had left messages in his bag of dirty laundry for his children to deliver to someone – he didn't specify who. Cortese's men found one letter, folded into a small tight package, wrapped in sellotape and sewn into the hem of his trousers. It appeared to be destined for Provenzano, so the officers photocopied it and replaced it.

In another letter, Lipari advised Provenzano to sell two villas and several apartments, as prosecutors were about to seize them.

In yet another, Lipari asked Provenzano for £16,000 to help him with his legal expenses but the notoriously tight-fisted godfather simply passed the request on to a wealthy entrepreneur who supplied the money.

Provenzano and Lipari didn't discuss only business. Provenzano once sent his *consigliere* the following passage from the Bible:

> Even so every good tree bringeth forth good fruit; but a corrupt tree bringeth forth evil fruit. A good tree cannot bring forth evil fruit, neither can a corrupt tree bring forth good fruit. Every tree that bringeth not forth good fruit is hewn down, and cast into the fire. Wherefore by their fruits ye shall know them.
>
> (Matthew 7:17–20)

Lipari responded with a breathless tribute, unintentionally highlighting the man of honour's failure to see any contradiction between their faith and their crimes:

> I was very much struck by the principle according to which a tree can be recognised by its fruit. I see that you spend much of your time reading, but your wisdom, not to say that of all of us, isn't shaped by reading which certainly helps a lot but a man also needs to be inclined to reflection and calm and to be altruistic in helping his fellow man. You have all these characteristics and so you face life as it comes, like a gift of God. Your faith is boundless and helps you enormously. God has illuminated you very much and I hope and pray that He will always protect you for your own good and for that of all those who are fond of you.

Lipari then got back down to business, reporting on kick-backs, threats and punishments.

A hidden police camera recorded a mafioso passing a letter to a relative of Provenzano's, after the two had embraced and kissed each other on the cheeks twice, in the lift of Palermo's main hospital. But then the trail went cold; no amount of surveillance could establish what happened to the letters after that. Following messengers closely enough to see them pass on the tiny packages proved impossible; they seemed to pass the letters on in crowded public places or in the offices of lawyers and accountants. Some of the suspects headed out to small towns similar to Corleone where everyone knew virtually everyone and the trail also went dead.

Cortese turned to American technology for help. Through the justice ministry in Rome, he borrowed a sophisticated, unmanned Predator aircraft, which American forces had used on secret reconnaissance missions against al Qaeda terrorists in Afghanistan and Iraq. For three weeks, investigators used the high-flying drone to track suspects believed to be carrying letters to or from Provenzano and to photograph several suspect locations near Palermo, but even this proved fruitless.

Provenzano's strategy of making the mafia 'invisible' began to pay off. In 1998, as Riina had long lobbied for the government of the centre-left prime minister Romano Prodi closed the maximum-security jails of Pianosa and Asinara off the Sardinian coast, where mafiosi had been held in strict isolation, to make way for luxury holiday resorts. That same year, a privacy law decreed that all records of phone calls more than five years old must be destroyed; this immediately hampered investigations into Riina's terror campaign of 1992–1993.

More laws that played into the secret society's hands followed. In 1999, another law decreed that from now on any testimony given to prosecutors by supergrasses, among others, would be thrown out unless repeated in court; this weighed heavily on mafia trials, as witnesses often lost their tongue when confronted by a boss. Yet another measure granted lawyers investigative powers similar to a prosecutor's, allowing them to question a witness to a crime even before the prosecutor did. This lay the witness open to intimidation by the lawyer's client.

These laws weren't enough for several bosses locked up in jail, who tried to negotiate directly with the state. The philosophy and theology student Aglieri, together with others, asked to meet the national anti-mafia prosecutor of the time, Pierluigi Vigna. They told him they were ready to dissociate themselves from the mafia – which would mean recognising their errors without having to admit their criminal responsibilities – and to recognise the authority of the state. But they left unsaid what they expected in return – most likely better jail conditions and a revision of their court cases at the very least. The prosecutor urged them all to go one step further and turn state's evidence, but they refused and the talks went no further.

In late 2000, thanks to a listening device hidden in the home of a farmer suspected of working for Provenzano near Mezzojuso, Cortese discovered that an unidentified elderly man, suffering from a prostate disease, was being cared for there by a senior doctor from a Palermo hospital. The device recorded the doctor telling his patient at the end of one visit: 'We'll see each other in January for the next check-up.' Cortese knew that Provenzano suffered from prostate trouble and the patient spoke with an accent which could well be from Corleone. Cortese became convinced that the patient was the godfather himself.

Cortese and a dozen officers raided the farm on the day of the next appointment. Guns in hand, they kicked down the door of the farm and leapt in through the windows. They shoved the doctor into a corner, grabbed the elderly patient and knocked him face down to the ground before slipping hand-cuffs on him. Then, grabbing him by the hair, they turned his head to have a good look at his face. Cortese swore under his breath in disappointment. The man looked nothing like Provenzano. But their catch was no mean feat: the figure stretched out at their feet was Benedetto Spera, number three in the mafia's hierarchy.

A few weeks later, Cortese found out just how close he had come to catching Provenzano. Another listening device in the visiting room at the jail where Spera was held recorded him confiding to his wife in a quiet voice: 'That day, he was there.' When Cortese raided the farm, Provenzano had been in a small villa only 200 yards away. The godfather had slipped away unnoticed.

After his narrow escape, Provenzano became more wary than ever. 'Watch out for lovers, they mean danger. And be especially on your guard with hunters. They could all be cops,' Provenzano never tired of saying. He consulted a handbook written by Captain De Caprio, who had arrested Riina, called *Action: A technique for fighting crime.*

The godfather became obsessed with police microphones and surveillance cameras. Using a miniature scanner, he would himself test a room or a car for bugs before getting down to business. Before one meeting, he wrote to his right-hand man Giuffrè to have his men inspect a farmhouse for any microphones and cameras, close to or away from the building. 'Make them check carefully and tell them not to talk either in their cars or in the house; tell them not to talk loudly when they're close to houses, whether they're new or in ruins. Thank Our Lord Jesus Christ,' Provenzano wrote.

Provenzano benefited from yet more laws welcomed by the mafia. One passed by the Prodi government in 2001 decreed that informers must reveal all they knew within six months of turning state's evidence; if they revealed evidence after that time, they risked being thrown out of the witness protection programme. Backers of the law, echoing Riina's denunciations in court, portrayed supergrasses as hardened criminals motivated by the allowances they received from the state and ready to commit new crimes.

Investigators protested that the time limit was much too short, especially for those who had to retrace a lifetime in crime. The investigators also pointed out that they needed much more time simply to win the trust of mafiosi, who had always seen the state as their enemy and who made their revelations gradually, especially when their evidence involved senior politicians. These protests were ignored.

The law also decreed that supergrasses must serve a quarter

of their jail sentence and hand over all their property to the state, including any that had been acquired legally or inherited. Widely seen both inside and outside the mafia as a sign the state was doing less and less to combat it, the law put a virtual stop to the wave of informers. With just one law, the state achieved what Riina had been desperately seeking with the murders of dozens of supergrasses' relatives – be they men, women or children.

In 2002, the new conservative government of Silvio Berlusconi revoked a requirement that an order for a mafioso to be held in isolation in prison should be renewed every two years; from then on, it would automatically be valid indefinitely. But the law effectively ended the isolation regime for such prisoners; they were no longer required to go for their hourly walk on their own but could now pass the time with up to four other inmates.

The law also gave prisoners the right to appeal against being held in isolation. Over the months that followed, more than a hundred bosses – including those convicted for Riina's terror campaign – won their appeals. As an official inquiry soon established, the isolation regime often became a farce: bosses chatted together during Sunday Mass, played football together and socialised not in groups of five but of more than a dozen. They still managed to send messages out of jail by passing notes to their wives or children when they embraced in the visiting-room, or by hiding notes in their clothes.

The government could not have cared less. As prime minister Berlusconi claimed in 2003: 'For us from the North, the mafia is a distant phenomenon; and when you take into account the fact that 90 per cent of mafiosi are in jail you can see organised crime is under control.'

7

The Fall of the Corleonesi

2002–2008

Provenzano and his Patron Saint

In the spring of 2002, Provenzano lost his closest lieutenant Giuffrè when police arrested the boss, known as 'Little Hand' because he had lost part of a finger on his right hand in a hunting accident. A few weeks later, while watching Pope John Paul II on television beatifying Padre Pio, a Capuchin friar famous for his stigmata and venerated as a worker of miracles, said to include the ability to be in two places at once, Giuffrè decided to turn state's evidence.

The former teacher in a technical school, who sat on the Cupola as head of the Caccamo clan just outside Palermo, explained that he wanted to save the lives of people whose murders had been decreed. He had decided to talk, he claimed, because the mafia's 'values' were no longer respected and he felt his place was no longer in it. Giuffrè confessed to a dozen murders, some of which he had carried out himself. He admitted he had approved the murders of several relatives of supergrasses, including Marino Mannoia's mother, sister and aunt.

Giuffrè described himself as 'born and raised in Provenzano's hands'. He joined the mafia in 1980 and started to work for Provenzano only two years later. He was the only one of the newer informers who had seen the godfather and was able to describe his face in detail, which allowed police to issue a new photofit. But despite two decades in Provenzano's service, Giuffrè had no idea where he lived.

Provenzano soon found out what Giuffrè had said about him. From a mole in the police, he obtained both the transcripts of the testimony and copies of the letters the defector had given prosecutors. When the godfather came across an account of Giuffrè's evidence in a newspaper article, he picked up a pair of scissors and cut out, one by one, nine letters from another page. He then glued the letters across the article, on top of his former friend's revelations.

The letters spelt out just one word: 'TREACHERY'.

Provenzano's mounting health worries – his prostate was increasingly painful – led him to consult Sicilian doctors, who told him he should have a check-up in hospital. The godfather was afraid a Sicilian or Italian hospital would be too risky and booked an appointment at a clinic in Marseille on the southern French coast. Provenzano made the long journey to Marseille in a truck in the summer of 2003, an escort car following. He travelled under the name of an accomplice, Gaspare Troia; Troia's son Salvatore accompanied him, together with the latter's Italo-French wife, who acted as his interpreter.

The evening before he was due to arrive at the clinic, Provenzano sought out a Sicilian restaurant near Marseille's harbour; called Don Corleone, it prided itself on serving authentic Sicilian specialities such as pasta with aubergines or cuttlefish ink. The menu poked fun at the godfather's organisation: among the starters were dishes called *omertà* (the law of silence), *cosa nostra* and a veal escalope renamed *scaloppina mafiosa*.

If Provenzano took offence, he showed no sign of it. Sitting underneath figures from Sicilian puppet theatre and a large photograph of the bandit Salvatore Giuliano hung on the walls, Provenzano ate sparingly but made a point of thanking the owner of the restaurant, a Corleone-born emigrant who had long ago settled in France. 'I'm pleased to have eaten our specialities. Today it's difficult to find them even in Sicily,' Provenzano told him.

Flattered, the owner uncorked a bottle for his guests and introduced himself. 'Alfredo Mauro, delighted,' he said.

'Provenzano, delighted,' the godfather replied.

'Like Bernardo?' the owner joked.

'The same family . . .' Provenzano replied laconically.

At the La Licorne clinic the following day, Provenzano told doctors that he suffered from hepatitis B and C, his legs felt 'heavy' and he had arterial problems and rheumatism. He said that he didn't smoke or drink, or take sleeping-pills. After the doctors had carried out the necessary tests, they recommended removing his prostate completely. Provenzano agreed and had the operation on a second trip. From then on, he had to use incontinence pads. He had to make a third trip late that same year for another operation, this time on a shoulder to treat a probable metastasis.

As he grew older and more frail, Provenzano became more and more obsessed with the aches and pains he suffered. In between trips to the French coast, he typed out a note to himself which began with the words: 'My sufferings'. Provenzano listed a benign prostate tumour, a cyst in the right kidney and what he described as 'an inflammation, an infection on my left hip, under the trouser-belt'. This mysterious infection depressed him, he complained, 'making my thoughts seem more heavy than they should'. He then detailed how to relieve his pains: 'Compresses of mallow directly on the hip or, better, four fingers from the trouser fastening'.

At the end of his third trip, he celebrated his return to Sicily with a dinner at a hotel on Palermo's seafront. Guests toasted the godfather's health with champagne and he gave a gift of £13,000 to the couple who had escorted him, paying in addition for their children to enrol at the city's French school.

A year later, a supergrass told investigators about Provenzano's trips. They questioned the doctors who had treated him and established that he was five foot six, weighed 148 pounds, had a false set of teeth and three scars on his body, one of them on his neck. Tissue taken from his shoulder, which the doctors had kept, yielded his DNA, which was checked against a blood sample which Provenzano's brother gave when he had an operation in Corleone in the same period.

For investigators, establishing Provenzano's DNA was the first concrete trace they had of his existence. It also meant there was no longer the risk that someone might offer them the body of a man resembling him, 'killing off' Provenzano so that he could remain alive and untroubled by pursuers.

Just over a mile from Corleone, off the road to the town of Prizzi, lies Horses' Mountain, which dominates a valley of gardens, vegetable plots and almond, pear and fig trees lying like an oasis of green in the surrounding desert of bleak hills and rocky outcrops. At 2,300 feet, the air in the valley is cooler than in Corleone and most of the homes there are owned by people who live in the town and come at weekends, especially during the stifling summers.

Among the few farmworkers who worked on Horses' Mountain in 2004 was Giovanni Marino, a shepherd well known in Corleone as the maker of delicious fresh ricotta cheese, which he made from a morning's milking and which his customers liked to serve still warm. Marino, who lived in the town, had no time for the health and hygiene diktats of European Union bureaucrats a world away in Brussels. He used sheep's milk that had just been milked, but not treated, and rennet, an enzyme from a kid's stomach, to coagulate the milk. The enzyme was obtained by making a kid feed off his mother, then killing it when its stomach was full; the partially digested milk would then be dried and preserved. Marino lived in Corleone but made his ricotta in a small farm on top of a hillock. The farm, 40 yards up a track off the dirt road which ran through the valley below Horses' Mountain, was no more than a small shack with a large barn of corrugated iron; sheep grazed in a small field just below.

The shack was just a converted sheep pen but Provenzano is believed to have made it his home in November 2004. The farm was far from an isolated hideout. People kept coming and going, buying ricotta from Marino and fetching fresh mountain water from a tap right next to the shack; it was considered the best spring water in the area. The godfather may have believed Saint Bernard, the patron saint of Corleone after whom he had been christened, would watch over him in this hideout. Visible from the shack, a statue of the saint at the top of a hill dominated the valley.

Cortese's work in tracking Provenzano's associates came to an abrupt halt in early 2005 when Palermo prosecutors overseeing the hunt for the godfather decided to order their arrests. The prosecutors drew up a list of 50 of Provenzano's lieutenants, from simple messengers and soldiers to businessmen, *consiglieri* and bosses. The prosecutors argued that arresting the suspects, most of whom were in Palermo, would be a decisive blow for the godfather, robbing him of an elaborate network which kept him always one step ahead of his pursuers. A weaker Provenzano might even be pushed into making a mistake. Cortese, however, was against making the arrests; he wanted to continue tracking the suspects in the hope they would lead him to his quarry. But prosecutors over-ruled Cortese and jailed them all.

Those sent behind bars included the 61-year-old Francesco Pastoia; at Provenzano's beck and call for the past three decades, he had acted mainly as a driver and executioner. The indictment for his arrest detailed a series of murders carried out without seeking the godfather's permission. In one bugged conversation at his home, Pastoia confided that he had violated several mafia rules and told a friend: 'We won't tell Provenzano; it's not the first time I've done this.' The boss said he had pocketed money destined for Provenzano and had even plotted to kill the son of one of the godfather's closest friends. Confident he would never be caught out, he boasted that his relationship with Provenzano was so close 'no one can divide us'.

After reading through the indictment in his cell, Pastoia hanged himself with a sheet – he knew what fate awaited him if he failed to take his own life. No mafioso attended his funeral and one night his tombstone was smashed to pieces and his coffin dug up and set alight – a posthumous warning to anyone who betrayed the godfather.

The arrests left Cortese with no more leads to follow. As the senior prosecutor Judge Grasso admitted: 'We'd burnt up our sources and our resources, we'd arrested all those who could have offered us new investigative leads.'

Cortese had to start again from scratch.

Cortese and his officers debated long and hard how to relaunch their hunt for Provenzano. What would he do now, they kept asking themselves? Where would he hide? Would he make a blunder? The officers all agreed that Provenzano must be feeling hounded by investigators and betrayed by supergrasses.

Cortese prided himself on his ability to think like the duplicitous Provenzano. Whenever he had to try to anticipate Provenzano's next move, he had taught himself to think of two options – a normal, predictable one and a surprise alternative. The logical step, he reasoned, would be for Provenzano to escape his pursuers by fleeing far away from Palermo, either to eastern Sicily or even to the Italian mainland.

But on the other hand, Cortese reflected, Provenzano might choose the one place where he thought no one would look for him. More isolated than ever, he would return to the fiefdom, where no one had been arrested, where he could rely on his blood family and the clan which had served him for a lifetime, where he could take the time necessary to rebuild his protection network.

Cortese decided to restart the hunt in Corleone. But rather than continue with the flying squad's 40-strong section, which was charged with hunting bosses, he set up a new, smaller team of detective inspectors to focus exclusively on Provenzano. Cortese picked the best officers he had worked with so far, as well as reinforcements from the elite SCO unit in Rome, the equivalent of the British CID. He wanted the new team to be ready to work at any time of the day or night and chose 24 men who were either single or whose families were far from Sicily, as well as one young woman. Unmarried and still living at home, she was nicknamed 'the Cat' because of her stealth on the job. She could sit for eight hours at a stretch, without moving, eavesdropping on conversations without ever missing a word.

The men and woman who would from now on hunt for Provenzano around the clock quickly became known as 'Team Cathedral' because their new headquarters were in a former chapel near Palermo's cathedral. Security could have been better: the cramped ground-floor offices had served as the neighbourhood police station until a few years earlier and the odd local rang the buzzer from time to time and had to be redirected to the police station a short walk away. Cortese's own office, which boasted a mural of saints and angels, was hardly safe; to clear the air of the smell from his cigars, he'd often leave open the metal door which opened out onto a small yard where his men left their scooters.

Pressing relentlessly for resources, Cortese equipped separate rooms for monitoring tapped conversations, watching videos from surveillance cameras and tracking cars with Global Positioning System (GPS) devices. In one soundproofed room, in unnatural stillness, four skilled eavesdroppers, using special filters to 'clean' tapes of background noises and amplify voices, would listen again and again to the words of mafiosi and their acquaintances, struggling to make out even the slightest whisper.

Cortese insisted on as many investigators as possible attending a daily briefing; his priority was to create a team spirit. He knew that the success of the mission and perhaps the lives of his men depended on each officer, out on the street, trusting his colleague to cover him at any time.

Team Cathedral became operational in March 2005. Cortese began by ordering his team to follow every move of Provenzano's partner Saveria, their son Angelo who lived with her and several close relatives. Surveillance cameras were hidden across Corleone for the first time. While their colleagues, including Cortese, kept watch, detectives slipped into the homes of Saveria and Provenzano's brother Simone to place electronic bugs.

Cortese kept his own visits to Corleone to the bare minimum. Photographs of him had appeared in the newspapers when he'd made big arrests in the past and he didn't want to run the risk of being recognised. But to see various spots for himself and to assess how to keep watch over them, he drove through Corleone a few times – always at night.

Team Cathedral and the Laundry Mystery

At 4 p.m. on the afternoon of 8 June 2005, Provenzano's brothers Salvatore and Simone sat down for a chat in the latter's kitchen. They talked of old family quarrels and complained that the godfather wasn't doing enough for them; they muttered about his two sons benefiting from 'all this benevolence simply because they're Provenzano's sons'.

A particularly embittered Salvatore complained that, after eight years during which they hadn't seen each other, Provenzano had sent a message through an intermediary saying he wanted to see him. 'Why the Hell did he get in touch . . . has he summoned me after eight years just so that we can have a row?'

Then Salvatore added: 'He's still here.'

'What?' Simone asked, startled.

'He's still here,' Salvatore repeated.

In the listening room at Team Cathedral headquarters 22 miles away in Palermo, the eavesdroppers on duty that afternoon exulted. They immediately tipped off Cortese, who had no doubt that the man Salvatore referred to only as 'he' was the godfather. The tactic of focusing on Provenzano's family was beginning to pay off.

Worried that information about the hunt might leak out and wreck it, Cortese stopped using phone intercepts. Monitoring a telephone number meant notifying a phone company, which would increase the risk of leaks. He would rely as much as possible on hidden cameras and microphones, and on old-fashioned, direct observation using powerful binoculars lent by the FBI.

Cortese gave orders for more surveillance cameras to be hidden in the town; one was placed on a streetlight opposite the house where Provenzano's companion Saveria and their son Angelo lived, and another inside the house, in a television set. Both cameras recorded a steady stream of visitors coming and going – relatives, colleagues of Angelo's and local people. Both Saveria and Angelo were far more active than they had been when the house had last been watched six years earlier.

But Cortese had no idea which of their visitors to follow. He knew he couldn't afford to waste time; Provenzano might suddenly find a new hideout far from Corleone with the aid of a new network as yet unknown to Cortese.

From his shack on Horses' Mountain, Provenzano ruled the mafia mainly by letter, using an electric typewriter and occasionally consulting a dictionary. He kept several rolls of sellotape within easy reach on his rough wooden desk, to seal his letters. On the back of a Texas Instruments calculator, the godfather known as 'the Accountant' stuck a note giving the euro's rate against the old Italian lira. He also kept a Bible to hand and near the desk hung two pictures, one of the Virgin and one of the Last Supper.

The letters Provenzano received were full of tributes to him. Among the warmest came from Messina Denaro, a mafioso for all seasons who had backed first the terror campaign under Riina and then Provenzano's more discreet strategy. Messina Denaro called Provenzano 'our maestro', pledged his 'undiminished esteem and affection' and signed himself 'your nephew' in his letters. In one, he wrote: 'You say that I'm better than you? No, I'm not better. I see myself in you and I believe in our Cause. I grew up with it and that's how things will be as long as I live.'

In another, Messina Denaro pledged that half of all he earned in extortion money would go to Provenzano. The boss asked for advice on managing public works contracts and resolving conflicts over territory between clans. 'I have faith in you, in your honesty and in your ability, as I previously had in T.T.R.,' he wrote – the initials stood for Riina.

But despite such proclamations of esteem, Provenzano's rule was beginning to be challenged. Bosses increasingly asked questions about his age and his health and some went as far as to plot behind his back. One of the most critical was Dr Antonio Cinà, a respected neurologist at Palermo's main hospital, who had cared for Riina and his family before treating Provenzano. Long a skilled *consigliere* of the Corleonesi, Cinà was exasperated by Provenzano's failure to make him head of a Palermo clan.

Dr Cinà found another discontented man of honour in the boss Nino Rotolo, a figure so powerful that Provenzano once wrote to him: 'You and I are equals.' Rotolo feared that he stood to lose influence and might have a war on his hands if Provenzano failed to prevent the return to Palermo of several mafiosi who had emigrated to America – relatives of the Corleonesi's enemies who had fled the purges of the early 1980s knowing they would be killed if they stayed. The Corleonesi banned them from returning at the time but now they wanted to come back.

Rotolo had written to Provenzano about the issue but received only non-committal replies. The godfather claimed he didn't have the authority to take a decision on his own and apparently realised that these mafiosi might seek revenge on their return. But he also reasoned that they would provide the mafia with more manpower. In a typically ambiguous passage, Provenzano wrote: 'For several reasons I can't express an opinion as my heart desires. My motto is: let God give them the certainty they made a mistake and then forgive them.'

Provenzano's fence-sitting and his hint that he might let bygones be bygones incensed Rotolo. He began to plan the killings of anyone who dared to return from America and ordered his men to find acid to dissolve the bodies. Rotolo, sentenced to life in jail, had won permission to serve his sentence in his elegant villa thanks to a medical certificate describing him as near death because he suffered from a serious form of high blood pressure. His illness didn't stop him regularly vaulting his garden wall to get to a shed of corrugated sheet-iron on his neighbour's land, where he received other mafiosi. They sat around a table on white plastic chairs and plotted extortion rackets, the appointment of friendly doctors to senior hospital jobs, cocaine-trafficking and murders.

Rotolo felt safe in the shed. He was sure that he could talk freely there, as he used an electronic device the size of a matchbox designed to scramble all radio wavelengths, supposedly making it impossible for any transmission of voices to be picked up by a police bug. Unknown to Rotolo, however, technology had moved on and a bug planted by police in a wall of the shed worked perfectly.

At one mid-morning meeting in September 2005, Rotolo and Cinà agreed it was high time Provenzano realised that at 72 he was too old to continue as godfather.

Cinà, who was due to meet Provenzano soon, outlined what he would tell him. 'I've been thinking about what I should tell him when I see him. I think I should first remind him of the huge responsibility he gave me in the past, the satisfactions I've had, but also the disappointments I'm suffering from . . .' Cinà said.

'Certainly,' Rotolo said.

'And then I can tell him: "You, you'll go down in the history books, but today who have you got on the horizon? Who can guarantee continuity? You're 70 years old, in ten years' time you may be dead and there's this idiot (the boss Salvatore Lo Piccolo) who's 60 and who's convinced he's your deputy. He thinks you told him that. But you've got to clear this thing up now, before you go away and retire." You know, I can tell him this because luckily we're on close terms . . .' Cinà said.

'Look, you've got to say all this in my name,' Rotolo said.

'In your name and in everyone's name,' Cinà said.

The two men were confident Provenzano would do as they demanded. They were agreed that a string of arrests had left him increasingly isolated. 'Look Nino,' Rotolo said, 'he's the one who's in need! Listen . . . he's got no one now!'

'Holy shit, everything's over for him!' Cinà exclaimed.

★

Three weeks later, Team Cathedral recorded a conversation between Provenzano's sons Angelo and Paolo in their cabin aboard the ferry *La Suprema* as it sailed to Genoa. Paolo had asked his brother to accompany him on a trip to Germany, where he was planning to settle. At dinner-time the brothers kept away from the ferry's restaurant and spread out on a folding table the food their mother had prepared.

As they ate, the 23-year-old Paolo, who had effectively been estranged from his father since the age of nine, complained that he had never had a proper talk with him. 'When I go to see him, it's only to sit pretty and do nothing. It's been the same thing ever since I was small . . . He says his dad beat him and that at the age of nine he had to go around selling things, while we've got everything. But when he asks you: "Have you ever needed anything?", does he even think you might reply: "Yes"?' Paolo said.

Angelo was angry with their mother Saveria. 'She's put up with all his decisions, she never had the courage to say: "I like this, I don't like this, let's do it this way, let's do it that way,"' he said.

'The fact is that we've had to put up with a whole lot of stuff and we still do . . . I've never said this to anyone, but how many people realise that what we've been through is even worse than if our father had died?' Paolo asked.

Over several months in late 2005, Cortese noticed confusing goings-on at Saveria's home in Corleone. One of the most regular visitors to the house was Giuseppe Lo Bue, a cousin and colleague of the godfather's son Angelo, who also worked as a hoover salesman. The camera hidden at the top of a streetlamp in front of the house would show him driving up to the house in an Audi A4 estate car; he would get out and carry an assortment of parcels and plastic bags into the house. Thanks to the mini-camera hidden in the television set in the house, Cortese discovered that the packages and bags contained trousers, shirts and sweaters. Lo Bue would emerge some time later with yet more packages and plastic bags. As he watched the videos again and again, Cortese wondered aloud: could this be the godfather's laundry? Try as he might, Cortese found it impossible to track what happened to a given package. Several days or even weeks would pass between packages arriving at the house. They went through so many different couriers and changed shape or wrapping so often that Cortese was stumped.

But late on the evening of 3 February 2006 one piece of the puzzle fell into place. Team Cathedral intercepted a conversation between Lo Bue and his wife Mariangela in which she reprimanded him tearfully.

'This isn't a family; I'm tired of seeing you only when you've got a spare moment,' Mariangela complained.

'For the moment, my love, the important thing is that the children mustn't want for anything but of course it would be better if we could spend more time together, but sometimes things are hard, you have to accept it . . .' Lo Bue replied.

'But Giuseppe, we've been living like this for eight months . . .'

'At least when you want to sit down for a rest for five minutes, you can. I can't even do that.'

'Alright, keep going then, let's see where it gets us. You do things because you've promised other people you will and you don't want to look bad . . .'

'You should be proud of your husband then if he doesn't want to look bad in other people's eyes . . . you should be proud . . .'

'I know what should make me proud of my husband and what shouldn't. I don't need you to tell me. And I also know I've got a husband who's hardly ever with me. I just hear his voice on the phone.'

'But if I make this commitment it's for everyone's sake.'

'We'll see, one day when you're alone . . .'

'Mariangela, now listen to me: maybe I'll be alone three years, four years, but afterwards I'd be with you again. I'll do this again and again to make sure you have everything you need. I don't think you've understood that.'

Cortese realised that Lo Bue was the lynchpin for a complex

courier network that he believed could only be serving Provenzano. It was taking up so much of Lo Bue's time that it was putting a strain on his marriage. The period of time Lo Bue had referred to spending alone – three to four years – corresponded to the time he would have to spend in jail if convicted of aiding and abetting the mafia.

The hunt inched forward over the next month. Cortese failed to discover just what 'things' Lo Bue had promised and to whom. But he did establish that several bags seemed to end up at the home of Lo Bue's father Calogero, just outside Corleone.

At five past midnight on 18 March 2006, one of Cortese's men saw Lo Bue walk out of Saveria's house with a plastic bag stamped with a supermarket's orange logo. Lo Bue carried the bag to his father's house. Cortese, exasperated by his lack of progress in piecing together the route taken by the bags, took a risk and deployed several men outside the house and in Corleone. Detectives in unmarked cars used what Team Cathedral called 'the conveyor-belt technique': a car would park in a given spot for a few minutes then leave, to be replaced by another which would in turn stop nearby, to be replaced by another and another.

After a day of watching, that evening a detective saw Lo Bue's father Calogero load the orange plastic bag into the boot of his car at his house, then drive off towards Corleone. Calogero stopped only a mile away from the town next to a silver Golf parked on a narrow road that was flanked on one side by open fields and on the other by a tall, rocky ridge. The detective tailing him had no choice but to stop some distance away, and from there he saw Calogero get out of his car and into the Golf. The latter was driven by an elderly, white-haired man the officer didn't recognise. He took down the Golf's number plate and was then told to stop his surveillance; he had seen the new man's face and driving on would have been too risky. An hour later a camera filmed Calogero returning home, this time carrying two plastic bags; there was no sign of the orange one. Cortese wondered if the Golf's driver could be the missing link in the chain of couriers.

Shortly after midnight, Team Cathedral established that the Golf belonged to the wife of the 70-year-old Bernardo Riina. He was no relation of Salvatore Riina, but he was first linked to Provenzano as far back as 1958. That year, he had given Provenzano an alibi which helped ensure his acquittal on a murder charge. Bernardo Riina was afterwards accused of criminal association and sent into internal exile. He had since returned to Corleone and in 2001 his name, in code, featured in a letter Provenzano's son wrote to the godfather.

Over the next ten days, Cortese placed two cameras outside Bernardo Riina's house and several more along roads on Corleone's outskirts. The cameras established that he drove out of the town almost every day, heading south-east.

Late one night, two detectives slipped into a wood five miles away from Corleone and walked at a steady pace until they reached a hillside above the town. After choosing a discreet vantage point, they set up a portable US-made Celestron telescope and instead of pointing it at the stars and planets, they aimed it at the sleeping town. A few days later, the telescope tracked Lo Bue visiting Bernardo Riina. Another few days passed before the telescope followed Bernardo Riina as he drove up towards a green valley where fruit and almond trees were in spectacular, colourful blossom just over a mile from Corleone. But trees blocked the telescope's vision and made it impossible to see just where he had gone.

The area was called Horses' Mountain.

On Horses' Mountain

Cortese found out that Bernardo Riina owned nothing on Horses' Mountain. Property records showed that his brother-in-law owned a few modest houses there but otherwise homes in the area were the property of farmworkers, shepherds and Corleone residents. It was the worst possible hunting ground for Cortese. Any member of Team Cathedral following a suspect risked being noticed instantly. The locals knew every face, every rock, every tree.

Cortese took the risk of deploying a handful of watchers who posed as telephone engineers, forest rangers and mushroom-hunters. On 5 April they tracked Bernardo Riina's Golf to a small sheep farm, which was no more than a shack and a barn on a small hill. The farm belonged to Giovanni Marino, a shepherd with a clean record; a few questions asked in town established that his ricotta cheese was much appreciated.

Cortese's first impression was that Marino was just another link in the chain of couriers who ferried bags to and from Provenzano. The farm certainly didn't look like a hiding place; the only apparent security was a gate off a dirt road that was left open most of the day and customers came there, often to buy ricotta and to fetch fresh mountain water from a tap next to the shack. Surely this couldn't be the refuge of the godfather, Cortese told himself. He considered giving up on the farm and looking elsewhere, but his instinct told him not to. Perhaps this was yet another example of Provenzano's tactic – wrong-footing his foes with an unpredictable move.

★

Cortese hesitated about using a camera to monitor Marino's farm. Repeatedly over the past few weeks, Team Cathedral had spotted lookouts who scanned the road to Corleone and nearby fields with binoculars, surely on the watch for any police presence. He would place a camera the next time a bag left the home of Provenzano's partner Saveria; the camera would tell him whether or not it ended up at the farm.

On the evening of 9 April, Team Cathedral's watchers saw Giuseppe Lo Bue leave the house carrying a small bag, which he took to his own home. That night, two detectives – their codenames were 'the Falcon' and 'the Bloodhound' – cautiously made their way up a hill at Horses' Mountain to a statue of Saint Bernard, patron saint of Corleone, which dominated the area. The statue was just a mile away from the farm.

Among some stones just below the statue of the saint, they hid a remote-controlled, infrared video camera, powered by bulky batteries weighing 55 pounds. The batteries lasted less than 24 hours, so they would have to be replaced every night. Cortese worried not only that Marino or another local might spot the camera, but also that some animal might knock it sideways or damage it. In a previous operation, a sheep had ripped away a microphone that was being used to pick up mafiosi conversations outside someone's house.

That same night a tiny, ten foot by ten foot shed at the foot of the hill and less than a mile away from the farm became Team Cathedral's new field headquarters. Cortese and four detectives – 'the Falcon', 'the Bloodhound', 'the Lynx' and 'the Fox' – squeezed themselves into the shed to watch a small monitor which relayed the images captured by the camera on the hill above them.

They couldn't risk being heard, nor could they venture out to stretch their legs, as the box was only a hundred yards from the road and several houses. There were two stools in the box, reserved for those whose turn it was to watch the screen. But with nothing else to do in that cramped space, the detectives stared at the screen even when it wasn't their turn. Cortese used his mobile phone, its ringing tone switched off, to keep in touch. On his orders, the bulk of Team Cathedral – 20 officers – were stationed in a safe house a few miles from Corleone, ready to intervene at any time.

The following morning, 10 April, watchers saw an acquaintance drive to Bernardo Riina's home, where he stayed for just ten minutes. It was impossible to establish whether he had dropped off a bag. Using the camera's zoom lens to scan the farm that day, the detectives noticed that part of the shack appeared to have been added on, as if to make it more comfortable for someone. But the shack looked empty; the door and the windows were permanently closed. Cortese immediately ordered checks on the farm's electricity consumption. They revealed that for almost all of the last ten years, the electricity consumption had remained very low. But from November 2004 onwards the amount had risen sharply, almost fourfold.

Watching the farm, however, showed that Marino arrived at the farm early in the morning, worked mostly outside in the open and left at midday to have lunch and presumably a siesta at home, before returning in the afternoon for just a few hours. How could he run up such a high electricity bill, Cortese wondered? If someone was hiding in the shack, it was likely he had moved in at the time the bill increased.

Several brief scenes intrigued Cortese that day. Marino climbed onto the roof of the shack to fumble with a TV aerial, probably intending to watch Italy's election night broadcasts that evening. While Marino was adjusting the aerial, the door of the shack was ajar but there was no sign of life inside. Later that day, Marino stood outside the door of the shack, looking at the door fixedly for five minutes; when he walked up to the door, it seemed to start opening even before he had touched the handle. Cortese told himself the door had perhaps been pushed open by the strong *scirocco* wind which was blowing hard that day. It also seemed odd to Cortese that Marino always locked the door to the barn where he made his ricotta, but never the shack's door.

Cortese and his four colleagues spent the day closeted inside their tiny shed without ever going outside, eating the sandwiches they had brought with them and relieving themselves in empty plastic water bottles cut in half. That evening, after Marino had left, more checks at the electricity board revealed that an appliance of some kind was still being used in the shack.

But the camera showed both the shack and the barn still engulfed in darkness.

Feeling stiff and exhausted after a second virtually sleepless night cooped up in the shed – with only Cortese, 'the Falcon' and 'the Bloodhound' stealing out up the hill to replace the camera's batteries – the detectives watched Marino arrive at his farm at 7.30 a.m. on 11 April.

'The Bloodhound' broke the edgy silence. 'If nothing happens today either, I'm not sure it's worth us going to change the batteries again tonight,' he said. Cortese said nothing and neither did the others. The next hour or so dragged on, the screen showing only the farm, a few bushes and some rocks. Nothing stirred.

At 8.57 a.m., something did happen. Marino walked up to the shack and stopped just outside the door with his back to it. He stood staring towards the statue of Saint Bernard; Cortese and his colleagues had the impression he was staring into the camera – straight at them – even though it was a mile away from the farm. Perhaps he was looking at the pastures where he would take his sheep, the detectives guessed. Or was he simply admiring the countryside? The detectives stared at Marino, looking for a clue as to what he was up to.

Careful to keep his voice down, 'the Lynx' said: 'There's something odd about him.'

At that moment, the detectives saw something move just behind Marino: a hand reached out from the doorway holding a small container, possibly a white bag.

Marino turned towards the door and took the container. The hand then withdrew out of sight.

'Bingo!' yelled 'the Falcon'. His shout made his colleagues jump and they quickly hushed him. But the euphoria brought all five detectives to their feet, embracing and slapping each other on the back, bumping up against each other in the tiny space and cheering quietly, each telling the other not to make any noise and to keep watching the monitor.

Now they knew someone was hiding in that shack. When Marino was standing outside the door the previous day, he must have been talking with whoever was inside.

The detectives talked in whispers about the next move. 'Let's go now, it's sure he's the one in the shack; it can't be anyone else,' one of them said. There was no need to say who 'he' was.

'Chief, let's call up the men. This is it, this is it, let's move quickly,' another echoed.

All four of Cortese's men were agreed: Team Cathedral had no time to lose and must raid the shack immediately.

Cortese was hugely tempted to rush into action without any further thought. But he refused to budge. He told his men that if it was Provenzano hiding in the shack, there was no reason for him to suspect they were onto him just then; there was no danger of him fleeing. 'Calm down, we've got everything under control. In an investigation, you can't just rely on your instinct,' Cortese said.

Cortese insisted on waiting to see if the bag which had been seen leaving Saveria's house two days earlier would arrive at the shack. Only then would he give the order to launch a raid. Cortese's chiefs in Palermo were ready to call up a massive force – helicopters to patrol the area, dogs to pursue any fugitives, firemen to enter a bunker or a blocked tunnel and dozens of police officers to put up road-blocks around Corleone. Cortese thought twice and then twice again about deploying such a force only to end up with egg on his face. He didn't want to think about the possibility that the bag could be taken somewhere else; or that anyone else could be hiding in the shack.

The detectives in the shed went back to staring at the screen.

An hour later, at 9.53 a.m., Cortese's mobile phone flashed. A detective from headquarters in Palermo told him that Bernardo

Riina had just left his home in a Land Cruiser. As Cortese told his men the news, he felt the adrenalin flow; the pieces of the jigsaw puzzle were falling into place. He and his men stared fixedly at the monitor as Palermo stayed on the line, tracking the Land Cruiser using cameras and surveillance teams: 'Now he's taken the road towards Horses' Mountain, up the hill . . .'

The Land Cruiser suddenly appeared on the screen, going through the open gate of the farm, up the short drive and stopping next to the barn. Bernardo Riina got out and walked round to the other side of the car. He opened the passenger door, leant inside and emerged holding the same small bag Team Cathedral had spotted being carried out of Saveria's house two days earlier.

The detectives embraced each other again, whispering: 'This is it, this is it!' until Cortese ordered them to be quiet and keep watching the monitor. They saw Bernardo Riina put the bag down on the ground, near the shack, and start chatting to Marino. The camera shifted away from the bag for a few moments. Soon afterwards, the camera swung back to the same spot.

The bag had disappeared.

As the monitor showed Bernardo Riina driving away, Cortese rushed out of the shed with 'the Falcon' and 'the Bloodhound', leaving only 'the Lynx' behind. As he jumped into a waiting car, Cortese ordered Team Cathedral to rendezvous at a previously agreed meeting place four miles away in a forest.

At 10.45 a.m., standing under a tree as the light rain bounced off the leaves above his head, Cortese briefed his 20-strong force. Most of them were in plain clothes and the rest in police uniform, with bulletproof vests and balaclavas.

Cortese's greatest fear was that the man in the shack – he still couldn't bring himself to call him Provenzano – might have a secret way out. If it was the godfather, perhaps he had ordered the shack to be built years earlier – Corleone was after all his fiefdom and had been all his life. Perhaps an armour-plated door and a tunnel under the shack would allow him to give his hunters the slip yet again. Cortese was so worried about this that in his briefing he insisted on the need to surprise the quarry. The hunters would drive up to the shack slowly – no tyres squealing – as if they had come to buy some ricotta. Only the lead car, in which he would ride, would drive up to the farm itself.

In just a few minutes, Cortese reminded his team – the plan was basic training for them – to deploy themselves in three consecutive rings around the target. The first security cordon would be made up of men ready to use brute force and smash their way into the shack if necessary; the second would have a more defensive role. He assigned 'the Cat', the only woman in his team, to the outer cordon simply because she ran the least risk of violence there. 'The Cat' accepted his decision with good grace but many of her male colleagues did not hide their disappointment at being stationed far from the target. He tried to ease their frustration, telling them that each member of the team had a vital role to play; they must above all remain lucid and stick to the plan.

'It's not because you can smell the prey that you have to act like uncontrollable hunting dogs,' Cortese told them with a smile.

The briefing over, Cortese got into the front passenger seat of a 4 x 4 car, together with three other detectives. Behind him came a van carrying all those destined to form the first security cordon. Closing the convoy was another car with another four officers. The rest of the team followed shortly afterwards. The convoy drove at a steady pace out of the forest then threaded its way through bare fields towards Horses' Mountain. As he drew nearer and nearer, Cortese felt his heart beating at a crazy rate but he did his best to appear calm to his men.

The voice of 'the Lynx' spoke in Cortese's earpiece. 'Marino's going in and out of the barn,' he said.

Good, Cortese thought to himself. The fact that the shepherd was at the farm would make things easier; if Marino wasn't there, the man hiding in the shack would be more watchful.

At Horses' Mountain, the convoy drove slowly up the dirt road which ran through the green valley, then the car carrying Cortese turned onto the track leading through the open gates of Marino's land up to the farm 40 yards away.

Cortese caught sight of Marino standing by the shack and the car was still moving when he catapulted himself out, gun in hand, and raced towards the iron door of the shack, which he could see was open just a crack. He saw Marino turn to face him. All he could think of was that he must stop the person closing the door on him. He swiftly shoved Marino aside as he ran. Closely followed by three agents, he reached the iron door just in time to see that the person inside was pulling it to; he could make out only the outline of a face.

A single thought flashed through Cortese's mind: if that iron door slammed shut in his face, he and his men would need at least 15 minutes to knock it down, allowing whoever was inside to escape through the underground tunnel if there was one.

He hurled himself against the door, shattering a pane of glass with his closed fist before bursting into the shack and reaching out to grab the wrists of the man standing in front of him – an elderly, wiry figure dressed in tattered jeans and a dark polo-shirt, a white scarf around his neck.

As an officer slapped handcuffs over the man's wrists, Cortese stared into his eyes and then at his face; after hours and hours spent staring at the only photograph of Provenzano, as a young man, and at pictures of his brothers and sons, Cortese was almost certain that this was the godfather. The man said nothing; he stared back with a defiant gaze, a mocking smile on his thin, bloodless lips. Cortese noticed the man looked as if he hadn't shaved in two or three days; his hair was silver, with large receding hairlines and some strands combed over the bald patches. Grey spectacles hung from a cord around his neck.

Cortese reached up, took hold of the white scarf and pulled it aside to uncover the man's neck. There on the pale, wrinkled skin was a scar, the scar left by the thyroid surgery that super-grasses had described. Three rosaries hung around his neck. Cortese knew how religious Provenzano was. He knew he had caught up with his quarry at last.

He said the words he'd been dreaming of saying for eight years: 'You are Bernardo Provenzano and I declare you under arrest.' Forced to sit on the double bed, his handcuffed wrists resting on his lap, Provenzano stayed mute, the arrogant half-smile still playing on his face. Cortese looked around him. There was a desk with an electric typewriter and sheets of paper laid out tidily on it. The rest of the shack was a mess, with clothes piled up untidily near the bed, which had no sheets on it, only a sleeping bag. A saucepan on a small camp stove caked with bits of food was streaked with the remains of boiled chicory. He remembered phone taps in which Provenzano's associates had talked of buying chicory. The dank smell of ricotta mixed unpleasantly with the sharp smell of the coffee Provenzano had just prepared. Religious icons and images of saints were spread around the shack.

Cortese and his men kept trying to make Provenzano say who he was. 'Why don't you tell us you're Bernardo Provenzano?' one officer pressed him.

'Tell us, what are you waiting for?' another echoed.

Provenzano was quiet for a moment longer, then turned his palms upwards in a gesture of resignation which contrasted with his bold stare. He hissed in a low voice: 'Why should I tell you, if you know it already?'

The ghost had become flesh and blood at last.

At 11.21 a.m., Cortese strode outside – the rain had stopped by then – shouting as loudly as his lungs would allow: 'Got him! We've got him!' The rest of Team Cathedral came running, yelling and hugging each other in delight. Cortese exchanged handshakes then walked a few yards away from the celebration. He made a couple of calls to his superiors in Palermo then looked around him, trying to piece together precisely what had happened just a few minutes earlier. He wanted to make sure that he would remember every detail of the raid. He stared at the shack, at the doorway through which he had first seen Provenzano and then turned to look at the statue of Saint Bernard up on the hill where his men had hidden a camera only 40 hours earlier.

Cortese sat down on a slab of rock. He thought of the eight years he had spent tracking the godfather, of the long days and nights and near-misses. He repeated to himself again and again, in tears: 'It's over.'

His men called him back into the shack, wanting to show him something. Inside, Provenzano was still sitting on the bed and still mute. The detectives handed a letter to Cortese which they had taken out of the typewriter. It was addressed to Provenzano's companion Saveria, whom he called '*Carissima amata* (My very dear love)'. In it, he asked her not to send him any more oven-cooked pasta.

As he looked around the shack more closely this time, Cortese was struck by how cramped and messy it was. The only spotless part was the new bathroom at one end. Daylight filtered in only through the open door as the windows had been obscured with black rubbish bags. A small television, which was broadcasting the results of the previous day's election, had been encased in cardboard to dim the brightness of the screen. Two pairs of head-phones lay near the television and an old-fashioned cassette player – tapes in the shack included Neapolitan songs and the soundtrack of *The Godfather II*. Cortese understood why no light and no noise had emerged from the shack.

On the desk next to his typewriter, the godfather had spread out his incoming and outgoing correspondence – the latter neatly folded and taped – and six rolls of sellotape. By his bedside lay a spare set of false teeth, a pile of medical leaflets on post-surgery impotence and other ailments, a book entitled *All foods from A to Z: Guide to a healthy and correct diet* and the breviary *Pray, pray, pray*.

Eighty-three small holy images, most of them representing Christ, were piled up in small stacks – Provenzano liked to give them to mafiosi. Several of the images lay among the pages of a medical encyclopaedia, the godfather apparently believing they would help ward off disease. The only signs of wealth were £30,000 in cash, of which £7,400 was hidden among socks and under-pants, and seven Scottish cashmere sweaters.

A news flash ran across the bottom of the television. 'The boss of bosses, the head of Cosa Nostra, on the run for 43 years, has been captured,' it read. 'Provenzano was hiding in a farm near Corleone, his birthplace.'

The godfather turned his head to look at the screen. 'You don't know what you're doing,' he murmured.

An armoured police car arrived shortly afterwards with an escort and Cortese told Provenzano to follow him out of the shack. Getting up from his bed, the godfather asked for his white scarf, which lay on a chair. Cortese gave it to him and Provenzano wrapped it around his neck, hiding his scar. Provenzano then asked for the copy of the Bible he had in his shack, but Cortese refused to let him take it.

In Palermo, when the convoy drew up outside the headquarters of Palermo's flying squad, a crowd shouted 'Bastard!', 'Murderer!' and 'Cuckold!' at Provenzano. He remained impassive, again smiling ironically as Cortese and other members of Team Cathedral hustled him in.

Shortly afterwards, the national anti-mafia prosecutor Pietro Grasso felt he had to try an approach he knew had almost no probability of success. He walked up to Provenzano and introduced himself. 'Listen, *Signor* Provenzano, I want you to know that if something can be done for this Sicily of ours, I will always be available,' Grasso said – a hint that he was ready to listen if the godfather ever decided to betray the law of silence. Provenzano gazed fixedly at Grasso. The prosecutor had the impression that Provenzano was straining to keep every muscle of his face immobile, anxious not to betray even the slightest hint that he might wish to accept the offer.

'Yes, but each according to his role,' Provenzano replied – he had no wish to turn state's evidence.

At a military airport outside Palermo, as Cortese escorted Provenzano to the helicopter waiting to fly him to a maximum-security jail in Terni on the mainland, the godfather unexpectedly turned towards his captor, offering his hand. Cortese shook it, expecting a weak handshake, but Provenzano's hand was firm. Neither man said anything.

Before he boarded the helicopter, Provenzano was heard to say to himself: 'Let God's will be done.' He then added: 'God help me.'

Provenzano was locked up in a 13 foot by 10 foot jail cell, watched by CCTV cameras 24 hours a day. His daily routine was to wake up at five or six o'clock in the morning and breakfast on coffee with milk and a glass of water. Banned from watching television, listening to the radio or reading newspapers, he spent much of the day writing or reading the Bible the prison authorities had given him, underlining passages as he read. Because of his prostate trouble, he ate mainly boiled rice, potatoes, vegetables and pasta with spices recommended by his doctors.

He kept in shape by walking up to two hours a day in the prison yard, doing gymnastics and using an exercise bicycle in a room next to his cell. He rarely talked to anyone and it was only after three days in jail that he first thanked a guard for bringing him his food, saying: 'May the Lord protect you.'

Nine days after his arrest, Cortese and four prosecutors travelled to the Terni prison in central Italy for a first formal interrogation. When Provenzano entered the room where the visitors were waiting for him, his lawyer motioned to him to take a seat. But the prisoner insisted on first being introduced to his visitors one by one, and shaking each by the hand. It was clear to those present that Provenzano recognised Cortese, but he didn't even bat an eyelid.

This time the prisoner gave his name in a steady voice – 'Bernardo Provenzano'.

He looked embarrassed when asked whether he was married. 'I wasn't able to,' he said in a regretful tone. 'It's something I plan to do soon.'

With both Provenzano and his heirs in prison – including Riina's brother-in-law Bagarella, Riina's eldest son and Brusca – the Corleonesi were finished. They are unique in the history of the mafia. Despite their peasant origins, over more than five decades they rose to challenge and overcome bosses in Palermo and across the rest of Sicily in an unprecedented purge. They transformed the brotherhood into a dictatorship. They launched an attack against the state which claimed 'distinguished corpses' while negotiating political demands. They sparked a haemorrhage of supergrasses and a crackdown by the state which saw hundreds of mafiosi jailed, finally switching strategies to lie low and make the mafia virtually 'invisible'.

Without the 'friends of the friends' whom they invariably found in every field – from businessmen to bankers, doctors, lawyers and politicians – the Corleonesi would have remained merely a rural clan. Instead they built up a vast fortune. Over a decade, the state has seized £4.5 billion from Provenzano and his lieutenants, but the godfather himself owned nothing. All his property was registered in the names of no fewer than 400 associates.

In 2006, the year Provenzano was arrested, the mafia was estimated to be collecting protection money from 70 per cent of businesses in Sicily and 80 per cent of those in Palermo. The earnings of the mafia and its two less powerful sister organisations, the Camorra in Naples and the 'Ndrangheta in Calabria, amounted to £42 billion a year – 10.5 per cent of Italy's GDP and more than the revenues of the country's biggest corporation, the oil and gas giant ENI. The figure excluded profits from drug-trafficking, which could be as high as £35 billion.

Riches aside, the legacy of the Corleonesi is a mostly disastrous one for the mafia. Although Provenzano succeeded in pulling the organisation away from Riina's campaign of terror, sweeping arrests have thrown it into turmoil, as replacing bosses is a long and often messy procedure. The power vacuum caused by the fall of the Corleonesi may see, in the absence of a clear successor to Provenzano, the most powerful clans agreeing to share control, with decisions taken at meetings of bosses – a return to the Cupola or regional commission first created in the mid-1970s.

One contender in the struggle for supremacy, the elderly

Palermo boss Salvatore Lo Piccolo – who had first opposed the Corleonesi but then jumped on their bandwagon – forged an alliance with former enemies of the clan who had escaped to America in the early 1980s and whom he now helped to return to Sicily. But Lo Piccolo soon saw his chances wrecked by the police, who arrested him and his son in 2007. After police surrounded a villa near Palermo, the clan head tried to flush a registry of extortion levies down the lavatory; he was captured before managing to do so.

Three months later, in early 2008, in an operation codenamed 'Old Bridge', police and FBI agents in America and Italy arrested 77 mafia suspects, many of them alleged allies of Lo Piccolo. The raids were the biggest since the break-up of the Pizza Connection drug-trafficking ring in the mid-1980s and netted among others the acting head of New York's Gambino family, John D'Amico, known as 'Jackie the Nose', and his deputy Domenico Cefalu, or 'Greaseball'. Investigators said the operation had prevented the outbreak of a new mafia war prompted by emigrants to Sicily seeking to fill the void at the top of the organisation.

The arrests were no doubt welcome news for another leading candidate – Matteo Messina Denaro, who in his mid-forties is more than 30 years younger than Provenzano. Messina Denaro is a bizarre mix of tradition and modernity. When his father, a respected boss, died in 1998, the family dressed the corpse in his best suit and laid him out, hands joined, on the bare earth of the estate where he had worked as a guard and then as a bailiff. The body was found by the police. Every year that followed, Messina Denaro placed a memorial notice to his father in a local newspaper, choosing passages from the Old Testament. But he also lived the life of a millionaire playboy, collecting girlfriends, designer clothes and Rolex watches – a lifestyle that could not be more different from that of the older generation that Provenzano and Riina belonged to. They clung to old-fashioned, rural values on marriage and a host of other issues. They wanted power for power's sake and accumulated wealth because in their eyes it represented power; they had no desire to flaunt their riches or to spend their money on a luxurious lifestyle.

The Corleonesi have been defeated, but the battle against the mafia is far from being won. Sadly that battle is not even being fought, save for the efforts of a tiny minority of courageous prosecutors and police officers. Falcone called them 'servants of the state' but the Italian state has asked nothing of them and simply uses them to hide the fact that it has yet to launch a determined, lasting strategy, not only to put mafiosi behind bars but also to persuade Sicilians that they can denounce the mafia's crimes without fear. The first people who need persuading are the thousands of bar-owners, shopkeepers, businessmen and industrialists who pay the mafia protection money.

Immediately after Falcone's murder, Palermitans hung white sheets from their windows and marched through the streets to demand an end to the brotherhood. But the days of widespread popular protests are long gone. Now the overwhelming majority of Sicilians appear resigned to the mafia ruling much of their lives. Political leaders have yet to show them an alternative. Falcone neatly summed up the state's efforts against the mafia: 'Emotive, episodic, inconsistent. Motivated only by the impression created by a given crime or by the effect that a particular initiative on the part of the government will have on public opinion.' In 2001, in a blatant admission of the state's failure even to contemplate eradicating the organisation, the government minister Pietro Lunardi said on television: 'The mafia has always existed and will always exist; unfortunately we will have to live with this reality.' Governments of both left and right have preferred to set other priorities, including terrorism and urban crime such as theft and prostitution.

The boss Giovanni Brusca once predicted: 'Cosa Nostra will disappear if the bosses lose their armies; if its strategy is no longer the winning one . . . and if certain Sicilian politicians stop wooing her.' But for the mafia to disappear, first and foremost Sicilians must trust the Italian state more than they fear the fraternity. As

Falcone wrote: 'The mafia is, essentially, nothing but the expression of a need for order, for the control of a state.'

Shortly after Provenzano's arrest, Cortese leafed through the Bible found in the shack. He noticed that the godfather had underlined the following passage:

> To every thing there is a season, and a time to every purpose
>   under the heaven:
> a time to be born, and a time to die;
> a time to plant, and a time to pluck up that which is planted;
> a time to kill, and a time to heal;
> a time to break down, and a time to build up;
> a time to weep, and a time to laugh;
> a time to mourn, and a time to dance . . .
> a time to love, and a time to hate;
> a time of war, and a time of peace.
>
> (Ecclesiastes 3:1–8)

Acknowledgements

This book couldn't have been written without the many people who helped me research it on trips to Sicily and Rome. I'm grateful in particular to all those who supplied me with more than 8,000 pages of court verdicts, arrest warrants, wiretap transcripts, supergrass testimony and other judicial documents. In Palermo, my thanks to the public prosecutors Maurizio De Lucia, Antonio Ingroia, Sergio Lari, Guido Lo Forte, Francesco Messineo, Giuseppe Pignatone, Michele Prestipino, Marzia Sabella, Lia Sava and Roberto Scarpinato; Francesco Accordino, former deputy-head of the Palermo police; Virgilio Alberelli, police spokesman; Piero Angeloni, head of the police's flying squad; Nonuccio Anselmo, author; Riccardo Avena of the *Giornale di Sicilia*; Enrico Bellavia and Salvo Palazzolo of *La Repubblica*; Giuseppe Cucchiara, former head of the flying squad; Peppino Lo Bianco of the *ANSA* news agency; Saverio Lodato of *L'Unità*; Professor Salvatore Lupo, Palermo University; Umberto Santino and Anna Puglisi, Centro Siciliano di Documentazione 'Giuseppe Impastato'; the staff of the Istituto Gramsci; and detective Salvatore Zuccarello of the flying squad.

In Corleone, I'm grateful to former mayor Pippo Cipriani; police superintendent Gianfranco Minisale; Dino Paternostro, editor, *Città Nuove*; and others who prefer not to be named.

In Rome, many thanks to Attilio Bolzoni of *La Repubblica*; Assunta Borzachiello of the Dipartimento Amministrazione Penitenziaria; Giovanni Colussi; Renato Cortese, former head of Team Cathedral; Fabrizio Feo of *TG3* news; Judge Pietro Grasso, national anti-mafia prosecutor; Riccardo Guido of parliament's anti-mafia commission; Francesco La Licata of *La Stampa*; Marco Minniti, former deputy-minister, Ministry of the Interior; Valeria Lupidi and Fernando Paladino, Servizio Centrale di Protezione; Giovanna Montanaro, author; Marcelle Padovani of *Le Nouvel Observateur*; Judge Alfonso Sabella, public prosecutor; Valeria Scafetta, author; Roberto Sgalla, spokesman for the Ministry of the Interior; and Judge Luca Tescaroli, public prosecutor.

I'm also very much in debt to the authors John Dickie, Peter Gomez, Leo Sisti and Francesco Silvestri; Nick Cornish, photographer; Francesco Dell'Aira, governor of Terni prison; and Benito Montorio, documentary-maker.

Both Clare Alexander, my agent, and Rupert Lancaster, my editor, were, as ever, stimulating and delightful to work with. Thanks also to Nicky Bull, Kerry Hood and Laura Macaulay at Hodder & Stoughton. Sean Ryan, foreign editor of *The Sunday Times*, kindly gave me the time necessary to finish when the deadline loomed. Warm thanks for their hospitality in southern Italy to Giovanna, Maria and Rita Punzo and Antonio Cristofari. I'm very grateful to my mother for making the time to go through the manuscript with a toothcomb and come up with a host of suggestions.

My heartfelt thanks to my wife Rita, who offered advice based on her own work against the mafia and put up with long absences, especially soon after the birth of our son to whom this book is dedicated.

John Follain is a journalist with a specialization in crime reporting. He has written about Italy as the Rome correspondent for the *Sunday Times* and the *Sunday Times Magazine* for the past ten years.

Notes on Sources

Prologue: 23 May 1992

p. 1 'After all . . . a super-prosecutor?' *La Licata*, p. 216.

p. 2 'Those who . . . to it.' Author interview with Giovanni Falcone, 11 November 1991.

p. 4 'I'm sorry . . . I'm sorry.' *Sentenza della Corte di Assise nei confronti di Pietro Aglieri* + *40*, Caltanissetta, 26 September 1997, p. 125.

1 Corleone 1905–1963

Dr Michele Navarra, 'Our Father'

p. 9 'this landscape . . . of 104°.' Lampedusa, Giuseppe Tomasi di, *The Leopard*, p. 123.

p. 12 'everything change . . . of corpses.' Leopoldo Franchetti, quoted in Falzone, Michele, *La mafia: Dal feudo all'eccidio di via Carini*, S. F. Flaccovio, 1984.

p. 13 'Speaking to . . . Sicilian towns.' Paternostro, Dino, *A pugni nudi: Placido Rizzotto e le lotte popolari a Corleone nel secondo dopoguerra*, p. 17.

p. 13–14 'We must . . . to Sicily.' Lupo, Salvatore, *Storia della mafia*, p. 123.

p. 16 The mafia . . . of security.' Mori, Cesare, *Con la Mafia ai ferri corti: le memorie del Prefetto di Ferro*, p. 158.

p. 17 'They are . . . and laws.' Barzini, Luigi, p. 279.

p. 17 'Across the . . . the mafia.' Tranfaglia, Nicola, *Mafia, politica e affari: 1943–91*.

p. 18 'I fear . . . obey them.' Anti-mafia commission, Rome parliament, *Mafia e politica*.

Luciano Leggio

p. 22   'How did . . . for 15,000.' *Giornale di Sicilia*, 25 May 1986.

p. 25   'are in . . . Catholic Church.' Falcone, Giovanni with Padovani, Marcelle, p. 43.

p. 25   'You must . . . of all!' Arlacchi, Pino, *Gli uomini del disonore*, p. 5.

p. 26   'I will . . . dear departed.' Fava, Giuseppe, *Processo alla mafia*.

Placido Rizzotto, 'the Northern Wind'

p. 31   'Wicked people . . . she reflected.' Paternostro, Dino, *Ecco la verità su me e Rizzotto*. *La Sicilia*, 20 March 2005.

p. 33   'He made . . . like me.' Paternostro, Dino, *A pugni nudi: Placido Rizzotto e le lotte popolari a Corleone nel secondo dopoguerra*, p. 41.

p. 34   '*Omertà* is . . . any names.' Witness account in Paternostro, Dino, *I Corleonesi*, p. 81, and author interview with Paternostro.

p. 34   'As another . . . for them.' Lewis, Norman, p. 110

p. 34   'At a . . . he predicted.' Paternostro, Dino, *A pugni nudi: Placido Rizzotto e le lotte popolari a Corleone nel secondo dopoguerra*, p. 40.

Leggio, Salvatore Riina and Bernardo Provenzano – 'the Holy Trinity'

p. 46   'Too poor . . . said later.' Interview with Mario Francese, quoted in Buongiorno, Pino, pp. 61–62.

Bullets and the Law of Silence

p. 49   'The next . . . what happened.' Palazzolo, Salvo and Prestipino, Michele, p. 281.

p. 50   'Mafiosi were . . . their home.' Fava, Giuseppe, *Mafia:Da Giuliano a Dalla Chiesa*, pp. 47–48.

p. 50   'One journalist . . . anyone dead?' Nese, Marco.

p. 52–53   'In this . . . the streets.' Lewis, Norman, p. 98.

2 The Rise of 'The Peasants' 1963–1974

Palermo: Challenging the Establishment

p. 59   'The politicians . . . and candidates.' Arlacchi, Pino, *Gli uomini del disonore*, p. 212.

p. 61   'The Corleonesi . . . Cosa Nostra.' Calderone.

p. 61   'Leggio wasn't . . . *gushed* money.' Angelo Mangano, quoted in Fava, Giuseppe, *Processo alla mafia*, p. 196.

p. 61   'My life . . . Palermo's salons.' *Giornale di Sicilia*, 3 August 1986.

p. 63   'Cosa Nostra . . . defector said.' Arlacchi, Pino, *Gli uomini del disonore*, p. 72.

'Be Wise' – Justice Mafia-Style

p. 65   'According to . . . former lover.' Paternostro, Dino, *Ecco la verità su me e Rizzotto*.

p. 67   'Drugs were . . . prisoner said.' Galluzzo, Lucio *et al*.

p. 67   'He and . . . one prisoner.' Arlacchi, Pino, *Gli uomini del disonore*.

p. 68   'Another chronicler . . . their hearts.' Linares, *Racconti popolari*, quoted in Mori, Cesare, *Con la mafia ai ferri corti: Le memorie del prefetto di ferro*, p. 51.

p. 66   'One day . . . robbing him.' Gruppo Abele, p. 321.

p. 68   'For the . . . be eliminated.' Scafetta, Valeria.

p. 70   'In the . . . in court.' Bolzoni, Attilio and D'Avanzo, Giuseppe, p. 79.

p. 72   'If the . . . doesn't exist.' Nese, Marco.

p. 73   'What I . . . local police.' Interview with Mario Francese, quoted in Buongiorno, Pino, p. 62.

p. 74   'For years . . . marry me.' Bolzoni, Attilio and D'Avanzo, Giuseppe, p. 30.

p. 74   'We got . . . serious people.' Interview with Giampaolo Pansa of *La Stampa*, in Buongiorno, Pino, pp. 65–65.

Death of 'the Cobra'

p. 75   'Cavataio is . . . innocent victims.' Arlacchi, Pino, *Gli uomini del disonore*, p. 70.

p. 76   'I'm risking . . . uniform on.' Palazzolo, Salvo and Prestipino, Michele, p. 11.

p. 76   'After a . . . the offices.' Arlacchi, Pino, *Gli uomini del disonore*, p. 81.

p. 78   'He now . . . longer grew.' Oliva, Ernesto and Palazzolo, Salvo.

p. 78   'Riina was . . . the time.' Pippo Calderone, quoted in Bolzoni, Attilio and D'Avanzo, Giuseppe, p. 124.

p. 78   'He found . . . each clan.' Bolzoni, Attilio and D'Avanzo, Giuseppe, p. 126.

p. 78   'Riina was . . . Buscetta, recalled.' Buongiorno, Pino.

p. 79   'Wait for . . . from Palermo.' Paternostro, Dino, *I Corleonesi: storia dei golpisti di Cosa Nostra*.

p. 79   'Leggio impressed . . . in Sicily.' Arlacchi, Pino, *Gli uomini del disonore*, p. 84.

p. 79   'Riina pretended . . . all weathers.' Bolzoni, Attilio and D'Avanzo, Giuseppe, p. 124.

p. 81			'Those of . . . Calderone said.' Arlacchi, Pino, *Gli uomini del disonore*, p. 89.

p. 81–82		'Leggio's habit . . . bother us.' Ibid, pp. 86–89.

p. 82–83		'He was . . . the air.' Ibid, p. 91.

p. 84			'In order . . . prince replied.' Ibid, p. 97.

On the Triumvirate

p. 86			'When they . . . informer said.' Antonino Calderone in Di Cagno, Giovanni and Natoli, Gioacchino, p. 25.

p. 86			'When asked . . . Rolex watch.' Padovani, Marcelle, p. 121.

p. 86–87		'Riina conducted . . . the hostage.' Arlacchi, Pino, *Gli uomini del disonore*, p. 6.

p. 88			'The two . . . supergrass said.' Antonino Calderone in Arlacchi, Pino, *Gli uomini del disonore*, p. 164.

p. 88			'One informer . . . towards others.' Scafetta, Valeria, p. 71.

p. 88			'On one . . . a cent?' Lodato, Saverio, *'Ho ucciso Giovanni Falcone': La confessione di Giovanni Brusca*, p. 51.

p. 90			'As Judge . . . man too.' Falcone, Giovanni with Padovani, Marcelle, p. 11.

'I Love Riina' – Ninetta Goes to Court

p. 91			'The boss . . . to anyone.' Padovani, Marcelle, p. 123.

p. 92			'The archpriest . . . takes communion.' Caruso, Alfio, p. 229.

p. 92			'Sheltering from . . . and discouraged.' *Giornale di Sicilia*, 27 July 1971.

p. 92–93		'Riina, she . . . a woman.' *Giornale di Sicilia*, 6 August 1971.

p. 94			'Despite her . . . church sacristy.' *Sentenza della Corte di Assise di Appello nei confronti di Salvatore Riina* + 7, Palermo. 13 December 2002.

p. 95			'According to . . . and thin.' Lodato, Saverio, *'Ho ucciso Giovanni Falcone': La confessione di Giovanni Brusca*, p. 129.

3 Forging a Dictatorship 1974–1983

Making Friends and Enemies

p. 100			'Riina likes . . . not Riina.' Gruppo Abele, pp. 324–325.

p. 100			'When some . . . trouble you.' Paternostro, Dino, *I Corleonesi: storia dei golpisti di Cosa Nostra*, p. 116.

p. 100			'Whether out . . . supergrass said.' Gruppo Abele, p. 325.

p. 101			'The Cupola . . . put it.' Cancemi, Salvatore, p. 24.

p. 101   'Every time . . . a stand.' Lodato, Saverio, *'Ho ucciso Giovanni Falcone': La confessione di Giovanni Brusca*, p. 65.

p. 104   'He once . . . to them.' Lodato, Saverio, *Dieci anni di mafia: La guerra che lo Stato non ha saputo vincere*.

p. 104   'A furious . . . the strings.' Tescaroli, Luca, *Le faide mafiose nei misteri di Sicilia*, p. 58.

p. 104   'Greco . . . nothing.' Arlacchi, Pino, *Gli uomini del disonore*, pp. 256–257.

The Last Stand of 'the Tiger'

p. 105   'One afternoon . . . join in.' Bolzoni, Attilio and D'Avanzo, Giuseppe, p. 132.

p. 108   'They never . . . their nature.' *Sentenza della Corte di Assise nei confronti di Pietro Aglieri + 40*, Caltanissetta. 26 September 1997, p. 816.

p. 108–109   'The testimony . . . public authorities.' Stajano, Corrado, p. 19.

p. 109–10   'Di Cristina's . . . boss joked.' Arlacchi, Pino, *Gli uomini del disonore*, pp. 159–160.

p. 110   'Riina's incredibly . . . the problem.' Ibid, p. 29.

p. 110–11   'In the . . . the rampage.' Riccobono quoted in Arlacchi, Pino, *Gli uomini del disonore*.

p. 111   'An ally . . . the wrong.' Arlacchi, Pino, *Gli uomini del disonore*, p. 279.

p. 111–12   'A few . . . said later.' Ibid, p. 281.

p. 113   'Bontate had . . . vote communist.' Testimony of Francesco Marino Mannoia to prosecutors Giancarlo Caselli and Guido Lo Forte, 3 April 1993, quoted in Tribunale di Palermo, *Integrazione*, 14 April 1993. And *Sentenza di primo grado nei confronti di Salvatore Riina + 31*, Palermo, p. 282. 15 July 1998.

p. 113   'When the . . . made public.' Gaspare Mutolo, quoted in Tribunale di Palermo, *Domanda di autorizzazione a procedere contro il senatore Giulio Andreotti*, 27 March 1993.

p. 113   'In a . . . legal costs.' Quoted in Abbate, Lirio and Gomez, Peter, p. 304 and Lodato, Saverio and Travaglio, Marco, p. 247.

Tommaso Buscetta, 'the Boss of Two Worlds'

p. 114   'A mafioso . . . a necessity.' Interview by Enzo Biagi in *Panorama*, *Mafia: Dentro i misteri di Cosa Nostra*, p. 35.

p. 115   'He wanted . . . reflected later.' Biagi, Enzo.

p. 115   'He obtained . . . interested in.' Lodato, Saverio, *Trent'anni di mafia*, p. 144.

p. 115–16　'Soon afterwards ... American underworld.' Commissione parlamentare d'inchiesta sul fenomeno della mafia e sulle altre associazioni criminali similari, *I boss della mafia*, pp. 295–315.

p. 116–17　'Now, in ... liked them.' Arlacchi, Pino, *Addio Cosa Nostra*.

p. 117　'One of ... sound,' he said.' *Sentenza della Corte di Assise di Appello nei confronti di Bruno Contrada*, Palermo, p. 159. 25 February 2006.

p. 117　'The boss ... the bill.' *Sentenza della Corte di Assise di Appello nei confronti di Bruno Contrada*, Palermo, p. 26. 25 February 2006.

p. 117　'When some ... he said.' Lodato, Saverio and Travaglio, Marco, p. 286.

p. 118　'One day ... become true.' Arlacchi, Pino, *Addio Cosa Nostra*, pp. 230–231.

p. 118　'On the ... for ever.' Ibid, p. 231.

p. 118–19　'With characteristic ... Buscetta explained.' Ibid.

p. 119　'His father ... respect commitments.' La Licata, Francesco, p. 27.

p. 119–20　'Growing up ... the mafia.' Falcone, Giovanni with Padovani, Marcelle, p. 21.

p. 120　'Falcone shrugged ... his memoirs.' Ibid, p. 22.

p. 120　'Thinking of ... at all!' Ibid.

p. 120　'When Falcone's ... live once.' Zingales, Leone, *Giovanni Falcone, un uomo normale*, p. 60.

p. 121　'For Falcone ... said later.' Lodato, Saverio, *Dieci anni di mafia: La guerra che lo Stato non ha saputo vincere*.

p. 121　'As he ... anti-personnel mine.' Falcone, Giovanni with Padovani, Marcelle, p. 27.

p. 121　'The president ... judge recommended.' La Licata, Francesco, p. 73.

p. 121　'I had ... Inzerillo said.' Buscetta testimony, vol. I, p. 92.

p. 121　'Falcone was ... got you.' Lodato, Saverio, *Trent'anni di mafia*, p. 54.

p. 122　'To his ... he said.' La Licata, Francesco, p. 76.

Purges and Banquets

p. 123　'What the ... systematic elimination.' Di Cagno, Giovanni and Natoli, Gioacchino, p. 33.

p. 123　'Giuffrè himself ... he said.' Ibid.

p. 125　'On the ... one's turn.' Bolzoni, Attilio and D'Avanzo, Giuseppe, p. 176.

p. 125　'To another ... these bastards.' Arlacchi, Pino, *Addio Cosa Nostra*, p. 234.

p. 125   'One of . . . the air.' *Richiesta di custodia cautelare nei confronti di Agate, Mariano + 57 persone*, Palermo, p. 648. 20 February 1993.

p. 126   'Buscetta commented . . . you're inside.' Arlacchi, Pino, *Addio Cosa Nostra*, p. 234.

p. 126   'A few . . . hurry up.' Falcone, Giovanni with Padovani, Marcelle, p. 66.

p. 127   'Eventually, Inzerillo's . . . and fired.' Biagi, Enzo.

p. 127   'A war . . . hears everything.' Buongiorno, Pino, p. 125.

p. 127–28 'As Judge . . . leaves undisturbed.' La Licata, Francesco, p. 9.

p. 128   'As an . . . ferocious men.' Testimony of Leonardo Messina to the anti-mafia commission, December 1992.

p. 128   'As Riina's . . . him immediately.' Buongiorno, Pino.

p. 128   'There is . . . do that.' Cancemi, Salvatore, pp. 34–35.

p. 128–29 '*Piano piano* . . . supergrass testified.' Testimony of Leonardo Messina to the anti-mafia commission, December 1992.

p. 129   'But as . . . the job.' Francesco Marino Mannoia quoted in Stille, Alexander, *Excellent Cadavers: The mafia and the death of the first Italian republic*, p. 309.

p. 129   'One of . . . against him.' Catania, Enzo and Sottile, Salvo, p. 190.

p. 130   'When the . . . island capital.' Lodato, Saverio, *'Ho ucciso Giovanni Falcone': La confessione di Giovanni Brusca*, p. 163.

p. 131–32 'As a . . . Riina introduced.' Testimony of Gaspare Mutolo to the anti-mafia commission, February 1993.

p. 132   'As the . . . and silence.' Lodato, Saverio, *'Ho ucciso Giovanni Falcone': La confessione di Giovanni Brusca*, p. 181.

p. 132   'Watching them . . . Brusca recalled.' Ibid.

p. 133   'Brusca drew . . . the wrong.' Ibid, p. 184.

p. 133–34 'Brusca himself . . . the weak.' Ibid, p. 187.

General Dalla Chiesa

p. 135–36 'Among the . . . his mouth.' Dalla Chiesa, Nando, p. 56.

p. 136   'Shortly after . . . to terror.' Ibid, p. 70.

p. 137   'As his . . . anyone else.' Ibid, p. 74.

p. 137–38 'In a . . . Chiesa said.' Ibid, p. 53.

p. 138   'One successful . . . Piedmontese General.' Ibid, p. 64.

p. 138   'That July . . . that long.' Ibid, p. 132.

p. 138–39 'A few . . . them down.' Ibid, p. 133.

p. 139   'Dismayed by . . . the fraternity.' Interview with Giorgio Bocca published by *La Repubblica*, 10 August 1982.

p. 139   'Asked how . . . a distance.' Ibid.

p. 139   'He explained . . . my sanction.' Ibid.

p. 139–40 'Clearly aware . . . he's isolated.' Ibid.

p. 140   'Exasperated by . . . General said.' Article by Roger Cohen, *The Wall Street Journal*, 12 February 1985.

p. 141   'When news . . . one shouted.' Lodato, Saverio, *Trent'anni di mafia*, p. 281.

Buscetta Plays for Time

p. 143   'The Corleonese . . . my neck.' Arlacchi, Pino, *Addio Cosa Nostra*, p. 36.

p. 143   'Buscetta said . . . too subtle.' Falcone, Giovanni with Padovani, Marcelle, p. 10.

p. 143–44 'That summer . . . its return.' Arlacchi, Pino, *Addio Cosa Nostra*, pp. 238–239.

p. 144–45 'The blow . . . years later.' Ibid, pp. 240–241.

p. 145   'Riina was . . . in acid.' Interview with *La Repubblica*, December 1992, quoted in Catania, Enzo and Sottile, Salvo, pp. 229–229.

p. 145   'I'm better . . . with it.' Biagi, Enzo.

p. 145   'Years later . . . Riina's orders.' Cancemi, Salvatore, pp. 59–60.

p. 145   'After turning . . . Buscetta said.' Ibid.

p. 145–46 'Badalamenti offered . . . the Corleonesi.' Arlacchi, Pino, *Addio Cosa Nostra*, p. 241.

p. 146   'Buscetta compared . . . Buscetta said.' Ibid, p. 234.

p. 147   'Riina was . . . seven executions.' *Richiesta di custodia cautelare nei confronti di Agate, Mariano + 57 persone*, Palermo, p. 486. 20 February 1993.

p. 148   'Riina is . . . tragic life.' Ibid.

Corleone Inc.

p. 149   'But the . . . by one.' Falcone, Giovanni with Padovani, Marcelle, p. 97.

p. 149   'Provenzano and . . . time either.' Cancemi, Salvatore, p. 38.

p. 149–50 'The informer . . . reason, always.' Scafetta, Valeria, p. 56.

p. 150–51 'When Riina . . . you're dead.' Grasso Pietro and La Licata, Francesco, p. 52.

p. 152   'For entrepreneurs . . . his territory.' Arlacchi, Pino, *Gli uomini del disonore*.

p. 153   'Appointments would . . . to him.' Antonino Giuffré, *Deposizione al procedimento penale N.124/97 RG a carico di Giuseppe Biondolillo + altri*, Termini Imerese, p. 48. 16 December 2002.

p. 154   'Two years . . . her audacity.' Madeo, Liliana, p. 71.

4 The 'Servants' of the State Fight Back 1983–1992

Judge Falcone in 'Enemy Territory'

p. 159   'I believe . . . he wrote.' Falcone, Giovanni with Padovani, Marcelle, p. 149.

p. 160   'One neighbour . . . Palermo's outskirts?' La Licata, Francesco, p. 84.

p. 160   'In the . . . that's all.' Ibid, p. 85.

p. 161   'Falcone 'suffered . . . Maria said.' Ibid, p. 77.

p. 161   'I'm not . . . enemy territory.' Falcone, Giovanni with Padovani, Marcelle, p. xi.

p. 164   'I want . . . he said.' Biagi, Enzo.

p. 164   'I must . . . interview me?' Falcone, Giovanni with Padovani, Marcelle, p. 27.

p. 164   'Nothing more . . . of life.' Ibid, p. 52.

p. 164   'We're both . . . each other.' Biagi, Enzo.

p. 165   'I knew . . . for them.' Falcone, Giovanni with Padovani, Marcelle, p. 52.

p. 165   'With him . . . Falcone said.' Ibid, p. 23.

p. 165   'Riina and . . . he said.' Stille, Alexander, *Excellent Cadavers: The mafia and the death of the first Italian republic*, p. 101.

p. 165   'Villainous men . . . their children.' Arlacchi, Pino, *Addio Cosa Nostra*, p. 12.

p. 165–66   'If I . . . loved ones.' Ibid, p. 13.

p. 166   'The death . . . he said.' Ibid, p. 14.

p. 166   'It's so . . . I could.' Biagi, Enzo.

p. 166   'A big . . . narcotics traffic.' Benedetto Buscetta debriefing by the US Narcotics Bureau, quoted in Sterling, Claire, *The mafia: The long reach of the international Sicilian mafia*, Hamish Hamilton, 1990.

p. 166   'Aware of . . . was now.' Stajano, Corrado, pp. 24–25.

The Maxi-Trial

p. 168   'This time . . . a friend.' La Licata, Francesco, p. 11.

p. 169   'They were . . . informer explained.' Cancemi, Salvatore, p. 28.

p. 169   'A few . . . to reply.' Ibid, p. 58.

p. 169   'Riina was . . . absolute supremacy.' Catania, Enzo and Sottile, Salvo, p. 189.

p. 171   'The most . . . Calò replied.' Jannuzzi, Lino, *Cosi parlò Buscetta*.

p. 171–72   'Leggio realised . . . Mutolo said.' Scafetta, Valeria, p. 72.

p. 172   'I don't . . . told her.' La Licata, Francesco, p. 140.

p. 172   'Judge Falcone . . . off you.' Ibid, p. 91.

p. 173   'The one . . . he said.' Cancemi, Salvatore, p. 64.

p. 173   'Provenzano and . . . an agreement.' Antonino Giuffrè, *Deposizione al procedimento penale N.124/97 RG a carico di Giuseppe Biondolillo + altri,* Termini Imerese, p. 48. 16 October 2002 p. 83.

p. 173–74   'From now . . . must die.' Di Maggio quoted in Catania, Enzo and Sottile, Salvo, pp. 193–194.

p. 174   'No, I . . . in Sicily.' Giovanni Brusca, *Deposizione al processo di appello per la strage di Capaci* (Falcone murder), Caltanissetta, p. 61. 2 July 1999.

p. 175   'If any . . . the table.' *Richiesta di custodia cautelare nei confronti di Agate, Mariano + 57 persone,* Palermo, p. 447. 20 February 1993.

p. 175   'He was . . . boss recalled.' Salvatore Cancemi in Gruppo Abele, p. 264.

p. 176   'In 1985 . . . £7 billion.' Estimates by the statistics agency ISTAT and the CENSIS research institute.

p. 176   'Falcone worked . . . the Atlantic.' Testimony of Nino Giuffrè, quoted in Abbate, Liro and Gomez, Peter, p. 183.

p. 177   'I'm a . . . nothing else.' La Licata, Francesco, p. 14.

p. 177   'It's a . . . the judge.' Giovanni Brusca quoted in Tescaroli, Luca, *I misteri dell'Addaura . . . ma fu solo Cosa Nostra?,* p. xxi.

p. 178   'At his . . . walking corpse.' Tescaroli, Luca, *Perchè fu ucciso Giovanni Falcone.*

p. 178   'By taking . . . informer explained.' Salvatore Cancemi in Gruppo Abele, p. 266.

p. 179   'When he . . . Buscetta said.' Lodato, Saverio, *Trent'anni di mafia,* p. 154.

p. 179   'I intend . . . and murderers.' Stille, Alexander, *Excellent Cadavers: The mafia and the death of the first Italian republic,* p. 130.

p. 179   'When their . . . the earth.' Di Cagno, Giovanni and Natoli, Gioacchino, p. 42.

p. 180   'I don't . . . with it.' Madeo, Liliana, p. 114.

p. 180   'The mafia . . . fire inside.' *Richiesta di custodia cautelare nei confronti di Agate, Mariano + 57 persone,* Palermo, p. 1862. 20 February 1993.

p. 180   'The fraternity . . . possible survivors.' Madeo, Liliana, p. 115.

p. 180   'Even though . . . women, no.' Arlacchi, Pino. *Addio Cosa Nostra,* p. 15.

'A Question of Courtesy' – Riina Fights to Keep his Promises

p. 182   **'Either you . . . your family.'** Catania, Enzo and Sottile, Salvo, p. 195.

p. 182   **'Riina felt . . . in Rome.'** Ibid, pp. 231–232.

p. 182   **'The judge . . . the Lord.'** Testimony of Gaspare Mutolo to the anti-mafia commission, February 1993.

p. 183   **'Vittorio Mangano . . . few kidnappings.'** Cancemi testimony of 26 January 1998, in Procura della Repubblica presso il Tribunale di Palermo, Direzione Distrettuale Antimafia, *Requisitoria del pubblico ministero, procedimento penale nei confronti di Gaetano Cinà e Marcello Dell'Utri.* 11 November 2004. published in Gomez, Peter and Taraglio, Marco p. 80.

p. 183   **'The message . . . Cancemi said.'** Ibid, pp. 281–83.

p. 183–84   **'Berlusconi's and . . . among clans.'** Ibid, pp. 283–300.

p. 184   **'I'm in . . . of it.'** Ibid, p. 324.

p. 184–85   **'Calogero died . . . your fault!'** Buongiorno, Pino, p. 79.

p. 185   **'Who does . . . sister protested.'** Ibid.

p. 185   **'There's nothing . . . mafia goes.'** La Licata, Francesco, p. 150.

p. 186   **'Sure, they . . . or otherwise.'** Falcone, Giovanni with Padovani, Marcelle, p. xi.

p. 186   **'What do . . . this button.'** La Licata, Francesco, p. 11.

p. 187   **'He felt . . . Falcone said.'** Ibid, p. 190.

p. 187   **'We were . . . supergrass said.'** Giovanni Brusca, *Deposizione al processo di appello per la strage di Capaci* (Falcone murder), Caltanissetta, p. 12. 1 July 1999.

p. 188   **'What drives . . . so-called 'heroes'.'** Author interview with Giovanni Falcone, 11 November 1991.

p. 189   **'It's a . . . of courtesy.'** Gaspare Mutolo's testimony to the anti-mafia commission of the Rome parliament, 9 February 1992.

p. 189   **I've had . . . get killed.'** *Richiesta di custodia cautelare nei confronti di Agate, Mariano + 57 persone*, Palermo, p. 388. 20 February 1993.

p. 189   **'Cosa Nostra . . . a state.'** Abbate, Liro and Gomez, Peter, p. 188.

p. 190   **'The godfather . . . nasty now.'** Madeo, Liliana.

p. 190   **'An animal . . . he's well.'** Testimony of Gaspare Mutolo to the anti-mafia commission, February 1993.

p. 191   **'My country . . . mafia's impunity.'** La Licata, Francesco, p. 209.

p. 191   **'But it . . . to pay.'** Quoted in Stille, Alexander, *Excellent Cadavers: The mafia and the death of the first Italian republic*, p. 350.

5 Mafia Terrorism 1992–1996

Giovanni Brusca is 'Operational'

p. 196   'I might . . . doubts disappeared.' Lodato, Saverio, *'Ho ucciso Giovanni Falcone': La confessione di Giovanni Brusca*, p. 32.

p. 196   'I've tortured . . . these things.' Ibid, p. 161.

p. 196   'We'd hit . . . of it.' Ibid, p. 162.

p. 197   'I found . . . killed three.' Ibid, p. 161.

p. 197   'We could . . . a widow.' Author interview with Alfonso Sabella, 29 November 2006.

p. 197   'This time . . . finished it.' Giovanni Brusca, *Deposizione al processo di appello per la strage di Capaci* (Falcone murder), Caltanissetta, p. 7. 16 June 1999.

p. 198   'Can we . . . no problem.' Ibid, p. 10. 1 July 1999.

p. 201   'I could . . . no problem!' *Sentenza della Corte di Assise nei confronti di Pietro Aglieri + 40*, Caltanissetta, p. 342. 26 September 1997.

p. 204   'If I . . . them pay.' Giovanni Brusca, *Deposizione al processo di appello per la strage di Capaci* (Falcone murder), Caltanissetta, p. 84. 2 July 1999.

p. 205   'The bosses . . . he reflected.' Ibid, p. 26. 1 July 1999 and Lodato, Saverio, *'Ho ucciso Giovanni Falcone': La confessione di Giovanni Brusca*, p. 105.

p. 205   'When the . . . said later.' *Sentenza della Corte di Assise nei confronti di Pietro Aglieri + 40*, Caltanissetta, p. 423. 26 September 1997.

p. 205–06   'One usually . . . to protect.' Falcone, Giovanni with Padovani, Marcelle, p. 162.

p. 206   'Giovanni is . . . kill me.' Lucentini, Umberto.

'I'm Racing Against Time' – Judge Borsellino

p. 207   'I'm putting . . . Cosa Nostra.' Cancemi, testimony of 29 January 1998, quoted in, *Decreto di archiviazione nei confronti di Silvio Berlusconi and Marcello Dell'Utri*, by Giovanbattista Tona, judge for preliminary investigations, Caltanissetta, p. 16. 3 May 2002.

p. 208   'What can . . . he said.' Bianconi, Giovanni and Savatteri, Gaetano, p. 85.

p. 208   'Stop. The . . . as possible.' Cancemi, Salvatore, p. 68.

p. 208   'This one . . . all up.' Ibid, p. 70.

p. 208   'To political . . . in hospital.' Giovanni Brusca, *Deposizione al processo di appello per la strage di Capaci* (Falcone murder), Caltanissetta, p. 30. 2 July 1999.

p. 208   'We have . . . Cosa Nostra.' Cancemi, Salvatore, p. 92.

p. 209–10   'Riina wasn't . . . were over.' Torrealta, Maurizio, *La trattativa. Mafia e Stato: un dialogo a colpi di bombe*, p. 155.

p. 210   'There was . . . his eyes.' Judge Salvatore Barresi, quoted in Stille, Alexander, *Excellent Cadavers: The mafia and the death of the first Italian republic*, p. 360.

p. 210   'I'm racing . . . to do.' Lo Bianco, Giuseppe and Rizza, Sandra, *L'agenda rossa di Paolo Borsellino*, p. 177.

p. 210   'Sleep, my . . . awake them.' Lampedusa, Giuseppe Tomasi di, pp. 122–123.

p. 211   'They created . . . whole system.' Testimony to the anti-mafia commission of the Italian parliament, 4 December 1993.

p. 211   'We were . . . a car-bomb.' *Reuters*, 20 July 1992.

p. 211   'I'm worried . . . you in.' Lo Bianco, Giuseppe and Rizza, Sandra, *L'agenda rossa di Paolo Borsellino*, p. 176.

p. 213   'Riina didn't . . . about it.' *Sentenza della Corte di Assise nei confronti di Giuseppe Graviano + 3*, Florence, p. 60. 21 January 2000.

p. 213   'It's time . . . the affair.' *Il Messaggero*, 29 February 1992.

The Clan's First Traitors

p. 216   'The evil . . . good lesson!' Cancemi, Salvatore, p. 42 and Cancemi in Gruppo Abele, p. 263.

p. 216   'Children have . . . my life.' Cancemi in Gruppo Abele, p. 265.

'Who was the Judas?' – Riina's Fall

p. 222   'But apparent . . . with anger.' Author interview with Guido Lo Forte, 22 November 2006.

p. 225   'Furnishings . . . there was.' Monticciolo, Giuseppe and Vasile, Vincenzo, p. 43.

p. 226   'They feel . . . he said.' Author interview with Francesco Iaccono, 16 June 1993.

p. 227   'Once more . . . protect us.' *Città Nuove*, February 1993.

Prayers, Politics and the Battle for Riina's Succession

p. 229   'As long . . . as before.' Bianconi, Giovanni and Savatteri, Gaetano, p. 143.

p. 230   'We had . . . and quiet.' Palazzolo, Salvo and Prestipino, Michele, p. 24.

p. 230   'Giving the . . . be done.' Grasso Pietro and La Licata, Francesco, p. 53.

p. 230   'Provenzano even . . . a diplomat.' Quoted in Bellavia, Enrico and Palazzolo, Salvo, p. 75.

p. 230   'Provenzano, however . . . we bother?' Cancemi, Salvatore, p. 43.

p. 232   'I've got . . . had abandoned.' Quoted by writer Gaetano Savatteri in Amenta, Marco, p. 123.

p. 232   'Please don't . . . there is.' Bellavia, Enrico and Palazzolo, Salvo, p. 164.

p. 232–33 'Mafiosi, be . . . not triumph.' Lodato, Saverio, *Trent'anni di mafia*, p. 338.

p. 235   'The mafia . . . completely even.' Bellavia, Enrico and Palazzolo, Salvo, p. 77.

p. 235   'The text . . . personal freedom.' Gomez, Peter and Travaglio, Marco, p. xxi.

p. 235   'According to . . . things done.' Abbate, Liro and Gomez, p. 220.

p. 236   'We'll need . . . and efficient.' Ibid, p. 222.

p. 236   'What is . . . the world.' Ibid, p. 217.

The Kidnapping of Giuseppe Di Matteo, Age 12

p. 238–39 'With his . . . to Hell.' Lodato, Saverio, *'Ho ucciso Giovanni Falcone': La confessione di Giovanni Brusca*, p. 145.

p. 239   'I hated . . . own hands.' Ibid, p. 147.

p. 242   'Brusca showed . . . up alive.' Ibid, p. 151.

p. 243   'I knew . . . the boy.' Ibid, p. 152.

p. 246   'I'd never . . . on him.' Monticciolo, Giuseppe and Vasile, Vincenzo, p. 70.

p. 247   'I was . . . Brusca said.' Lodato, Saverio, *'Ho ucciso Giovanni Falcone': La confessione di Giovanni Brusca*, p. 163.

p. 249   'In a . . . sulphuric acid.' Monticciolo, Giuseppe and Vasile, Vincenzo, p. 142.

p. 250   'Guarding Giuseppe . . . very evening.' Ibid, p. 144.

p. 254   'It was . . . got out.' Lodato, Saverio, *'Ho ucciso Giovanni Falcone': La confessione di Giovanni Brusca*, pp. 144–145.

p. 254   'Does repenting . . . don't know.' Ibid, p. 144.

p. 255   'Giuseppe was . . . any more.' Author interview with Alfonso Sabella, 29 November 2006.

p. 256   'As soon . . . us all.' Caruso, Alfio, p. 562.

p. 256   'I understand . . . hundred books.' Lodato, Saverio, *'Ho ucciso Giovanni Falcone': La confessione di Giovanni Brusca*, p. 160.

6 The Mafia Turns 'Silent' 1995–2002

'Enough Massacres; Enough Murders' – Provenzano's Rule

p. 259   'Break their balls.' Bellavia, Enrico and Palazzolo, Salvo, p. 43.

p. 259–60   'There was ... been given.' Monticciolo, Giuseppe and Vasile, Vincenzo, p. 163.

p. 260   'I'm sure ... in Corleone.' Ibid, p. 170.

p. 260   'There is ... supergrass Contorno.' Ibid, p. 165.

p. 260   'According to ... a friend.' Testimony of Giovanni Brusca, quoted in Bellavia, Enrico and Palazzolo, Salvo, p. 43.

p. 261   'When Monticciolo ... or hesitating.' Monticciolo, Giuseppe and Vasile, Vincenzo, p. 175.

p. 261   'The new ... all over.' Palazzolo, Salvo and Prestipino, Michele, p. 24.

p. 262   'The search ... European Union.' Grasso Pietro and La Licata, Francesco, p. 57.

p. 262   'The point ... things quietly.' Bellavia, Enrico and Palazzolo, Salvo, p. 26.

p. 262–63   'We have ... be eliminated.' Antonino Giuffrè, *Deposizione al procedimento penale N.124/97 RG a carico di Giuseppe Biondolillo + altri*, Termini Imerese, p. 140. 16 October 2002.

p. 263   'Someone who ... betray twice.' *Richiesta di custodia cautelare nei confronti di Agate, Mariano + 57 persone*, Palermo, p. 503. 20 February 1993.

p. 263   'Its capacity ... the old.' Falcone, Giovanni with Padovani, Marcelle, p. 92.

p. 263   '*Basta* (Enough) ... young soldiers.' Abbate, Liro and Gomez, Peter, p. 26.

p. 264   'Why can't ... want that.'* Quoted in Bellavia, Enrico and Palazzolo, Salvo, p. 62.

p. 264   'Was capable ... a sheet.' Lodato, Saverio, *'Ho ucciso Giovanni Falcone': La confessione di Giovanni Brusca*, p. 175.

p. 266   'There's no ... obeys orders.' Author interview with Pietro Grasso, 29 November 2006. Grasso refused to reveal the mafioso's identity.

p. 266   'I can't ... one letter.' Bellavia, Enrico and Palazzolo, Salvo, p. 69.

p. 266   'God willing ... in another.' Palazzolo, Salvo and Prestipino, Michele, p. 30.

p. 266   'In one . . . Provenzano wrote.' Oliva, Ernesto and Palazzolo,
            Salvo.

p. 266–67   'I ask . . . of evidence.' Procura della repubblica presso il tribunale
            di Palermo, *Attività integrativa di indagine depositata dal p.m. in
            data 24.1.2007*, fig. 58.

Brusca Confesses

p. 269   'What can . . . his computer.' Author interview with Renato
            Cortese, 28 November 2006.

p. 269–70   'The depot . . . bulletproof jackets.' Lodato, Saverio, *Trent'anni
            di mafia*, p. 396.

p. 270   'But one . . . the morning.' Author interview with Salvatore
            Zuccarello, Palermo police, 22 November 2006.

p. 271   'Massacred me . . . upside down.' Lodato, Saverio, *'Ho ucciso
            Giovanni Falcone': La confessione di Giovanni Brusca*, p. 190.

p. 271–72   'He confessed . . . involved in.' Author interview with Alfonso
            Sabella, 29 November 2006.

p. 272   'Palermo and . . . last decades.' Lodato, Saverio, *'Ho ucciso
            Giovanni Falcone': La confessione di Giovanni Brusca*, p. 166.

p. 272   'All I . . . their pain.' Ibid, p. 201.

p. 272   'I've decided . . . she wrote.' Lodato, Saverio, *Trent'anni di mafia*,
            p. 398.

p. 272–73   'Concern over . . . Cipriani said.' Author interview with Pippo
            Cipriani, 22 November 2006.

p. 274   'In May . . . he said.' Bellavia, Enrico and Palazzolo, Salvo, p. 40.

p. 274   'In another . . . he talks!' Procura della Repubblica di Palermo,
            Direzione Distrettuale Antimafia, *Richiesta di custodia cautelare in
            carcere nei confronti di Riina Giuseppe Salvatore + 24*, June 2002.

p. 275   'What good . . . manager said.' Bellavia, Enrico and Palazzolo,
            Salvo, p. 25.

p. 275   'We're moving . . . to boss.' Quoted by the supergrass Giuffrè in
            Abbate, Liro and Gomez, Peter, p. 237.

p. 275–76   'Dissatisfaction with . . . he said.' Quoted in Abbate, Liro and
            Gomez, Peter, p. 242 and in Bellavia, Enrico and Palazzolo, Salvo.

Searching for a Ghost

p. 277   'Until the . . . for both.' Grasso Pietro and La Licata, Francesco,
            p. 42.

p. 278   'What fascinated . . . complete opposite.' Author interview with
            Renato Cortese, 28 November 2006.

p. 278   'Corleone is . . . put it.' Ibid.

p. 279   'You'll understand . . . strict control.' Quoted in Abbate, Liro and Gomez, Peter, p. 282.

p. 279   'How can . . . on me?' Bellavia, Enrico and Palazzolo, Salvo, p. 30.

p. 281   'I was . . . and punishments.' Quoted in Caruso, Alfio, p. 606.

p. 282   'Cortese turned . . . proved fruitless.' Author interview with Marzia Sabella, 17 November 2006.

p. 284   'Watch out . . . of saying.' Abbate, Liro and Gomez, Peter, p. 21.

p. 284   'Make them . . . Provenzano wrote.' Palazzolo, Salvo and Prestipino, Michele, p. 9.

7 The Fall of the Corleonesi 2002–2006

Provenzano and his Patron Saint

p. 289   'He had . . . in it.' Testimony of Antonino Giuffrè, omicidio brothers Giuseppe and Salvatore Sceusa on 19 June 1991, hearing 8 October 2002, p. 14.

p. 291   'As he . . . trouser fastening.' Procura della repubblica presso il tribunale di Palermo, *Atti irripetibili depositati dal p.m. all'udienza del 31.1.2007; rif. Sequestro del 13.4.2006 a carico di Provenzano Bernardo*, p. 39.

p. 294   'We'd burnt . . . investigative leads.' Grasso Pietro and La Licata, Francesco, p. 42.

Team Cathedral and the Laundry Mystery

p. 298   'You say . . . I live.' Quoted in Bellavia, Enrico and Mazzocchi, Silvia, p. 224.

p. 298–99 'I have . . . for Riina.' Quoted in Abbate, Liro and Gomez, Peter, p. 288.

p. 299   'For several . . . forgive them.' Ibid, p. 278.

p. 300   'At one . . . Cinà exclaimed.' Ibid, p. 279.

p. 301   'Three weeks . . . Paolo asked.' Ibid, p. 292.

p. 302   'But late . . . understood that.' Quoted in Bellavia, Enrico and Mazzocchi, Silvia, p. 177.

On Horses' Mountain

p. 315   'Shortly afterwards . . . state's evidence.' Grasso Pietro and La Licata, Francesco, p. 27.

p. 316   'Nine days . . . do soon.' Ibid, p. 61.

p. 317   'In 2006 . . . £35 billion.' SOS Impresa, Confesercenti, *Le mani della criminalità sulle imprese*, report by national retailers association, 2006.

p. 319   'Emotive, episodic . . . public opinion.' Falcone, Giovanni with Padovani, Marcelle, pp. 139–140.

p. 319   'Cosa Nostra . . . wooing her.' Lodato, Saverio, *'Ho ucciso Giovanni Falcone': La confessione di Giovanni Brusca*, p. 166.

p. 320   'The mafia . . . a state.' Falcone, Giovanni with Padovani, Marcelle, p. 56.

Bibliography

Archival sources

General

Sentenza della Corte di Assise nei confronti di Angelo La Barbera + 116, Catanzaro. Lower court verdict on murders in Palermo and nearby towns 1950s–1960s. 22 December 1968.

Sentenza di primo grado nei confronti di Luciano Leggio + 63, Bari. Lower court verdict on murders in Corleone 1950s–1960s. 10 June 1969.

Rapporto giudiziario di denuncia a carico di Greco, Michele + 161, Palermo. Account by the police and the *carabinieri* of the first two years of the 1981–1983 mafia war. 12 July 1982.

Richiesta di custodia cautelare nei confronti di Agate, Mariano + 57 persone, Palermo. Indictment for murders carried out in 1981–1991. 20 February 1993.

Sentenza della Corte di Assise di Appello nei confronti di Francesco Adelfio + 96, Palermo. Appeal court verdict on murders in Palermo 1980s–1990s. 20 November 2003.

Bruno Contrada

Sentenza della Corte di Assise di Appello nei confronti di Bruno Contrada, Palermo. 25 February 2006.

Rosario Spatola drug-trafficking case

Sentenza istruttoria nel procedimento penale contro Rosario Spatola + 119, Palermo, by Judge Giovanni Falcone. 25 January 1982.

Murder of Rocco Chinnici

Sentenza della Corte di Assise nei confronti di Salvatore Riina + 14, Caltanissetta. 14 April 2000.

Sentenza della Corte di Assise di Appello nei confronti di Salvatore Riina + 14, Caltanissetta. 24 June 2002.

Memoria del pubblico ministero al giudice per le indagini preliminari, Palermo. Report by prosecutors Giuseppe Pignatone, Michele Prestipino Giarritta, Maurizio de Lucia and Antonino di Matteo on the murder of Judge Rocco Chinnici. 1 October 2004.

Giulio Andreotti

Domanda di autorizzazione a procedere contro il senatore Giulio Andreotti, Palermo. 27 March 1993. Addenda of 14 and 20 April 1993.

Sentenza della Corte di Assise nei confronti di Giuseppe Calò + 5, Perugia. Lower court verdict. 24 September 1999.

Sentenza della Corte di Assise di Appello nei confronti di Giuseppe Calò + 5, Perugia. 17 November 2002.

Sentenza della Corte di Appello nei confronti di Giulio Andreotti. Appeals court verdict on Andreotti. 2 May 2003.

Sentenza della Corte di Cassazione nei confronti di Giulio Andreotti, Rome. Supreme Court verdict on Andreotti. 28 December 2004.

Murder of Carlo Alberto Dalla Chiesa

Sentenza di primo grado nei confronti di Antonino Madonna + 3, Palermo. Verdict on murder of General Carlo Alberto Dalla Chiesa. 22 March 2002.

Maxi-trial

Ordinanza sentenza contro Giovanni Abbate + 706, Palermo. 8 November 1985.

Marcello Dell'Utri

Procura della Repubblica presso il Tribunale di Palermo, Direzione Distrettuale Antimafia, Requisitoria del pubblico ministero, procedimento penale nei confronti di Gaetano Cinà e Marcello Dell'Utri. 11 November 2004.

Sentenza di primo grado nei confronti di Marcello Dell'Utri + 1, Palermo. 11 December 2004.

Murder of Salvo Lima

Sentenza di primo grado nei confronti di Salvatore Riina + 31, Palermo. Lower court verdict on murder of Salvo Lima. 15 July 1998.

Sentenza della Corte di Cassazione nei confronti di Giuseppe Graviano + 7, Rome. Supreme Court verdict on murder of Salvo Lima. 2 October 2003.

Murder of Giovanni Falcone

Sentenza della Corte di Assise nei confronti di Pietro Aglieri + 40, Caltanissetta. 26 September 1997.

Sentenza della Corte di Assise di Appello, Caltanissetta. 7 April 2000.
Sentenza della Corte di Cassazione nei confronti di Pietro Aglieri + 32, Rome. 18 April 2003.

Murder of Paolo Borsellino

Sentenza della Corte di Assise nei confronti di Vincenzo Scarantino + 3, Caltanissetta. 27 January 1996.
Sentenza della Corte di Assise nei confronti di Salvatore Riina + 17, Caltanissetta. 13 February 1999.
Sentenza della Corte di Assise nei confronti di Mariano Agate + 26, Caltanissetta. 9 December 1999.
Sentenza della Corte di Assise di Appello nei confronti di Mariano Agate + 26, Caltanissetta. 7 February 2002.
Sentenza della Corte di Assise di Appello nei confronti di Salvatore Riina + 16, Caltanissetta. 18 March 2002.
Sentenza della Corte di Cassazione nei confronti di Mariano Agate + 9, Rome. 17 January 2003.
Sentenza della Corte di Cassazione nei confronti di Salvatore Riina + 14, Rome. 12 March 2004.

Murder of Ignazio Salvo

Sentenza della Corte di Assise nei confronti di Leoluca Bagarella + 2, Palermo. 11 January 1996.

Baldassare di Maggio

Sentenza della Corte di Assise di Appello nei confronti di Baldassare di Maggio + 18, Palermo. 6 April 2002.

Arrest of Salvatore Riina, family

Sentenza della Corte di Assise nei confronti di Giovanni Riina + 8, Palermo. 23 November 2001.
Sentenza della Corte di Assise nei confronti di Salvatore Giuseppe Riina + 4, Palermo. 31 December 2004.
Sentenza di primo grado nei confronti di Mario Mori e Sergio de Caprio, Palermo. 20 February 2006.

Bombings in Florence, Milan and Rome

Sentenza della prima Corte di Assise di Appello nei confronti di Umberto Maniscalco + 2, Florence. 11 June 1997.

Sentenza di primo grado nei confronti di Leoluca Bagarella + 25, Florence. 6 June 1998.

Sentenza della Corte di Assise nei confronti di Giuseppe Graviano + 3, Florence. 21 January 2000.

Sentenza della prima Corte di Assise di Appello nei confronti di Leoluca Bagarella + 22, Florence. 13 February 2001.

Decreto di archiviazione nei confronti di Silvio Berlusconi and Marcello Dell'Utri, by Giovanbattista Tona, judge for preliminary investigations, Caltanissetta. 3 May 2002.

Sentenza della Corte di Cassazione, Rome. 6 May 2002.

Sentenza della Corte di Assise nei confronti di Giuseppe Graviano + 1, Florence. 23 April 2004.

Murder of Father Giuseppe Puglisi

Sentenza della Corte di Assise di Appello nei confronti di Giuseppe Graviano + 2, Palermo. 13 February 2001.

Kidnapping of Giuseppe di Matteo

Sentenza della Corte di Assise di Palermo nei confronti di Leoluca Bagarella + 66. 10 February 1999.

Bernardo Provenzano

Ordinanza di applicazione e di rigetto di misure cautelari nei confronti di Bernardo Provenzano + 20, by Renato Grillo, judge for preliminary investigations, Palermo. 6 November 1998.

Comunicazione notizia di reato relativa all'attività investigativa svolta per la cattura del latitante mafioso Provenzano Bernardo, report to prosecutors by the Sezione Catturandi of the Palermo police flying squad. 8 February 2001 (printed in Bellavia, Enrico and Mazzocchi, Silvana, *Iddu: la cattura di Bernardo Provenzano*, Baldini Castoldi, 2006).

Ordinanza di custodia cautelare in carcere nei confronti di Lorenzo Agosta + 29, Palermo, by Gioacchino Scaduto, judge for preliminary investigations. 24 January 2002.

Ordinanza di custodia cautelare in carcere nei confronti di Andrea Impastato e Filippo Lombardo, Palermo, by Gioacchino Scaduto, judge for preliminary investigations. 30 October 2002.

Ordinanza di custodia cautelare in carcere nei confronti di Michele Aiello, Giuseppe Ciuro and Giorgio Riolo by Giacomo Montalbano, judge for preliminary investigations, Palermo. 4 November 2003.

Sentenza nei confronti di Vito Alfano + 16, Palermo, by Roberto Binenti, judge for preliminary investigations. 12 December 2003.

Rapporto giudiziario di denuncia a carico di Carmelo Gariffo + 29, Palermo. Report by the *carabinieri* police. 10 April 2004.

Arresto del latitante Provenzano Bernardo, report to prosecutors by the SCO unit and the flying squad of the Palermo police. 12 June 2006 (printed in Bellavia, Enrico and Mazzocchi, Silvana, *Iddu: la cattura di Bernardo Provenzano*, Baldini Castoldi, 2006).

Fermo di indiziati di delitto nei confronti di Andrea Adamo + 51, Palermo, by prosecutors Giuseppe Pignatone, Michele Prestipino, Domenico Gozzo, Maurizio de Lucia, Antonino Di Matteo, Roberta Buzzolani. 20 June 2006.

Relazione di consulenza grafica, Palermo, by court-appointed experts Lorenzo Rinaldi and Pasquale Gismondi. 12 October 2006.

Atti irripetibili, Palermo. Report by prosecutors on letters seized from Bernardo Provenzano. 31 January 2007.

Testimony by informers

Leonardo Vitale, to Palermo prosecutors, police and *carabinieri*, 30 March 1973.

Stefano Calzetta to Palermo prosecutor Rocco Chinnici and others, 12 March 1983–28 February 1985, 5 vols.

Vincenzo Sinagra to Palermo prosecutor Vittorio Aliquò and others, 30 November 1983–30 April 1985, 2 vols.

Tommaso Buscetta to Palermo prosecutor Giovanni Falcone and others, July–August 1984, 3 vols.

Salvatore Contorno to Palermo prosecutor Giovanni Falcone and others, October 1984–June 1985.

Antonino Calderone to Palermo prosecutor Giovanni Falcone and others, 19 March 1987–25 June 1988, 4 vols.

Francesco Marino Mannoia to Palermo prosecutor Giovanni Falcone and others, 8 October 1989–19 June 1990.

(Copies of the above all available at Cambridge University Library)

Commissione parlamentare di inchiesta sul fenomeno della mafia e sulle associ- azioni criminali simili, Audizione del collaboratore di giustizia Antonino Calderone, 11 November 1992. *Audizione del collaboratore di giustizia Tommaso Buscetta*, 19 November 1992.

Audizione del collaboratore di giustizia Leonardo Messina, 4 December 1992.

Audizione del collaboratore di giustizia Gaspare Mutolo, 9 February 1993.

Giovanni Brusca, *Deposizione al processo di appello per la strage di Capaci* (Falcone murder), Caltanissetta. 16 June 1999, 1 July 1999, 2 July 1999, 3 July 1999.

Salvatore Cancemi, *Deposizione al processo d'appello per la strage di Capaci* (Falcone murder), Caltanissetta. 22 October 1999.

Antonino Giuffrè, *Deposizione al processo di appello a carico di Salvatore Biondino.* 8 October 2002, 10 October 2002, 23 January 2003, 24 January 2003.

Antonino Giuffrè, *Deposizione al procedimento penale N.124/97 RG a carico di Giuseppe Biondolillo + altri,* Termini Imprese. 16 October 2002, 17 October 2002, 25 October 2002, 26 October 2002.

Antonino Giuffrè, *Deposizione al processo di assise a carico di Rizzo Rosolino,* Palermo. 3 April 2006.

Newspapers

Corriere della Sera (Milan)
Giornale di Sicilia (Palermo)
La Repubblica (Rome)
La Sicilia (Catania)
La Stampa (Turin)
L'Ora (Palermo)

Interviews

Anti-mafia prosecutors, Palermo:
Maurizio De Lucia
Antonio Ingroia
Sergio Lari
Guido Lo Forte
Francesco Messineo
Giuseppe Pignatone
Michele Prestipino
Marzia Sabella
Lia Sava
Roberto Scarpinato

Anti-mafia prosecutors, Rome:
Pietro Grasso
Alfonso Sabella
Luca Tescaroli

Pippo Cipriani, former mayor of Corleone, Palermo
Renato Cortese, former head of Team Cathedral, Rome
Giuseppe Cucchiara, former head of police flying squad, Palermo
(All carried out in November 2006 and February 2007)

Books

Abbate, Lirio and Gomez, Peter, *I complici*, Fazi, 2007.

Amenta, Marco, *Il fantasma di Corleone*, Rizzoli.

Andreatta, M., 'La mafia corleonese e la sua continuità', in *L'associazionismo a Corleone. Un'inchiesta storica e sociologica*, eds Paolo Viola and Titti Morello, CD-ROM edited by Istituto Gramsci Siciliano, Palermo, 2004.

Anselmo, Nonuccio, *Corleone Novecento*, 4 vols, Palladium Editrice, Corleone, 1998 and 2000.

Arlacchi, Pino and Buscetta, Tommaso, *Addio Cosa Nostra: la vita di Tommaso Buscetta*, Rizzoli, 1994.

Arlacchi, Pino and Calderone, Antonio, *Gli uomini del disonore*, Mondadori, 1992.

Aurelio, Angelici, Galasso, Alfredo, Petruzzella, Francesco and Roccuzzo, Antonio, *Uno sguardo dal bunker: cronache del maxiprocesso di Palermo*, Ediprint, Siracusa, 1987.

Aymard, Maurice and Giarrizzo, Giuseppe, *La Sicilia*, Einaudi, 1987.

Barbacetto, Gianni, Gomez, Peter and Travaglio, Marco, *Mani pulite: la vera storia*, Editori Riuniti, 2002.

Bartolotta Impastato, Felicia, *La mafia in casa mia*, La Luna, Palermo, 1987.

Bellavia, Enrico and Palazzolo, Salvo, *Voglia di mafia*, Carocci, 2004.

Bellavia, Enrico and Mazzocchi, Silvana, *Iddu: la cattura di Bernardo Provenzano*, Baldini Castoldi, 2006.

Biagi, Enzo, *Il boss è solo*, Mondadori, 1986.

Bianconi, Giovanni and Savatteri, Gaetano, *L'attentatuni: storie di sbirri e mafiosi*, Baldini Castoldi, 1998.

Boffano, Ettore, *Il procuratore. Gian Carlo Caselli*, Baldini Castoldi, 1995.

Bolzoni, Attilio and Lodato, Saverio, *C'era una volta la lotta alla mafia*, Garzanti, 1998.

Bolzoni, Attilio and D'Avanzo, Giuseppe, *Il capo dei capi*, Mondadori, 1993.

Bongiovanni, Giorgio and Cancemi, Salvatore, *Riina mi fece i nomi di . . .*, Massari, 2002.

Bowden, Mark, *Killing Pablo: The hunt for the richest, most powerful criminal in history*, Atlantic Books, 2002.

Buongiorno, Pino, *Totò Riina: La sua storia*, Rizzoli, 1993.

Calderoni, Pietro and Savatteri, Gaetano, *Voci del verbo mafiare: Aforismi di Cosa Nostra*, Tullio Pironti, 1993.

Cancemi, Salvatore, *Riina mi fece i nomi di . . .: Confessioni di un ex boss della Cupola a Giorgio Bongiovani*, Massari, 2002.

Cancila, Orazio, *Palermo*, Laterza, 2000.

Caponnetto, Antonino, *I miei giorni a Palermo*, Garzanti, 1992.

Caruso, Alfio, *Da cosa nasce cosa*, Longanesi, 2005.

Catania, Enzo and Sottile, Salvo, *Totò Riina: Storie segrete, odii e amori del dittatore di Cosa Nostra*, Liber, Milan, 1993.

Cavallaro, Felice, *Il caso Contrada*, Rubbettino, 1996.

Chinnici, Giorgio and Santino, Umberto, *La violenza programmata: omicidi e guerre di mafia a Palermo dagli anni '60 ad oggi*, Franco Angeli, 1991.

Clare, Horatio (ed.), *Sicily: Through writers' eyes*, Eland, 2006.

Commissione parlamentare d'inchiesta sul fenomeno della mafia e sulle altre associazioni criminali similari, *I boss della mafia*, Editori Riuniti, 1971.

Commissione parlamentare d'inchiesta sul fenomeno della mafia e sulle altre associazioni criminali similari, *Mafia, politica, pentiti: la relazione del presidente Luciano Violante e le deposizioni di Antonio Calderone, Tommaso Buscetta, Leonardo Messina, Gaspare Mutolo*, Rubbettino, 1993.

Dalla Chiesa, Alberto, *Michele Navarra e la mafia del corleonese*, La Zisa, Palermo, 1990.

Dalla Chiesa, Nando, *Delitto imperfetto*, Editori Riuniti, 2003.

Davis, John H., *Mafia Dynasty: Rise and Fall of the Gambino Crime Family*, HarperCollins, 1994.

D'Elia, Sergio and Turco, Maurizio, *Tortura democratica: Inchiesta sulla 'Comunità del 41bis reale'*, Marsilio, 2002.

Deliziosi, Francesco, *Don Puglisi*, Mondadori, 2006.

Di Cagno, Giovanni and Natoli, Gioaccino, *Cosa nostra ieri, oggi, domani*, Dedalo, 2004.

Falcone, Giovanni with Padovani, Marcelle, *Cose di Cosa Nostra*, Rizzoli, 1991.

Falzone, Gaetano, *Storia della mafia*, Flaccovio, Palermo, 1984.

Fava, Giuseppe, *Mafia: Da Giuliano a Dalla Chiesa*, Editori Riuniti, 1984.

Fava, Giuseppe, *Processo alla mafia*. Ites, 1971.

Fiume, Giovanna and Lo Nardo, Salvo (eds), *Mario Francese: una vita in cronaca*, Gelka, Palermo, 2000.

Follain, John, *A Dishonoured Society*, Little, Brown, 1995

Galluzzo, Lucio, Nicastro, Franco and Vasile, Vincenzo, *Obiettivo Falcone*, Tullio Pironti, 1989.

Gomez, Peter and Travaglio, Marco, *L'amico degli amici*, Rizzoli, 2005.

Gruppo Abele, *Dalla mafia allo stato*, Edizioni Gruppo Abele, 2005.

Hess, Henner, *Mafia*, Laterza, 1973.

Hill, Greg, *On the Run: A Mafia Childhood*, Warner, 2005.

Imposimato, Ferdinando, *Un juge en Italie*, Editions de Fallois, 2000.

Ingrasci, Ombretta, *Donne d'onore: Storie di mafia al femminile*, Bruno Mondadori, 2007.

Jamieson, Alison, *The Antimafia: Italy's fight against organised crime*, Macmillan, 2000.

La Licata, Francesco, *Storia di Giovanni Falcone*, Feltrinelli, 2002.

Lampedusa, Giuseppe Tommasi di, *The Leopard*, Harvil, 1992.

Lewis, Norman, *The Honoured Society: The Sicilian Mafia Observed*, Eland, 1984.

Lo Bianco, Giuseppe and Rizza, Sandra, *Il gioco grande*, Editori Riuniti, 2006.

Lo Bianco, Giuseppe and Rizza, Sandra, *L'agenda rossa di Paolo Borsellino*, Chiarelettere, 2007.

Lo Bianco, Giuseppe and Viviano, Francesco, *La strage degli eroi: vita e storia dei caduti nella lotta contro la mafia*, Arbor, Palermo, 1996.

Lodato, Saverio, *Trent'anni di mafia*, Rizzoli, 2006.

Lodato, Saverio, *La mafia ha vinto: intervista a Tommaso Buscetta*, Mondadori, 1999.

Lodato, Saverio, '*Ho ucciso Giovanni Falcone': La confessione di Giovanni Brusca*, Mondadori, 1999.

Lodato, Saverio and Travaglio, Marco, *Intoccabili*, Rizzoli, 2005.

Lucentini, Umberto, *Paolo Borsellino*, San Paolo Edizioni, 2003.

L'Unità (ed.), *Mafia e potere: Cosa Nostra raccontata da Tommaso Buscetta, Leonardo Messina e Gaspare Mutolo davanti alla Commissione parlamentare antimafia*, 1993.

Lupo, Salvatore, *Andreotti, la mafia, la storia d'Italia*, Donzelli, 1996.

Lupo, Salvatore, *Storia della mafia dalle origini ai giorni nostri*, Donzelli, 2004.

Madeo, Liliana, *Donne di mafia*, Mondadori, 1994.

Marchese, Antonino, *Corleone: L'identità ritrovata*, FrancoAngeli, 2001.

Marino, Giuseppe, *I padrini*, Newton Compton, 2006.

Martorana, Giuseppe and Nigrelli, Sergio, *Così ho tradito Cosa Nostra. Leonardo Messina: la carriera di un uomo d'onore*, Musumeci, Aosta, 1993.

Martorana, Giuseppe and Nigrelli, Sergio, *Totò Riina: Trent'anni di sangue da Corleone ai vertici di Cosa Nostra*, Musumeci, 1993.

Matard-Bonucci, Marie-Anne, *Histoire de la mafia*, Editions Complexe, 1994.

Mignosi, Enzo, *Il Signore sia coi boss*, Arbor, 1993.

Montanaro, Silvestro and Ruotolo, Sandro (eds), *La vera storia d'Italia*, Tullio Pironti, 1995.

Monti, Giommaria, *Falcone e Borsellino*, Editori Riuniti, 2006.

Mori, Cesare, *Con la mafia ai ferri corti: Le memorie del prefetto di ferro*, Flavio Pagano, 1993.

Mori, Cesare, *Tra le zagare oltre la foschia*, La Zisa, 1988.

Nese, Marco, *Nel segno della mafia: Storia di Luciano Liggio*, Rizzoli, 1975.

Newark, Tim, *The Mafia at War*, Greenhill, 2007.

Oliva, Ernesto and Palazzolo, Salvo, *Bernardo Provenzano: il ragioniere di Cosa Nostra*, Rubettino, 2006.

Olla, Roberto, *Padrini*, Mondadori, 2003.

Orlando, Leoluca, *Fighting the Mafia and Renewing Sicilian Culture*, Encounter Books, 2003.

Padovani, Marcelle, *Les dernières années de la Mafia*, Gallimard, 1987.

Pantaleone, Michele, *Mafia e politica 1943–1962*, Einaudi, 1962.

Pantaleone, Michele, *Mafia e droga*, Einaudi, 1966.

Paternostro, Dino, *A pugni nudi: Placido Rizzotto e le lotte popolari a Corleone nel secondo dopoguerra*, La Zisa, 1992.

Paternostro, Dino, *I Corleonesi: storia dei golpisti di Cosa Nostra*, published with L'Unità, 2005.

Paternostro, Dino, *L'antimafia sconosciuta: Corleone 1893–1993*, La Zisa (Le Pietre), 1994.

Pepino, Livio, *Andreotti la mafia i processi*, Edizioni Gruppo Abele, 2005.

Pinotti, Ferruccio, *Poteri forti: la morte di Calvi e lo scandalo dell'Ambrosiano*, Rizzoli, 2005.

Puzo, Mario, *The Godfather*, Signet, 1978.

Puzo, Mario, *The Sicilians*, Random House, 1984.

Rabb, Selwyn, *Five Families: The Rise, Decline and Resurgence of America's Most Powerful Mafia Empires*, Thomas Dunne Books, 2005.

Renda, Francesco, *Storia della Mafia*, Sigma, 1963.

Santino, Umberto, *L'alleanza e il compromesso*, Rubbettino, 1997.

Santino, Umberto, *La mafia interpretata*, Rubbettino, 1995.

Savatteri, Gaetano, *I siciliani*, Laterza, 2005.

Scafetta, Valeria, *U baruni di Partanna Mondello: storia di Mutolo Gaspare, mafioso, pentito*, Editori Riuniti, 2003.

Sciascia, Leonardo, *A ciascuno il suo*, Einaudi, 1988.

Sciascia, Leonardo, *Candido: ovvero Un sogno fatto in Sicilia*, Einaudi, 1977.

Sciascia, Leonardo, *Il giorno della civetta*, Einaudi, 1972.

Sisti, Leo, *L'isola del tesoro: Provenzano e Ciancimino, corleonesi doc*, BUR, 2007.

Stajano, Corrado (ed.), *Mafia: L'atto di accusa dei giudici di Palermo*, Editori Riuniti, 1992.

Stancanelli, Bianca, *A testa alta: Don Giuseppe Puglesi, storia di un eroe solitario*, Einaudi, 2003.

Stille, Alexander, *Excellent Cadavers: The mafia and the death of the first Italian republic*, Jonathan Cape, 1995.

Stille, Alexander, *The Sack of Rome*, Penguin Press, NY, 2006.

Suddovest documenti (ed.), *Delitto Lima: L'atto di accusa di giudici di Palermo*, Suddovest, Agrigento, 1992.

Tescaroli, Luca, *I misteri dell'Addaura: . . .ma fu solo Cosa Nostra?*, Rubbettino, 2001.

Tescaroli, Luca, *Perchè fu ucciso Giovanni Falcone*, Rubbettino, 2001.

Tescaroli, Luca, *Le faide mafiose tra i misteri di Sicilia*, Rubbettino, 2003.

Torrealta, Maurizio, *La trattativa*, Editori Riuniti, 2002.

Torrealta, Maurizio, *Ultimo, il capitano che arrestò Totò Riina*, Feltrinelli, 1999.

Tranfaglia, Nicola, *La sentenza Andreotti*, Garzanti, 2001.

Tranfaglia, Nicola, *Mafia, politica e affari 1943–2000*, Laterza, 2001.

Turone, Sergio, *Politica ladra: Storia della corruzione in Italia: 1861–1992*, Laterza, 1992.

Ultimo, *La lotta anticrimine: Intelligence e azione*, Laurus Robuffo, undated.

Vecchio, Angelo, *Luciano Liggio*, Antares Editrice, 1994.

Vecchio, Angelo, *Totò Riina*, Antares Editrice, 1997.

Vecchio, Angelo, *L'ultimo re dei Corleonesi*, Antares Editrice, 2006.

Violante, Luciano, *I corleonesi: Mafia e sistema eversivo*, L'Unità libri, 1993.

Zingales, Leone, *Giovani Falcone, un uomo normale*, Aliberti, 2007.

Zingales, Leone, *Il padrino ultimo atto: Dalla cattura di Provenzano alla nuova mafia*, Aliberti, 2006.

Zingales, Leone, *Provenzano: Il re di Cosa Nostra*, Luigi Pellegrini, 2001.

Zingales, Leone, *Rocco Chinnici: L'inventore del pool antimafia*, Limina, 2006.

Index

4/11 6
2/15 (10) 11/14
9/19 (12) 2/19